READING FOR STUDENTS *with* SPECIAL NEEDS

Second Edition

FRANK J. GUSZAK

University of Texas

KENDALL/HUNT PUBLISHING COMPANY
4050 Westmark Drive Dubuque, Iowa 52002

Library of Congress Catalog Card Number: 97-74466

ISBN 0-7872-4446-5

Printed in the United States of America
10 9 8 7 6 5 4 3 2 1

Table of Contents

1

READING FOR STUDENTS WITH SPECIAL NEEDS

Reading for Students with Special Needs, the title of this book and chapter, suggests discussions limited to students with major reading difficulties. Such is not the case. Rather, students with special needs are all of the pupils in a given classroom, from the most able reader to the least able. Because each pupil has the potential to develop his/her skill further, this book is intended to help teachers to understand wide ranges of reading capabilities found in the elementary school.

By the time a child enters first grade, reading variability has already manifested itself. Some pupils are reading two or three years above first grade level while others struggle to read their own names.

Some of the reasons for initial reading variance can be seen in the children's age. Before a child can enter first grade in many states, that child must have reached his or her sixth birthday before September 1. This means that the children with August birthdays will have just turned six while those with September birthdays will be seven years of age. Immediately, it is apparent that we are working with children who vary a whole year in age. When we discover that some of these pupils started preschool at the age of three while others may have never experienced kindergarten, it is further apparent as to why they arrive at first grade with such apparent differences in literacy.

Curiously, the range of reading differences will be smaller on the first day of first grade than it will ever be again. With each passing day and year, the range expands rapidly . While some wish to eliminate this range and carry all of the pupils at the same level, such is not the nature of human individual differences. With nurturing intellectual experiences the range should broaden. This is just as it should be because individual differences will exert themselves in the area of reading just as they exert themselves in physical development. The highest readers should fly while other readers must be nurtured slowly as they progress through the stages of literacy.

A helpful way of viewing the normal or expected range of reading that might be found in each grade level is the simple formula that suggests that the normal range is two-thirds of the age of the pupils in a given grade. Thus, the following ranges would be typical of elementary level pupils.

Grade 1:	2/3 of 6 years of age	=	**4.0**	years
Grade 2:	2/3 of 7 years of age	=	**4.6**	years
Grade 3:	2/3 of 8 years of age	=	**5.3**	years
Grade 4:	2/3 of 9 years of age	=	**6.0**	years
Grade 5:	2/3 of 10 years of age	=	**6.6**	years

Grade 6:	2/3 of 11 years of age	=	**7.2**	years
Grade 7:	2/3 of 12 years of age	=	**8.0**	years

After seventh grade, the range of differences tends to narrow because the very low readers have either been placed in special classes or have dropped out of school.

That reading variability is the norm rather than the exception in our graded schools needs to be understood by parents and teachers. With an understanding of this reality, we shouldn't view extremely high or low readers as a curse but rather as pupils in need of the best programs we can provide.

In viewing the normal reading range of reading achievement in a **third grade class**, we refer back to the older, vocabulary controlled basal readers. The so-called average readers would read somewhere between a second reader - two (2/2) and a third reader - two (3/2). We would find our gifted readers reading from one to four grade levels above the average readers while our disabled readers would be reading from a second reader (2/1) level to no reading level at all.

A graphic view of this range in grade three would reveal the following:

Grade 3 – 2/3 of age 9 = 6 years of reading differences :

(RR. refers to reading readiness, no reading skills; PP refers to the first three preprimers made up of about 100 words total; P refers to the primer of the first grade; 1/2 refers to the first reader or last book of the first grade. The first number of the other books designates the grade level intended for that book.)

While this book is concerned with more effective programming for the gifted and disabled readers that occupy the opposite ends of the normal reading distribution, it is also concerned with all the pupils in the normal range. It is critical that a wide array of readers be present in a classroom if that classroom is going to function as a literary environment. The responsibilities of strong and weak readers to one another will be one of the important parts of this program that emphasizes cooperative learning.

As this book is written, the previous dominant form of reading instruction in America, the **basal reading program,** has been replaced by the **"whole language program"** which has sought to replace "anthology" type books of controlled vocabulary with "authentic" children's books (Goodman, Bird, & Goodman, 1991; Stephens 1991). Concomitant with the new movement is an increased move to **"on level"** reading where all students experience teacher direct instruction from the same book. This instructional stance has taken the position that 1) good literature will make reading more interesting and 2) the range of differences can be spanned by high quality teacher direction and pupil rehearsal. Consequently, all the pupils in a grade level are placed in the same literature books and asked to read at the same pace (Jones et. al., 1985). With "on level whole language" reading adopted by more and more **regular classrooms** (classrooms with special students included), concerns are raised about those students who have difficulty with the authentic literature books chosen for their particular grades. With "controlled vocabulary" in disrepute (Milligan, 1993), what types of materials will be used with slower readers?

STUDENTS WITH SPECIAL NEEDS

One of the realities of any instruction today is the use of "labels". In an effort to provide more effective interventions for different students, the proliferation of categories has emerged in the past two decades. Consequently, pupils are tested to determine if they can best be served under the auspices of the various new programs. Although every student can be considered a student with special needs, the concern here is that exceptional pupils' special needs are not lost in the labels discussion. Included in the array of students with special needs are those who might be classified as gifted readers as well as those who would be labeled as disabled readers. The classifications are not intended for discrete discussions of learning disabilities but rather as indicators of some of the most frequent classifications of special students.

In order to personalize the instruction of pupils, I have chosen the following six pupils who will be followed through the book so that the reader can have some idea of how their reading needs might be met. Five pupils have labels that suggest some type of difficulty classification while the sixth pupil, Stan, is a gifted reader. All six pupils are classmates in a heterogeneous, regular, self-contained third-grade classroom that we shall see at the end of the book. Thus, we can illustrate how a teacher with a wide set of reading levels can subsequently plan and manage an individualized program.

Gifted and Disabled Readers

Grade	**Pupil Names**	**Description**	**Common Term**
3rd	**Stan**	**Gifted Reader**	**GT**
3rd	Mary	Learning Disabled	LD
3rd	Robbie	Dyslexic	DX
3rd	Tanya	Attention Deficit	ADD
3rd	Greg	Mentally Retarded	MR
3rd	Sam	Mentally Retarded	MR

Gifted Readers. Definitions of giftedness usually depend upon unique traits, but the gifted reader is the one who is reading at the 80th or 90th percentile in terms of standardized test scores (Au & Mason, 1990). These pupils typically find traditional instruction boring and often try to substitute other books at every opportunity. Although many gifted readers with different traits could be chosen, one pupil—**Stan**—has been chosen to illustrate this very important dimension. After reading the following information about Stan, the focus will shift to his four classmates with reading deficits.

Grade -	Third Grade
Age -	8 years 3 months
Reading Achievement -	90 th percentile
Math Achievement -	85 th percentile
IQ -	120
Family -	both parents and two siblings

Stan, a very able third grader, has been chosen because able students represent about 20 per cent of the overall body of students. Although their giftedness in reading varies, their patterns of placement and work are often illustrated by the things that Stan does in the course of each reading day.

A gifted reader in a traditional self-contained third-grade classroom, Stan can read sixth-grade level books with good comprehension. Despite his advanced reading ability, he is expected to participate in the weekly reading program using the adopted third-grade literary readers which are often three years below his reading level. Typically, he does the following things each day:

Reads a 6–9 page story
Completes 5–9 journal pages (workbook)
Completes 6–8 phonic worksheets

In his five clock hours of reading each week, Stan spends approximately 20 minutes a day in the total group reading activities with his teacher and eighteen other pupils. The teacher normally reads the story aloud to the class on Monday, reads it with them on Tuesday, and has them read it individually on Wednesday. Each day's reading is enhanced with activities and materials provided by the publisher. Included in these daily activities are specific skills lessons in word analysis and comprehension.

With about 40 minutes of planned seat work each day divided between journal (workbook) pages and dittoed skill sheets, Stan and the others in the class are supposed to spend about 200 minutes a week on these activities. Because he works through the assignments so easily, Stan normally completes these tasks in about five minutes each day and has the remaining 35 minutes for working on other things or reading. Normally, he chooses to read from the favorite mystery book that is usually in his pocket. He loses himself in this book and thus continues to develop his abilities to read mystery books.

Stan leaves his classroom for the gifted classroom (which is called High Flyers) every Tuesday and Thursday mornings at 10:00 where he does a number of activities incorporating higher level thinking skills for about an hour. The content of the work in the gifted classroom varies each six weeks and is considered to be an enrichment to the program.

When asked about reading instruction, Stan has no big problems with it because he gets to spend most of his time in the pursuit of independent reading. In this sense, he is ahead of a lot of his gifted reading peers across the country because they are subjected to more workbook pages than he has to do. Stan does a lot of free reading and he appreciates the opportunity.

Disabled Readers. When we use the term disabled readers, we suggest that these readers have problems that interfere with their acquisition of reading skills. Comprising an estimated 13 to 16 percent of the school population (according to the US. Department of Education, 1984), these pupils struggle to do elemental reading tasks. Although labels have seldom been productive in terms of outlining specific cures for these pupils (Shepard, Smith, & Vojir, 1983), I have chosen to use these labels because many people use and misuse them. The misuse, I feel, comes in terms of suggestions from some special-interest reading groups that maintain that they have the only successful approach to a given problem.

Prior to the days of special education and gifted classes, students with special needs who were admitted to schools were often given the same assignments as their grade level peers. Teachers often didn't know what to do with them. Consequently, many were allowed to stay until they dropped out or were passed on to another grade. Under the provisions of **The Education for All Handicapped Children Act (Public Law (PL) 94-142 (1975),** handicapped students were to be given a special type of education that called specifically for the handicapped to be:

1) given **individualized instruction** and **mainstreamed,**

and

2) educated as much as possible in the **least restrictive environment (LRE).**

The wording of the law relative to special education students was very clear. It stated the following:

> **in order to receive funds under the Act every school system in the nation must make provisions for a free, appropriate public education for every child... regardless of how seriously he may be handicapped.**

With this law in effect, there was new hope that children with learning problems might be assisted in meaningful ways that would allow them to partake more successfully in the educational process and subsequently obtain the necessary skills with which to participate effectively in a literate society.

Specifically, a four step referral process was outlined for pupils with any of the following thirteen types of disabilities: autism, deaf-blindness, deafness, hearing impairment, mental retardation, multiple disabilities, orthopedic impairment, chronic or acute health problems (like a heart condition or epilepsy), serious emotional disturbance, specific learning disability, speech or language impairment, traumatic brain injury, and visual impairment. Of this number, only a few disabilities, such as deafness or blindness can be measured by objective tests. The referral process contains the following provisions:

The Four Steps in the Referral Process

Step 1: Comprehensive individual assessments occur within 30 school days from the time special education receives the referral information. This is done so that the **admission, review, dismissal (ARD) committees** can have the necessary information to make an educational decision for the pupil.

Step 2: Admission, review, and dismissal (ARD) committees composed of specialists, teachers, principals, and the pupil's parents meet to determine the existence of a handicap and what special needs exist. If a need is determined, the process moves to the next step.

Step 3: The **individual educational plan (IEP)** is drawn up if the student qualifies in the ARD conferences for special education services. Pupil goals and objectives are set, services to be provided outlined, and parental consents obtained before services are started.

Step 4: After the services have been progressing, the ARD committee **meets at least annually to review pupil progress toward the educational goals and objectives of the IEP** and makes any necessary changes. This step is to evaluate the program for the pupil to determine if gains are being made.

This four-step identification process initiated the development of individual learning plans that were intended to uniquely benefit those pupils included in the legislation. While many pupils have undoubtedly been helped to become effective readers and learners, it's apparent that others have not been successful because of inappropriate plans and/or implementations.

Because of text length, the complete array of literacy techniques for all the handicap categories will not be the focus of this text. Rather, the focus will be upon how five pupils in a traditional reading program can be subsequently placed into an individualized classroom that will provide them with success. You have already briefly met Stan, the gifted reader, and his classmates (Mary, Robbie, Tanya, Greg, and Sam, pupils with reading problems). Each of the latter five pupils has been designated with one of the following labels that will now be discussed: learning disabled, dyslexic, attention deficit disorder, and mentally retarded.

Learning disabled (LD). This generic term refers to a heterogeneous group of disorders that are characterized by great difficulties in the acquisition and use of all communication skills (listening, speaking, reading, writing). These problems are intrinsic and are presumed to be the result of some central nervous system dysfunction. Typically, learning disabled individuals are those who have substantial gaps between expected and actual achievement levels in at least one academic area that are not attributed to mental retardation or emotional disturbance. According to the United States Department of Education (1984), approximately five percent of school age children are learning disabled.

By far, the largest class of special education students are the 49.9 % that are labeled "learning disabled" (*Newsweek*, December 13, 1993). This is so because the federal definition for inclusion in this classification states that there must be "a severe discrepancy between achievement and intellectual ability." Because state departments of education specify what tests will be used to determine learning disability, there is a wide range of variance between the pupils who inhabit this classification. Yesseldyke (*Newsweek*, December 13, 1993) indicates that more than 80 percent of all schoolchildren in America could qualify as learning disabled according to one or more of the various definitions now used.

Mary, a seemingly normal third grader in Stan's class, fits the common learning disabled profile of dissonance between ability and achievement because she has problems in dealing with any symbolic material (reading, writing, or mathematics). When she didn't learn to read in the first grade, she was retained a year in the hopes that a second year of beginning reading would be more helpful. Unfortunately, the second year seemed to make little difference in her reading. Now in her fourth year of school, Mary remains essentially a non-reader.

Grade -	Third Grade, retained in second
Age -	9 years 6 months
Reading Achievement -	6 th percentile
Math Achievement -	40 th percentile
IQ -	100
Family -	both parents, only child

Mary's teacher is frustrated when she attempts to help Mary. In the course of the school year, the teacher has given her extra help in order that she might read with the whole class. Because Mary is virtually a non-reader, she seldom follows the class reading or discussion.

When Mary's turn comes up in the small reading groups that are formed by the teacher for additional practice, the other pupils prompt her and give her all the words. Mary appears frustrated and seeks to withdraw when such activities occur.

When the students do worksheets and workbook pages, Mary usually manages to get her name and little else on the page. She spends a lot of time playing with her pencil and stacking things up on her desk.

Having experienced nearly four years of frustration, Mary doesn't seem to realize that reading can be a satisfying experience. Because of this and her own frustrations, the teacher has referred Mary to the ARD committee. After reviewing her IQ test scores, the committee finds that Mary is not disabled mentally. Rather, it is determined that she is learning disabled. Because of her low reading scores she will be provided with a special phonics program in her classroom three times a week.

Dyslexia (DX). This label designates a disorder of constitutional origin manifested by a difficulty in learning to read, write, or spell. Despite conventional instruction, adequate intelligence, and the necessary socio-cultural factors, these students have great difficulty in functioning in the print world of the classroom and reading (Texas Education Code Section 21.924).

The cause of dyslexia is uncertain but one promising area of investigation has been the possibility that particular areas of the brain are damaged or in disruptive competition with one another (Obrzut, Obrzut, Hynd, & Pirozzolo, 1981). Autopsies of dyslexics have revealed a jumbling of brain myelinated neurons (Clark & Gosnell, 1983). Another strong possibility indicates that inheritance may cause the problem through the passing on of a dominant gene on chromosome 15 (Smith, Kimberling, Pennington, & Lubs, 1983). Whatever the cause may be, dyslexia is often diagnosed as the cause of reading difficulties.

Robbie, one of the third graders, has been identified as a "dyslexic" by his parents, the family physician, and the school psychometrist. Some of the data that supported the labeling was:

Grade	-	Third Grade, retained in first
Age	-	9 years 1 months
Reading Achievement	-	10 th percentile
Math Achievement	-	80 th percentile
IQ.	-	110
Family	-	single parent, one brother

Because Robbie has high intelligence, high math achievement, no history of birth complications, a strong supportive family, there appeared to be no other rational explanation of his reading problem other than "dyslexia." When his high math achievement is viewed against his low reading achievement he seems to be a prime candidate for that label.

Robbie's reading was characterized by several symptoms commonly attributed to dyslexics—reversals of letters and words, inability to remember words, difficulty with concentration, difficulty with hand-to-eye coordination, and directional confusions.

Like Mary, Robbie is a member of the whole group reading experience associated with the "whole language" adoption. He, too, is frustrated by the school work. Unlike Mary, he is somewhat difficult to manage and represents an ongoing behavioral problem in the classroom. He seems to like to get attention by doing things that make the other children laugh.

Despite his classification as a "dyslexic," Robbie's parents have resisted his placement in a class for learning disabled pupils. Rather, they have sent him to commercial tutoring programs after school and to special summer reading clinics. Neither intervention appears to have helped much and his parents are becoming even more concerned.

When asked about reading, Robbie answers with a clear "I hate it." This feeling is pretty apparent when he is asked to do anything that resembles reading in and out of the classroom.

Attention Deficit Disorder (ADD). A rather recent descriptor of pupil behaviors (Bales, 1985), the attention deficit disorder (ADD), refers to a rapidly growing group of approximately 800,000 children who display inappropriate attention and impulsivity (Dworetzky, 1990). Such children fail to finish assignments and appear not to listen to instructions. They are easily distracted and demonstrate impulsive behaviors such as calling out in class. Some of these children also demonstrate hyperactivity.

In addition to being inattentive and impulsive, such children appear to move about excessively. They seem to be driven all the time by some internal mechanism. Although the underlying cause of the disorder is unknown, many researchers feel that it is induced by allergic reactions to food additives. Some physicians prescribe drugs such as amphetamines or Ritalin. Curiously, some of the stimulants have actually helped hyperactive children toward calmness and attention. Another theory suggests that hyperactivity is a learned disorder (conditioned by the environment) and that it can be treated as effectively by behavior modification as it can by medication (Pelham, 1977; Wulbert & Dries, 1977).

Recently, any child who appeared to be very active has seemingly been tagged with this label and given amphetamines or Ritalin. The problem is rather great because there is still considerable debate about the long term effects of such drugs.

Tanya, a third grader, has been labeled ADD by her physician, teacher, and parents. At this time, her school has no provisions for ADD students in their special education program. She has trouble staying in her seat and the teacher feels that she has to keep telling her to sit down and get busy. Tanya is good-natured about the requests and obeys, but the pattern of getting up or off-task is rather continuous.

Grade -	Third Grade
Age -	8 years 8 months
Reading Achievement -	50 th percentile
Math Acheivement -	30 th percentile
IQ -	95
Family -	single parent, three sisters

As a less successful reader in the class, Tanya's performance is best characterized as "streaky." She does some things very well but then appears not to understand what is going on about her. She is seldom aware of the place in the reader when she is asked to read aloud and has a poor record of completing achievement tests.

Tanya's doctor has her on Ritalin, a drug that is supposed to calm her down. The teacher feels that she can tell when Tanya is taking Ritalin because her behavior appears to be more calm.

Tanya thrives on attention and wants the teacher to see her work often. She seems to like books even though her reading achievement is very erratic.

Mentally Retarded (MR). Children who are termed *mentally retarded* supposedly have significantly lower intellectual functioning than their peers. They also display deficits in adaptive behavior as manifested in the developmental period (Grossman, 1977). The government estimates that approximately 1.9% of school-age children are mentally retarded (U.S. Department of Education, 1990).

One of the most troubling aspects of special education has to do with this category because of the fact that more than twice as many blacks as whites are classified as mentally retarded. (*Newsweek*, 54, December 13, 1993 based on US. Dept. of Education Office of Civil Rights 1990 Survey of Schools). Among the reasons for such are conditions of poverty and "culturally biased IQ tests used to classify students. "

For purposes of illustration, we shall view the true stories of Greg and Sam. Although classified in the same category, it will soon be apparent that the boys have very different needs.

Greg, a third grader with Downs syndrome, has been tested with the prerequisite individual intelligence test and has been found to be functioning in the mid 70s. Because he has no other adaptive behavior deficits, he continues in the regular classroom in all subjects. Research documenting the success of pupils like Greg in regular classrooms has been done (Madden & Slavin, 1983).

Grade -	Third Grade
Age -	10 years, 2 months
Reading Achievement	- 12 th percentile
Math Achievement	- 30th percentile
IQ -	75
Family -	both parents, two siblings

Research by Rynders (Dworetzky, 1989) and his colleagues at the University of Minnesota with 30-month-old Downs syndrome children proved that an early intervention communication program could be highly successful in producing pupils who could read. Of the 13 pupils who participated in the early start program, 11 were reading at or above second grade level comprehension later in their school years.

In apparent recognition of the early intervention programs like the Minnesota program, Congress passed Public Law 99-457 in 1986 to provide early intervention programs for handicapped children. Essentially, this extension of Public Law 94-142 meant that states could begin helping handicapped children from birth.

Like the previous special needs students, Greg attempts to read along with the whole group. Unfortunately, his primer level reading skill is too far below the level of the books being read by the class. His unique reading needs don't appear to be met by the whole class reading scenario.

Greg's mother, a teacher, has read to him since he was an infant and has continued to read with him at home on a regular basis. Probably because of his early literacy start, he has continued to take a great deal of pleasure in books.

When asked about reading, Greg reflects positively about books. When he speaks of his favorite books, he always includes the Dr. Seuss books, which were read to him extensively as a toddler. He still likes to read these books just for fun when time permits.

Although he's not able to function in the low reading group, Greg's primer level reading skill provides a hopeful reminder that other pupils like him can succeed and possibly gain functional reading skill. Research has shown that many Downs syndrome children have a good chance of achieving (Turkington, 1987) when given proper support.

Sam, a black third grader struggling to read, was forced to move out of his regular class to a class of mentally retarded children because of an invalid intelligence test. Because there was little academic work in reading and math in the special class, Sam's scores plummeted even further down. When his mother saw her son's self confidence going down with his achievement, she found a reading specialist who ran new tests. The new tests revealed normal intelligence and below average achievement.

Grade	-	Third Grade
Age	-	9 years, 7 months
Reading Achievement	-	40th percentile
Math Achieve.	-	50th percentile
IQ	-	95
Family	-	single parent, three siblings

It seemed that Sam's real problem was a visual one in that he had trouble focusing his eyes. When the problem was corrected he was able to return to his original class where he prospered. Thus, Sam's problem illustrates the ever present danger of misdiagnosis.

PROGRAMS FOR STUDENTS WITH SPECIAL NEEDS

The Admissions, Review, Dismissal (ARD) committee makes very important decisions about how a given child is to be dealt with in a school program. This committee determines when a pupil will be admitted to or dismissed from a special program. For the students admitted, the committee decides whether the individual educational program (IEP) can be accomplished in a regular classroom, regular classroom/consultation, itinerant services, resource services, content mastery services, resource services, or a self-contained special education classroom. Each of these situations is briefly described.

Regular Classroom. More and more reading programs for special students are carried out in the setting of the regular classroom by the regular teacher of that classroom because of the perceived value of **inclusion** (keeping students main streamed as much as possible). Individual educational programs (IEP) provide either special materials or the means by which to adapt current plans to the targeted special pupils. For reading, such adaptations might include: extended time for completing assignments, shortening assignments, requiring alternative texts and materials, allowing oral tests, allowing the student more frequent breaks, and changing the pace of learning to allow for individual differences.

Stan, Mary, Robbie, Tanya, Greg, and Sam, pupils with special needs, reside in a regular classroom along with their gifted reader friend, Stan. Mary, Greg ,and Sam have undergone the ARD process. While Greg was not placed in the program because of his lack of qualifications, Mary was given an individual education plan (IEP) that called for instruction three times a week by the classroom teacher in synthetic phonics. Sam, with visual help, was able to continue in the regular classroom.

Regular Classroom/Consultation. When the ARD committee feels that the teacher may need special help, they will specify that a specialist in special education work with the classroom teacher as a consultant to establish program directions called for by the IEP. In the previous example of the regular program, the teacher was assigned the task of helping **Mary** three times a week with a special synthetic phonics program but was not given sufficient help to insure that she knew how to operate the program. Possibly, the ARD committee didn't realize the help that the teacher would need.

Itinerant Services. Itinerant services by a special education teacher are sometimes a part of an educational plan. These special teachers may come to the regular classroom regularly to work with special children or may make suggestions to the regular teacher about how to work with special children.

When **Robbie's** IEP was first established, it was decided to include him in his classroom. To assist him with his DISTAR Program (Englemann & Bruner, 1969), the special education teacher was to visit him three times a week during his twenty minute reading class. After a semester of operation, the ARD committee reconvened at the request of the special teacher and heard the recommendation of that teacher that the plan be ended because Robbie was not experiencing the success they had anticipated. Quite likely, the special teacher may not have experienced success because she was not trained in the delivery of the program. While the plan didn't work for Robbie, it had obviously worked for other teachers and pupils.

The role of itinerant teachers in special education is an important one because of the growing problem of **"pull out programs"** (programs offered outside the regular classroom) that continue to take pupils from their base classrooms for long periods of time. Because of the serious problems resulting from the lack of accountability for a pupil's learning, some states are mandating that special services must take place in the regular classroom. California has taken a stand against the "pull out programs" and has mandated that all such services must be subsequently brought into the regular classroom. At this time the movement for **"inclusion"** has been growing rapidly.

Another option for the itinerant teacher is to provide the regular classroom teacher with disabled children, demonstrate instructional techniques, conduct workshops, and arrange for visits to model programs.

Resource Services. Resource services are those that are provided by a special education teacher outside of the regular classroom. Exceptional children receive services in a resource center for a portion of the day. This resource teacher will also consult with classroom teachers regarding instruction within the classroom.

Although **Robbie** might subsequently be moved to a resource room soon for reading instruction, he has not yet experienced that. One of the reasons that he has not been placed in a resource room is that his parents will not provide their consent for such a placement. Many parents feel that once their children are placed in resource rooms and other such pull-out programs, they are endangering the pupils' chances of staying with their peer groups. These parents feel that their children will be labeled and ostracized from many of the important groups and happenings in a school.

Content Mastery Classrooms. Some schools provide a separate room for pupils with special needs during the various subject fields. In schools, any pupil may be assigned to this room without the four step referral procedure. The students bring their assignments or reading materials to this room, and a special teacher provides them with individual help in any content or skills subject. In such programs, a qualified pupil with difficulties in his third reader workbook might get special assistance from the teacher assigned to the content mastery classroom. Sometimes, paraprofessionals assist content mastery teachers in these classrooms.

Because content mastery classrooms operate on the assumption that the sending classroom teacher best knows what the pupil needs, its success depends in large part on the accuracy of that assumption. At best, it is a valuable assist to the classroom teacher. At its worst, it is simply another mindless workbook or copy situation.

Decisions about pupil placements are made every day when parents or teachers become disenchanted with what is happening in a special classroom. Sometimes the decisions result in pupils being taken out of success situations. Yet, there are other times when the ARD committee decides that the results indicate that a child can be better served in his own classroom. What is needed for making such decisions are better determinations of the kinds of reading achievement that can be expected in different time intervals as well as better means of measuring and documenting the reading progress of individual pupils. Specific means of detailing reading progress via rate, word recognition, and comprehension are discussed later in the text.

Self-Contained Special Education Rooms. If pupils cannot prosper in any of the previous arrangements and classes are available, pupils can be placed in homogeneous classes of exceptional children.

> Removal from the regular classroom or resource room to a self-contained special education room (where the student spends the main part of his time) should only happen if the ARD committee decides that one of the following situations exists:
>
> 1) The recommended curriculum or instruction can't be implemented in the regular classroom or resource room with supplementary aids and services if students without handicaps are present,
>
> or
>
> 2) the student has not achieved satisfactorily in the regular class despite an appropriate IEP, correct instructional modifications, and **appropriate aids and services.**

ALL THE OTHER KIDS

Although the focus of this chapter has been those pupils with special needs, there are a lot of other good- and poor-reading pupils occupying the example third-grade class of this book as well as other classes across the country. Many of these pupils are failing to meet their reading potential.

Sadly, many pupils who begin first grade already reading are systematically prevented from reading because many teachers feel the need to cover a specified program, whether basal oriented or whole language centered. Some basal centered teachers require all the pupils to complete a readiness book and its accompanying workbook pages before they read another book, even though some of them are already reading. Some whole language teachers persist in teaching a given trade book and ignore the fact that some of the pupils have already read that book and a number of others.

Whereas good readers may be needlessly delayed, poor readers are often asked to do the opposite—swim in a reading current that is too swift. Although many are capable learners, they are left behind by the reading curriculum that is dictated by a school calendar that calls for a story per week with all the trimmings (whether it's a basal story or a trade book chapter). Once these pupils get behind, they continue to experience the phenomenon known as the **"cumulative deficit"** that suggests that "the farther you go, the farther behind you get." We can never close the deficit between good and poor readers nor should we try to do such. Still, we can launch non-achievers onto paths of success that will have them moving up each year in reading achievement rather than moving backward.

All students—special and regular—need a chance to participate in reading programs that are tailored to them as individuals. This book describes one such program that has produced a successful track record.

SUMMARY

From the first day of first grade, when children arrive nearly a year apart in age and everything else, their reading differences continue to vary further as they progress through the grades. Although variability is natural and good, it needs to be understood. Able readers must be allowed to move even farther than they are currently moving and disabled readers must show steady reading increases.

Typically, exceptional pupils are given labels such as gifted readers or disabled readers Disabled readers include the following: LD—Learning Disabled, DX—Dyslexic, ADD—Attention Deficit Disorder, and MR—Mentally Retarded. The disabling conditions may exist in combinations with other conditions to the point that the pupil may be considered to be multiply handicapped. Some folks would have us believe that there are only a few instructional options for disabled learners.

Planning for the reading growth of disabled readers is the task of an ARD (admission, review, dismissal) committee that determines how, when, and where approved pupils will be provided for in terms of the IEP (individual educational plan). While these plans have definite programs that these pupils are supposed to follow in the least restrictive environment (LRE), the programs don't always work as intended. Also, parents don't always avail themselves of possible programs.

To illustrate what happens to special needs students, this chapter describes Stan, a gifted reader and his unchallenging reading program. At the opposite end of the spectrum, four learning disabled students are described in order to indicate their handicapping conditions and some of the provisions made for their reading instruction. Mary, Robbie, Tanya, and Greg , seem to be having little success in their regular third-grade class where they join three other similar pupils daily in the literature reader (whole class). Sam, although misdiagnosed as mentally retarded, prospers when his problem is discovered to be a correctable visual one. Robbie, the focus of a team teaching effort wherein the special education teacher came in three times a week to work with him, didn't seem to progress under that arrangement. Resource rooms may or may not be possibilities for Robbie and Greg in the near future. Many parents have grave concerns about permitting their children to go to resource rooms or self contained special education classrooms for fear that their children will be stereotyped as being "slow."

STUDY SUGGESTIONS

1. Make an appointment to visit with a classroom teacher to discuss the range of reading levels found in that teacher's classroom. Ask about the tests that are used for determining the reading levels as well as the means that are used for referring pupils to **Admission, Review, Dismissal (ARD)** conferences. Ask if it is possible to see an old **Individual Educational Plan (IEP)** with the pupil's name scratched out. If it is, study the descriptions of the problem and the proposed solutions. Note how the student's progress or failure to read was measured.
2. Make another appointment with a special education teacher to discuss the types of problems that teacher encounters in the course of a given day. Ask if you might see an old IEP with the pupil's name scratched out. Note what kind of reading program intervention was prescribed as well as any recorded measures of the pupil's success or failure in the prescribed program.
3. Ask your local school administrator about any special provisions that are being made to determine whether students have **dyslexia** or an **attention deficit disorder.**

2

RELEVANT RESEARCH ON READING INSTRUCTION

Hundreds of research reports annually deal with the reading process as well as the means by which pupils learn to read (Adams, 1990; Pearson, Barr, Kamil, & Mosenthal, 1984). Despite a lack of clarity on the nature of the process and the best means of producing readers, there are nonetheless a number of ideas that are strongly supported by the results of available research. This chapter attempts to detail some of the more crucial concerns under the following categories; Learning to Read: The Great Debate; Models of Reading; Emergent Literacy; Reading-Writing Connections; The Concept of Fit; Connected Reading; and Rehearsal Effects.

Learning to Read: The Great Debate

Because the words of our English language are derived from a 26-letter alphabet, the first American reading teachers sought to teach reading by initially teaching some of the sounds commonly associated with the alphabet and then spelling out words that students subsequently read in the New England Primer (Smith, 1963). In the mid-1800s, when the emphasis shifted to elements of controlled vocabulary, a major change in reading instruction was apparent (Smith, 1963). In essence, the great debate as to whether pupils should be taught initially with sounds and letters or words in sentences had begun. The debate as to whether reading instruction should be driven by the code (alphabet and sounds) or the message (meaning-based approach) has become increasingly sophisticated over the years.

Chall's 1967 book *Learning to Read: The Great Debate* (reissued in 1983) brought research to bear on the hotly disputed topic of how to start reading instruction (Flesch 1955, 1981). After reviewing the historical studies comparing **meaning first approaches** with **code emphasis (phonics) approaches,** Chall concluded that the code emphasis programs were superior. Her conclusion, though, seems flawed because she essentially demonstrated that most of the historical research upon which she based her findings was subject to poor control groups, inadequate descriptions of the experimental methods, limited controls of the experimental conditions, and questionable measurement instruments (Carbo, 1987; Rutherford, 1968).

Because of Chall's stature in the reading field and the desire of a large segment of the population for an intensive phonics program, her suggestions were well received by the educational community that invested millions of dollars in supplemental phonics programs in the 1970s and 1980s to boost what was happening in the dominant basal reader program.

The battle lines were drawn between the phonics and meaning folks. In time, more sophisticated explanations of the reading process would be generated. Terms such as bottom-up processes, top-down processes, and interactive processes would appear.

Bottom-up was the term used to refer to the views of early cognitive psychologists who viewed reading as a process whereby information was initially processed as letters, and then as sounds, and so on up to the higher cognitive steps, with meaning finally emerging as the end product (Sperling 1967; Sternberg, 1969; Theios, 1973). The instructional implications of this view called for the learning of the letters, their associated sounds, word synthesis, and finally sentence synthesis. In other words, reading starts with the building blocks of letters and their sounds and proceeds upward toward meaning. Many reading programs are based on such a progression (Flesch, 1955, 1981; Gatengo, 1969; Spalding, 1962; Sullivan, 1963).

Top-down theorists viewed reading as a holistic process whereby higher level processing directed the flow of information down through the lower level responses (Goodman, 1976; Hochberg, 1970; Kolers, 1972; Smith 1978). From this view, reading was a hypothesis-testing procedure in which the reader formed and tested an hypothesis throughout the reading act. Consequently, the reader used only the graphic information necessary to confirm the hypothesis. For readers possessing a great deal of prior information about the text, the confirmation might be very rapid, thus permitting unusually fast reading performances. Goodman (1976) illustrated how readers utilize semantic (meaning), syntactic (word order) and graphophonic (letters and their sounds) cues to construct meaning.

Whereas the "bottom-up" folks would start with the sounds of letters (usually vowels first), the "top-down" advocates would start with story materials in which the pupils could predict what was being said in print. Although the best predictable materials were the pupils' own language experience stories (Allen, 1966), predictable trade books came into great favor. Today, publishers produce a wide variety of predictable texts in the vein of Martin's *Brown Bear, Brown Bear, What Do You See?* (1967, 1983) where the pupils initially discover a pattern, as in the following example:

> Brown Bear, Brown Bear, what do you see?
> I see a red bird looking at me.
> Red Bird, Red Bird, what do you see?
> I see a yellow duck looking at me.

Interactive is the term used to describe the interplay of the top-down and bottom-up models. While research continues in the effort to describe the reading process, it seems safe to say that the process is neither exclusively bottom-up nor top-down, but rather is in teractive. In an extensive analysis of the pertinent literature, Stanovich (1980) found that both theories fail to explain the actions of good and poor readers. Consequently, he and others have developed research designs that support the interactive explanation. Stanovich has found that the processes are not only interactive but compensatory in that the poor reader who is deficient in word analysis (bottom-up) skills may overuse context (top-down) skills.

> Interactive models, best exemplified in the work of Rummelhart (1976), assume that a pattern is synthesized based on information provided simultaneously from several knowledge sources. The compensatory assumption that a deficit in any knowledge source results in a heavier reliance on other knowledge sources, regardless of their level in the processing hierarchy. Thus, according to the interactive-compensatory model, the poor reader who has deficient word analysis skills might possibly show a greater reliance on context factors. In fact, several studies have shown this to be the case. (Stanovich, 1980, p.63)

Although the work of many investigators, including Rummelhart (1976), Stanovich (1980), Juel (1980), and others, supports the model of reading as an interactive and compensatory action, such research does not provide instructive data to beginning reading teachers who want to know how pupils should be introduced to reading. Information on competing theories and their implications for instruction is offered by Calfee and Drum (1986).

Arguably, the most prominent position about learning to read has been Chall's predominantly bottom-up approach. This position drew major support from the **Follow Through** studies of the 1970s, in which the children of preschool **Headstart** programs were followed into the primary grades. In trying to determine which of these programs produced the highest results, the programs emphasizing academic skills, and more particularly code emphasis, were clearly ahead and their students remained on top throughout their school tenure (Adams, 1990; Becker & Gersten, 1982). Issuing from this finding was the view that reading should be initially a **code emphasis** (phonic approach) and the position that such an emphasis was best accomplished through **direct teach**. The position has received recent support from an extensive review of the literature (Adams, 1990). Probably the most apparent approach has been the *Hooked on Phonics* (Gateway Educational Products) program that has been advertised extensively on radio and TV. This is advertised as a "do-it-yourself" phonics program that is supposed to help children as well as adult illiterates. I have not seen any research to support the advertising claims.

Lest anyone think that the decision is complete, it's important to note that one of the most successful Follow Through programs also featured a heavy emphasis upon **connected reading** (Meyer, 1983). Noting this, Chall (1983) commented that "It would appear, then, that an early opportunity to do meaningful connected reading in addition to learning how to decode is needed to integrate both abilities." Thus, the very significant term **connected reading** was added to the terms **code emphasis** and **direct teach.** You will be reading more about the importance of connected reading later in this chapter and book.

Emergent Literacy

Emergent literacy is rapidly replacing the term "**reading readiness**," which appears to have outlived its usefulness. In the 1930s, the term "reading readiness" was used to support the notion that everyone wasn't ready to learn to read at the same time. Unfortunately, the term became synonymous with reading readiness tests, reading readiness workbooks, reading readiness classes, and a host of other tasks that suggested that mastery of discrete skills was necessary before engaging pupils with meaningful reading contexts. Many students were not allowed to begin reading instruction until they achieved certain reading readiness test scores, mastered specific sound-to-symbol patterns, or learned to follow certain types of instruction (Durkin, 1983). Currently, some school districts are requiring students to pass phonemic awareness tests in kindergarten before they are "passed" to first grade (Adams, 1990).

Emergent literacy, simply put, refers to what beginning readers and writers are doing with literacy tasks as they grow up. We have long recognized that beginners come with very different reading and writing experiences. Some are already responding to print in kindergarten while others are a great distance from such. To better understand the differences the children bring to school it is worthwhile to view some of the experiences that cause the emergence of literacy. Specifically, the following kinds of children are more likely to demonstrate emergent literacy skills:

> Children who have used language extensively
>
> Children who have been read to extensively.
>
> Children who have had musical and other repetitive experiences that allow them to deal with familiar songs, rhymes, jingles, and symbols.
>
> Children who have people who show them how writing works (typing children's names, wish lists, stories, etc.)

Children who have used language extensively. Children want to know. Thus, we see them constantly asking "why" about all the things around them. As we answer their questions, they generate more informed questions that allow them to create their model of how the world works. Children who don't have extensive opportunities to ask questions and have those questions answered will fail to develop properly in their language and understanding. Many projects have been initiated to offset language deprivation and create an early impact in the home environment. These projects involve willing parents in learning how to verbally interact with their children, answer their questions, and take them to higher levels of thinking.

Children who have been read to extensively. The most important home literacy factor is a parent's reading aloud to children (Anderson, Hiebert, Scott, & Wilkinson, 1984). This pleasurable experience makes no demands upon children but launches them, nevertheless, into the world of language and literature.

Although home reading is the most important stimulus to subsequent reading success, reading has invariably begun when children note the intriguing signs and labels that dominate their existence. Children read soft drink logos, gum wrappers, cereal boxes, grain types, graffiti words, road signs, clothes labels, tennis shoe labels, and a host of other things in every setting (Link, Tompkins, & Shaw, 1980). Words catch their attention from early on and they continue their questions with the oft repeated "what does that say?" They repeat their questions if they are answered. If not, they are unsure and have already begun to develop an uncertainty about the written symbols of their environment.

Some children, who have their questions answered, also benefit from folks who will read many quality books to them in the course of growing up. *'Twas the Night Before Christmas* was a book that was etched into the very existence of many of us as we were growing up and heard this enchanting story at Christmas time. From there, we listened in rapture as we heard the classics of such beloved fairy tales as *Cinderella, Little Red Ridinghood, Hansel and Gretel, Jack and the Beanstalk, Snow White,* and *Pinnochio.*

Besides just reading the stories to children, clever adults do those innovative things that make books come alive. Daddy will growl as he read the wolf's refrain from *The Three Little Pigs :* "Little Pig, Little Pig, Come out or I'll blow your house down." To this day, we can scarcely resist the refrain "Not by the hair of my chinny-chin-chin." This pleasurable social event builds a desire and interest in reading. If this exposure is continued, children develop both vocabulary and a sense of story structure that helps them learn to read (Elley, 1989; Teale, 1981).

These great readers would pause to build the emotion of the moment and stop to ask children what was going to happen next. Such language play invited children at the earliest ages into the wonderful give and take of literary language (Martinez & Roser, 1985; Sulzby & Teale, 1986).

By motivating children to interact with picture book stories, Whitehurst et al. (1981) found that overall language development was increased substantially. Such discussions were also significant to children's subsequent appreciation of language and literature (Snow & Ninnio, 1986).

Children who have had musical and other repetitive experiences. Some of the rich literature experiences of children's books are made more meaningful by the child's rhythmic recitation. Who can ever forget that "You'd better watch out; you'd better not cry; you'd better not pout—I'm telling you why..." When the print is matched with melody, an indelible trace is placed in our memory.

You will notice that most preschoolers delight in the sharing of the favorite nursery rhymes such as *Baa Baa, Black Sheep* and *Humpty Dumpty.* As soon as you start the first line, these three- and four-year-olds who have experienced the rhymes are out in front of you, saying the patterns they love and enjoy so much. Bradley and Bryant (1983) hypothesize that these pupils are demonstrating **phonemic awareness** (the ability to differentiate significant speech sounds). Seemingly, phonemic awareness which is deemed essential to learning to read is seeded in the children's knowledge of nursery rhymes.

Using a version of the "shared book" experience, Brown, Cromer, and Weinberg (1986) used familiar stories, rhymes, and songs with rural South Carolina kindergartners and realized higher year-end test scores. Shared book experiences have become regular parts of kindergarten and first grade programs throughout this country.

Some years back, when we were working with some lower-socioeconomic status (SES) beginners in reading, we decided to put their book to music. Our music was pretty strange and we were obviously embarrassed when we sang it the first time to them. Our embarrassment disappeared when we discovered that our not-so-original lyrics and tune were a musical hit with our young audience. The children loved to sing things that they could follow along in print. From that day forward for the balance of the summer, the children insisted that we sing the song with them at the end of the morning before they went home. To our further surprise, some of the children would even come to class early each day to sing the song and point at the words on the chart before class started.

This familiar rhyme puts reading to music.

Children who have people who show them how writing works. Although some of the people on *Sesame Street* (Children's Television Workshop) and other educational programs show the children how writing works, the best teachers are those people who take the time to help the child write a Christmas list, a food list, a cousin's name, a friend's name, the name of a dinosaur, or anything else the young author wants to have recorded.

A nursery school director once called me to come and see the two-year-old girl who was reading all her classmates' names off their disposable diaper boxes. Upon my arrival, the prodigy was brought forth and put to the test. To my wonder and their pleasure, she proceeded to read the diaper boxes of approximately ten of her peers in the nursery. When I was asked how it happened, I had to say that I didn't know but that I strongly suspected that she was one of those unique children that had a high degree of interest in symbols. She also had someone who would answer her questions and help her to verify the testing she was obviously doing in terms of how written language works. Needless to say, the little girl was sort of a legend in her own time at that nursery school.

Some parents and preschool teachers find that some children want to go beyond the lists and short transcribing processes and do things like titling their pictures, writing the names on pupil-drawn inventions, and actually writing letters or stories for the children. These parents and teachers are often surprised by how much information is recalled by the children who have dictated a letter or a story.

With the advent of the personal computer, some children are taking over much of the process themselves. Commercial programs like International Business Machines' (IBM) **Writing to Read** have permitted pupils to move quickly into production.

For years the language-experience approach (LEA) has been praised for its value in showing pupils the connections between oral and written speech (Allen & Allen, 1966; Ashton-Warner, 1963; Stauffer, 1965). Despite questions about its value as a complete program for developmental reading (Guszak, 1985; Stahl & Miller, 1989), language-experience remains a most valuable introductory means for print match experiences. Language-experience has maintained a dedicated set of followers for many years.

The Reading-Writing Connection

Increasing attention has been given to the connections between reading and writing. For many children there is a sense of message in their earliest markings (Clay, 1979). That is, the student has the awareness that symbols carry meaning. While some of a child's earliest writings may carry little meaning because of his inability to control the symbols, it is very clear that some of the most important content of the pupil's reading is his own thinking: He wants to tell his story so that he and others can read it (Calkins 1986).

As previously indicated, the language experience approach to reading (Allen & Allen, 1966) has operated on the connections between what the author wanted to say and the inscribing of that message by a helper. With the advent of the IBM **Writing to Read** program, technology has given many young writers unique opportunities to write what they are not yet capable of producing with their limited handwriting skills. While the research supports for the *Writing to Read* program appear to be lacking (Freyd & Lytle, 1990), some promising possibilities seem to be present.

Still, there are many sound-to-symbol associations that must be learned before the student has a reasonable chance of understanding his message. The parallel process is available for the young writer who learns to encode certain letters for sounds on paper. From invented spellings, some children can initiate the reading process from their writing. Routinely, I have observed kindergartners writing stories of more than 40 words.

Some pupils, because they lack either motor coordination or phonetic spelling capablity (the ability to match letters and their sounds), are unable to operate in the IBM program because they cannot handle the invented spelling. These children need to match a meaning with a larger graphic representation, such as a word, a sentence, or even a story. They can later reconstruct the smaller units, such as the following example:

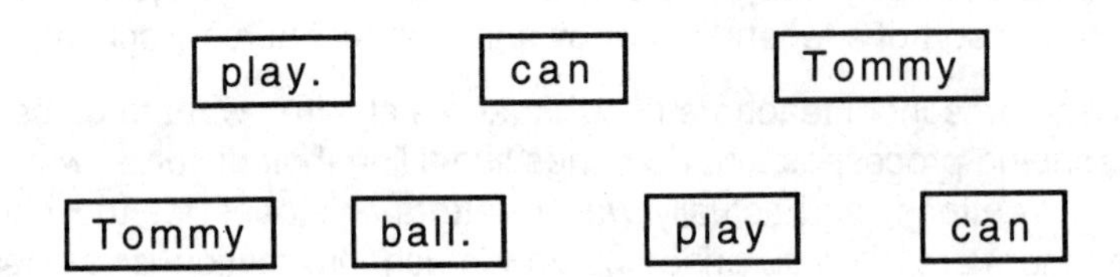

Many children enjoy making sentences about themselves and the important things in their lives. I have found that beginners like to make very long sentences that stretch across a great deal of space. I vividly remember one child who asked for word cards to be made for him so that he could create the following run-on sentence:

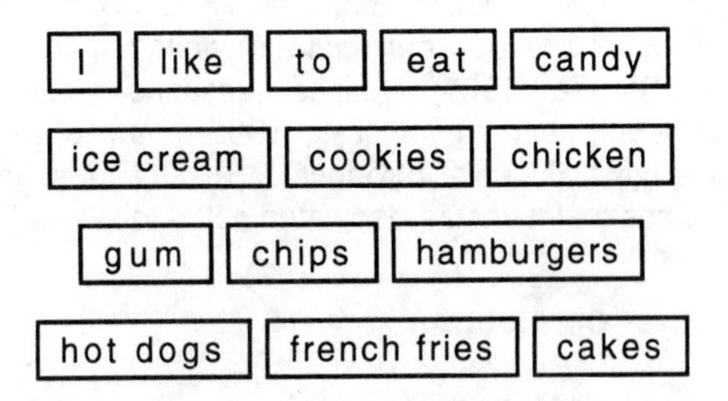

After this young reader had completed the sentence, he wanted to keep it together so that he could add new things to it. The teacher wisely suggested that he tape it together so that he could keep it and unroll it whenever he wanted to read it and show it to people. Our youthful reincarnation of Faulkner thought that was a good idea, and took it upon himself to show the sentence to any visitor that would happen to come near him in the course of the next few weeks.

Technology has made it possible for humans to speak into computers and have their messages encoded in print almost immediately on the screen. The ready availability of such technology would be a significant bridge between speaking and writing, because the speech could be easily coded for subsequent reading. It seems that this would be the ultimate language experience approach for all—a computer that instantly displays any words as you speak them into its microphone. Perhaps learning to read would then become such a simple task that little time would have to be invested in instruction.

The Concept of Fit

One of the most profound aspects of reading instruction has been the concept of how reading materials fit students. Kilgallon (1942) first discussed the concept of *fit* and reading difficulty in terms of word recognition and comprehension. This concept was popularized by Betts (1946), who developed criteria for determining a pupil's independent, instructional, and frustrational reading levels. This was determined by having the pupil read aloud and answer comprehension questions over the material read. Betts' criteria have been the subject of ongoing debate (Beldin, 1970; Guszak, 1985; Powell, 1970) ever since they were first introduced. The criteria for determining independent, instructional, and frustrational reading levels as outlined originally by Betts are indicated in the following chart:

INFORMAL READING INVENTORY CONCEPTS (Betts)

Reading Level	Word Recognition	Comprehension
Independent	99%+	90%
Instructional	95%	75%
Frustrational	90%	50%

Lest we think that the above percentages are infallible, it is important to state that they were just a beginning. Beldin (1970) found that theoretical support for Betts' percentages were lacking. Powell (1970) went even farther and conducted research to see what the word recognition percentages would look like to obtain a minimum comprehension of 70 to 75%. He found that pupils reading preprimer through second-grade materials could comprehend sufficiently with word recognition as low as 83%. Yet, Powell found that pupils reading third-grade (or higher) materials had to have a considerably higher word recognition success in order to sustain the 70 to 75% comprehension. Such findings provided the beginnings of further research into the necessary percentages for different levels of readers.

Whether the students are scored on their first or second readings of a selection makes a tremendous difference (Brecht, 1977). Brecht found that nearly 70% of the subjects could raise their placement level if they read silently before reading orally. In his original study, Betts based his judgments on the students' performance on the second reading. Such findings are consistent with a wealth of information about the effects of rehearsal upon reading skill (Dowhower, 1987). As you will subsequently read, our beginning readers demonstrate sharp differences in their first and second readings.

One of the more interesting studies was that done by Roberts (1976) who observed the performances and subsequent reading attitudes of pupils who were presumably over placed by the Betts criteria. She found that many did quite well in the supposedly frustrational material. She concluded that the Betts criteria were not backed by sufficient evidence to justify their use. Still, the research did not indicate that the concepts of independent, instructional, and frustrational were inappropriate for use.

In classroom studies, a different view has emerged that supports the validity of placing pupils in relatively easy materials (Berliner, 1981). Gambrell, Wilson, and Gantt (1981) found that student reading achievement was benefited by low error rates of 2 to 5%. Beck (1981) makes a strong case that readers should read extensively from easier materials as well as take on the challenge of more difficult materials periodically. Readers have opportunities to develop fluency in the easier materials while they acquire new knowledge and reading strategies in the more challenging text in Clay's Reading Recovery program (Clay, 1979). For years, easy reading has been the centerpiece of our reading programs as children begin their reading day with independent level text (Guszak, 1978, 1985). We have found that many beginners insist upon rereading some stories and books because they want to feel comfortable and unchallenged.

Even as the Betts criteria themselves are problematic, there are basic concerns with issues such as what constitutes an oral reading error (Goodman & Goodman, 1977; Weber, 1970), what constitutes comprehension (Goodman & Goodman, 1965; Hoffman & Baker, 1981; Leu, 1982; Wixson, 1979), and whether other factors, such as rate, should be considered in the judgment (Guszak, 1985; Salmon, 1990).

I feel that the fluency or rate with which a pupil reads materials reveals rather clearly whether pupils are having meaning or word recognition difficulties with text. Consequently, the concept of minimum rates has been used and is gaining recognition (Hoffman & Crone, 1989; Hoffman et al., 1984). By listening to beginners read, a teacher can easily assess the number of words read per minute, and thereby determine whether the pupils need more rehearsal with the materials at hand. I will argue repeatedly that rate is a more valuable monitoring dimension than word recognition. Also, it is much easier for a classroom teacher to obtain rate checks than to calculate the word recognition percentages of a large number of children. You will be reading a great deal about rate in the balance of this text.

Although minimum rate standards have marked a host of research studies (Dowhower, 1987; Moyer, 1976, 1982; Neil, 1980; Samuels, 1979), very little has been said about a *definitive* lower threshold: We simply do not know how slowly pupils can read and still succeed. Some ideas for what that minimum might be have been generated by Guszak (1985), Blair (1980), and Salmon (1990). Further information about the relative performance of pupils with minimal rates was seen in Dowhower's research (1987) which revealed how pupils with very low rates could improve their rates through certain interventions.

Initially, we started out with rate minimums of 45 words per minute for beginning readers but soon found that such rates were too slow. We discovered that If pupils were going to approximate any kind of normal speech in their oral reading, they had to operate considerably faster than 45 words per minute. Consequently, we came up with what we felt were the very lowest **minimum** rates that were necessary for pupils at the beginning reading levels. It's important to emphasize the word minimum because we are not referring to good or average rates, but rather to the very slowest rates possible for success at reading in the levels given. You will note that as a rule-of-thumb, the rate increases ten words for each grade level. This is so because pupils must become increasingly fluent as they read more difficult books.

The rule-of-thumb can be extrapolated to higher level books if you wish. The problem is that higher level readers must read so much faster than the beginners. They must also develop a wide set of speeds for the varying reading tasks.

Minimum Oral Rates for Beginning Readers

1st-Grade Materials:	60 words per minute
2nd-Grade Materials:	70 words per minute
3rd-Grade Materials:	80 words per minute

When these rates are used, the teacher has a quick means of assessing word recognition. Thus, fitting the proper book to the pupil becomes the first important decision faced by a teacher who is attempting to support the pupil's reading development. This will be discussed at length later in the book.

Connected Reading

Allington (1977) raised the critical question when he asked "If they don't read much, how they ever gonna get good?" His survey of Chapter I classes revealed that, on average, the pupils read 43 words of connected text in the course of a day. In a similar study with low reading groups, Allington (1980) found that low readers read less than half the amount of the more able readers.

Seeking to find how much time was spent in connected reading in the course of a day by the normal readers, some surprising findings were noted in a number of studies that sought to describe what was happening at the various elementary grade levels.

Berliner (1981), in a study of the time spent by fifth graders "engaged" in reading, found that many classrooms spent less than one hundred hours in reading during a whole school year. Presumably, the hour referred to all of the reading activities in the course of the day. When you realize that there are normally about 180 school days in the year, it suggests that pupils read for approximately half an hour per day.

Greenwood, Delquardi, and Hall (1981), by contrast, found that fourth graders spent about fifteen minutes of each school day engaged in silent reading. Although there is a drastic difference between the findings of these two studies, they do, taken together, give us an estimate of fifteen to thirty minutes for the average amount of time that students are engaged in silent reading each school day.

Two other teams of investigators, each studying the number of minutes spent on silent reading during the reading period itself, found results that were even more alarming. Kurth and Kurth (1987) found that students in first, third and fifth grades engaged in silent reading for only about ten minutes during a 60-minute reading period. Ysseldyke and

Algozzine (1982-1983) found that second, third, and fourth graders engaged in silent reading in school for about eight minutes per day.

Looking back, we see that the amount of time a pupil spends reading silently in the elementary grades is probably no more than half an hour per day, and could be as short as eight minutes per day. Whether such small doses of reading are enough to enable elementary students to develop good reading habits and skills remains a key question. In posing this question, I am especially concerned that special students may need much more connected reading time than they encounter in the course of any given school day. I have no hard data on the amount of time that special students are engaged in connected reading in the typical classroom, but my hunch is that it is no more than ten minutes per day. Indeed, based on my observations of many different classrooms, I would say that ten minutes per day is a generous estimate of time spent in connected reading.

Before we become too upset about the apparent lack of connected reading time for children, it is imperative to support the intuitively obvious case that connected reading can and does make a difference. Studies of out-of-school reading and in-school reading that support this case will be discussed briefly in the following paragraphs.

In their study of 155 student self-reports of out-of-school activities, Anderson, Wilson, and Fielding (1988) found that book reading was the best predictor of several measures of reading achievement, including gains in reading achievement between second and fifth grades. The authors' main question and answer are quoted directly as follows:

> **Does reading, particularly book reading, cause growth in reading proficiency? The fact that book reading was a significant predictor of growth suggests that the answer is *yes*.**

Further support for the position of home reading can be seen in reports such as *Becoming a Nation of Readers: The Report of the Commission on Reading* (Anderson, Hiebert, Scott, & Wilkinson, 1985) and *What Works: Research About Teaching and Learning* (U.S. Department of Education, 1986).

Evidence that supports the importance of book reading to the improvement of reading proficiency is found in the research of Elley and Mangubhai (1983). Using a **book flood** technique, the authors placed libraries of English storybooks in the classrooms of Fiji children and found that they made much larger gains on achievement tests than the children in the comparison classrooms. The advantage continued to appear in subsequent years. (This unique study, which had a dramatic effect upon the acquisition and use of varied books in classrooms, will be discussed further in Chapter 3.)

The idea that students who read books extensively would improve in their reading proficiency seems so logical that one might wonder why Elley and Mangubhai would have thought that a study like theirs (1983) would be meaningful. However, many different studies of the relation between book reading and gains in reading proficiency have not found such clear-cut support for the developmental value of the sustained sort of reading that occurs when students read books. For example, several studies of McCracken's (1971) Sustained Silent Reading have failed to demonstrate the effectiveness of this approach (Anderson et al., 1988; Miller, 1980). That sustained reading would not improve reading ability is hard to believe, but the findings of these studies clearly show that such is the case.

However, in spite of the conflicting findings of the Anderson study, theoretical support for the value of sustained reading to a student's reading development is not limited to the results obtained in Fiji. Taylor, Frye, and Maruyama (1990), in a carefully controlled study of how much time pupils spent on reading during the reading period at school, found that those who spent more time reading enjoyed significantly greater gains in their reading achievement. Their study tracked the progress of 195 students in Grades 5 and 6. Because of the significance of this study to the main premise of this book, it will be discussed in greater detail in Chapter 3.

For now, I would like to note that Taylor's group found no significant relation between time spent on silent reading at home and achievement gain. Rather, the superior achievement gains were specifically related to the greater amount of time spent on connected reading at school. The Taylor study serves as a strong support of the value of connected reading at school. It provides teachers with a great deal of hope that their efforts can result in significant change in spite of certain home situations. Of course, more study needs to be undertaken on the relative values of home reading and school reading for at-risk readers.

Teachers facing the challenge of helping at-risk readers catch reading may find that merely increasing the time allotted for connected reading may not be sufficient to make these students into good readers. Because many of these pupils lack the elemental skills needed for connected reading, they must reread their materials in order to develop the reading skills that will allow them to benefit from more and more reading. Consequently, the subject of rehearsal becomes the focus of our interest in those pupils who have initial difficulty in learning to read.

Rehearsal Effects

Although connected reading at home or at school is certainly a form of reading rehearsal, the meaning of rehearsal here refers to having the student repeat reading a selection until the student can read the selection fluently with understanding (Chomsky, 1978; Cunningham, 1978; Dowhower, 1987; Moyer, 1976; Samuels, 1979).

Undoubtedly, we have all rehearsed various skills in order to develop mastery. Many of us have routinely had students reread a passage until the students can read the passage with some degree of accuracy. Even the traditional reading strategy of reading silently before reading orally has given credence to the rehearsal effect. Rehearsal began to take on a new dimension when Samuels (1979) and others (Chomsky, 1978; Moyer, 1976) started to relate the rehearsal to some type of criterion performance. The criterion performance for Samuels was 85 words per minute: Students would reread materials until they reached that level. Samuels' research revealed that students could transfer the effects of their improved reading to other materials once they had reached the criterion level in their initial materials.

Theoretical support for the rehearsal procedure can be found in whole language theory (Clay, 1985; Holdaway, 1979; Hoskisson, 1975a, 1975b), information processing paradigms (Samuels & LaBerge, 1983), and verbal efficiency theory (Perfetti & Lesgold, 1979).

Strong support is available to show that positive results occur in reading rate and word recognition accuracy between the first and last reading of the same passage (Carver & Hoffman, 1981; Chomsky, 1976; Dahl & Samuels, 1979; Herman, 1985; Neil 1980; Rashotte and Torgensen, 1985). Evidence exists in some of these studies that the fluency gains carry over to novel passages.

Dowhower (1987) described the effect of two rehearsal procedures on second grade transitional (see Chall, 1983) readers with practiced and unpracticed passages. She found that the transitional readers' rate, accuracy, comprehension and prosodic reading were significantly higher after the repeated reading practice whereby they reached a criterion rate of 100 words per minute. She found that the **tape-assisted rehearsal** condition provided special benefits to those transitional readers who were slower than the others. These latter pupils were able to make dramatic gains with the tape assist that allowed them to move to the simple rehearsal mode later.

Dowhower's study adds weight to the mounting evidence in support of the rehearsal process. Details relative to the use of rehearsal will be forthcoming in the chapters to come.

SUMMARY

The great debate as to whether reading is primarily bottom-up (starting with letters and sounds and building upward) or top-down (starting with meaning and progressing toward smaller units) is no longer valid. It's apparent that reading is an interactive process with both the meaning and graphic elements providing inputs into the complicated process. Although the bottom-up view has had strong support from Chall as well as the Follow Through studies, connected reading has been regarded as the most effective input by many. Because direct teach code emphasis programs have not been compared with effective individualized programs featuring extensive connected reading, there is really no valid basis for the comparison of the two approaches to beginning reading.

The study of emergent literacy has advanced the recognition that literacy is emerging years before a student enters a formal school program. In setting aside the misused concept of reading readiness, emergent literacy proponents seek to make us more aware of the elements of children's emerging literacy. As we look at creating the means that support the emergence of literacy, we seek to help the child meet the following needs: to use language extensively, to experience the joys of listening to stories daily, to handle predictable books and play with them, to delight in musical and other language repetition experiences, and to have people around them who show them how writing works by writing down their messages and notes.

Reading and writing are not separate skills; rather, they are intertwined aspects of literacy. We read what we write and write what we read. Technological programs as well as curricular programs must recognize the interrelatedness and make it possible for students to participate extensively in the reading-writing processes.

That books must fit the skills and interests of the pupils who are reading them is an old concept. Still, the practices of many reading programs ignore what research has shown us about the importance of reading easier materials as well as the dangers of trying to read materials that are too difficult.

It seems almost impossible to learn to read or write if you don't read or write. Still, a lot of evidence suggests that pupils are doing embarrassingly little reading and writing. Rather than devoting instructional time to doing workbook pages and practicing isolated skills, it's apparent that a new commitment to engaged time in reading and writing activities must be generated for all children.

Practice makes perfect, according to the old adage. Appropriate practice certainly makes for better readers when slow readers reread their materials to the point of mastery or automaticity. Countless studies support the efficacy of rehearsal for lower level readers.

STUDY SUGGESTIONS

1. Ask several friends how they believe that people learn to read. See if their descriptions most closely resemble the top down, bottom up, or interactive concepts of reading acquisition. Summarize your findings and share them with your instructor and classmates. Compare notes with your classmates to see what things they found out about adults' perceptions of how they learned to read.

2. Read a story to a preschooler and note the child's responses to the story. Watch to see if the child is interested in the story and pays attention. Hand a picture type book to the child upside down and see if he turns it right side up. Ask the child to read the picture book to you to see whether or not he invents a story to go along with the pictures in the book. If the child does invent a story, note how the story corresponds to the pictures in the book. If the child states that he cannot read, don't push him to invent but rather have him tell you about the meanings of some of the pictures.

3. Recite some common nursery rhymes and see if the pupil joins you in the process. If they child does join you, allow him to finish the lines of certain ones. If the child wants to take over the process and say the rhymes, allow him to do so and attempt to see how many rhymes that he has learned.

3. You might want to keep a journal for the semester in which to record your observations to the tasks at the ends of chapters. If so, it would be well to record the date of each journal entry and the amount of time spent on the task at hand. Record any questions in your journal so that you may ask your instructor or peers about when you come to class.

3

BASIC PRINCIPLES AND PROGRAMS THAT WORK

The selected research from Chapter 2 is combined with additional research to develop a set of five reading program principles. The principles could apply to any reading program, but their inclusion seems particularly important to those students with special program needs.

After the five principles are explored, the reader is presented with brief descriptions of successful programs that have used the principles with very different populations.

FIVE BASIC PRINCIPLES FOR READING INSTRUCTION

From the preceding research discussions and our observations of reading instruction, five principles seem uniquely critical to the process of learning to read.

Reading is caught, not taught.

Reading is caught principally from books.

Reading is caught from books that fit.

Reading is caught when books that fit are read regularly.

Reading is caught when books are shared.

Although the principles could be combined into a single principle, it seems worthwhile to view the implications of each.

Reading is Caught, Not Taught

Much of the current research would argue that reading is taught rather than caught—that teachers teach students to read rather than students learning to read by practice (Brophy & Good, 1990; Lehr, 1986; Osborn, Wilson, & Anderson, 1985). Citing the Follow Through research studies of the 1970s, Brophy and Good (1990) support the favorable findings for direct teach of code emphasis. It must be remembered, though, that highly structured, direct teach types of programs such as DISTAR were being compared with some laissez-faire types of reading programs. Also, the so-called experimental projects did not use true experimental designs (Samuels, 1981). To the best of my knowledge, none of the comparisons that support the direct teach approach have been comparisons with effective individualized programs such as the one being provided in this text. In comparisons, pupils in our individualized programs have produced better results than those in direct teach programs. Some of the most dramatic programs supporting this will be discussed later in this chapter.

Whereas the instructional aspects of reading are stressed in most reading texts (Au & Mason, 1990; Durkin, 1989 ; Stoodt, 1989), the basic position of this book argues that reading is not taught but rather that it is principally caught through extensive experiences with books and reading. Emergent literacy research provides us with insights as to how this process begins in the earliest years (Dyson, 1990; Sulzby, 1985; Teale, 1986).

Marie Clay (1976a) was curious to discover why non-English speaking Samoan children learned to read English better than their English-speaking Maori counterparts. She discovered that the Samoan children were daily participants in a reading tradition whereby the family gathered each day for Bible reading sessions.

Just as the Samoan children "caught" reading by participating in the family literacy experience with the Bible, other children catch reading in a variety of ways and emerge rapidly on the literacy ladder. Some acquire it as they travel through their neighborhoods and observe signs, logos, and print items in various forms. Rural children acquire it by learning the names of feeds, seeds, fertilizers, weed killers, defoliants, and the other print forms that invade food and fiber cultures. Other children require little more than the redundant advertisements and programs that they see on their commercial television in their long days of TV watching.

Because the evidence is so overwhelming that reading is caught in a variety of environmental circumstances, I'm convinced that it is too important to be taught using the traditional basal reader conventions described in the first chapter of this book. Rather, daily experiences with good literature must be the key.

While many people would agree that reading can be caught in supportive environments such as those of the Samoan children observed by Marie Clay, many express doubt as to whether schools can reach children soon enough or with sufficient intensity that the children develop an appreciation for literacy. Legislators must think that early identification and programming are important because the Congress has developed a law that provides intervention to specially handicapped children prior to their third birthday.

While early intervention is desirable, such is not always possible. Therefore, supportive school environments can generate reading through two important inputs: providing extensive listening opportunities where children hear appropriate literature, and providing extensive opportunities for children to read and write about books.

Literary environments require the active sharing of literature as a daily procedure. While some educators consider this to be a value unique to the lower grades, I feel that the practice is appropriate through all grades. There appears to be no upper limit: We see enthusiastic listeners of all ages. In fact, one of the favorite activities of my summer graduate courses are the daily sessions in which individuals share a unique book or book part with others. We have experienced a range of emotions in the process.

While listening to and interacting with others about literature is a great generator of reading interests (Snow & Ninnio, 1986; Whitehurst, 1988), it's somewhat akin to walking by a bakery and smelling the delightful aromas without actually tasting. Tasting involves touching and devouring, just as reading involves readers by immersing them in the story, the characters, and the actions so that they feel that they are themselves in the story. Listening programs must naturally expand into reading programs by permitting pupils' opportunities to touch and taste the books on their own.

Teachers who love and share books with children have often opened the world of literature to many who never knew the satisfactions found in books. After a book is read, the children wish to pick the book up on their own and relive the most exciting and stimulating pages. They wish to read sequels of the story. They wish to see what else the author has written.

Even before the advent of television, there were individuals who received no satisfaction from reading a book. They might be situated in the midst of the most extensive library in the world, yet they would play cards, flip coins, or indulge in some other non-literary activity. These people, and there are many, have probably not been bitten by the reading bug, so to speak. To help such people realize the neat things in books, Lyman Hunt (1969) envisioned a strategy he called USSR—Uninterrupted, Self-sustained, Silent Reading. Hunt believed that many people had not experienced the joy and satisfaction of reading because they had never sat down long enough to give it a fair chance. By allowing pupils the opportunity to select something they wanted to look at or read and disallowing any other activity, he sought to hook pupils on reading. To make the environment supportive of reading, Hunt directed the teacher or leader to read, too, and explicitly stated that no one was to bother anyone—including the teacher. Working on the theory that such a period of time given to reading daily would allow the bonding of books and people, Hunt started with five-minute sessions and progressed to longer reading periods as the natural interests were developed.

Hunt's ideas about bringing books and people together in school settings have been copied by many and given new names (McCracken, 1978). While it seems safe to say that USSR in some form exists in every state, it's equally safe to say that it has not proven to be as successful as one might hope (Anderson et al., 1980; Cline & Kretke, 1980). The problem seems to be with the implementation of the plan rather than with the concept behind USSR.

One of the key principles in the USSR concept, as developed by Hunt, was that everybody should read at the same time. This meant that teachers would provide the modeling to show their pupils that reading was important to them. In school settings, the initial fervor over USSR caused principals to require that everybody, from the principal to the custodian read at the assigned time. While this seemed to be a good idea, it also seemed to be a part of USSR's undoing. Most school people could not keep their commitment to USSR. Principals had to answer phone calls, secretaries had to meet parents, teachers had to fill out lunch reports, and so on. USSR became a less frequent affair—sometimes used only once a week. Thus, the continued exposure to reading was lost.

When USSR or one of its descendants (SSR, DEAR) has been faithfully maintained on a daily basis at a fixed time with active teacher models, I have seen obvious benefits in terms of pupils catching the book habit. Such classrooms provide observational evidence that some nonreaders can become readers over a period of time. Some will not, though, so we must go further with the other principles.

Reading is Caught from Books

> **Each child enters school on his fifth birthday in New Zealand. And he goes home that day with a gift from the teacher which is a symbol of himself as a young scholar, a new book. (Guthrie, 1983c, p.124)**

When our first scholar was a toddler, he carried his *Baby's First Book* proudly as one of his most prized possessions. He shared it with us and would reach down and touch the individual pictures and tell us what they were. For him, the road to literacy was already started.

Whereas the five-year-old New Zealander happily announced his new book on his return from the first day of school, our first grader brought home a tattered first preprimer as his first book from school in December. This book was preceded by what seemed to be ten pounds of ditto and workbook pages.

While beginners in New Zealand are excited about books and reading, many of their counterparts in the U.S. report that reading in school is boring. They equate reading with the one hour period that is called "reading" in the course of each school day.

Although school reading may be called "boring" by some pupils, it's apparent that reading has probably not been boring to children in the following environments:

Home Bible reading (Clay, 1976),
Home story reading (Edwards, in press),
Television *(Captain Kangaroo, Reading Rainbow),*
Nursery school reading.

Clay's (1976) account of the Samoan children's reading success as a result of the daily family reading of the Bible is but one of many similar happenings in fundamental religions where the families spend significant amounts of time reading and reflecting on biblical or other scriptural passages.

Because of the recognized power of home story reading, major projects such as **Reading is Fundamental (RIF)** have been initiated in most states to provide books and training for parents on how to read to their children. Such programs have meant that preschool literacy experiences have been provided for those families who did not have the resources for buying books for their children. While research is limited as to the benefits in terms of reading achievement, there are hopeful findings.

Television has provided programs such as *Mister Rogers' Neighborhood, Captain Kangaroo,* and *Sesame Street* that have provided book sharing experiences with children. One of the more recent programs, *The Reading Rainbow,* has made books its exclusive focus and has shared the finest in contemporary children's literature over the Public Broadcasting System for several years. The benefits of programs like *The Reading Rainbow* are difficult to measure but it seems apparent that the effects on the sales of children's book has been amazing since U.S. citizens spend millions of dollars annually on children's books.

Always the standby for nursery programs, book reading has always been at the center of the curriculum. It's estimated that book reading constitutes at least a fourth of the daily quiet activities in nursery school curricula.

That many pupils are catching reading from their preschool experiences is well documented (Teale, 1986). What needs to be realized is that these experiences must be continued right into the formal schooling experience in kindergarten and first grade if readers are to build on the foundation that has already been laid in many circumstances. Even if the foundation has not been laid, the need for book reading is all the more important and must be the driving force of reading instruction.

For reading to be caught, a wide array of trade books must be present in the classrooms of kindergarten and graded classrooms. Of course, the opportunities must be provided for them to share these books in meaningful ways so that they view them as friends, much like the toddler who carries his precious book around.

Reading is Caught from Books that Fit

The concept of **fit** seems simple-minded. Few adults would consider purchasing shoes or clothing that didn't fit, yet some of these folks would never pause to consider whether a book fits a given child's interests , experiences, and reading capabilities.

Interest is a tricky thing because pupils can be interested in certain books but may still be unable to read them with sufficient satisfaction or ease. While their interest may build bridges that allow them to succeed, it's not a sure thing. While interest should be one of the key judgments in reading a book, it must be realized that interest may often be the byproduct of the success of reading a book. This is a critical point that must be considered whenever pupils are provided with opportunities to read books.

Reading capabilities refers to the skills arsenal a pupil brings to any given book. This skills arsenal may be counted in terms of instant sight words, word analysis patterns, word structures, and a host of other things. What is important is that the arsenal has to be measured against the skills required to read any given book. Consequently, if we provide a student with an arsenal of skills that is normally associated with the end of first grade and ask him to read a third grade level book we may see an instant mismatch that can't be remedied even though he is interested in the book and knows something about it.

As seen in Chapter 2, the concept of "fit" in terms of books was initially articulated by Kilgallon (1942) and popularized by Betts (1946) when he referred to pupil reading skills as **independent, instructional,** and **frustrational** (see Chapter 2). Since then, the concepts have been widely discussed and a variety of criteria applied to each (Ekwall & Shanker, 1983; Gonzales, 1975; Guszak, 1985; Hunt, 1969; McCracken, 1966; Powell, 1968). While many reading authorities subscribe to the concept of fit as first described by Betts and Kilgallon, others feel that the constructs have little value for reading instruction.

It is most common to hear the term "frustrational level" associated with a pupil's reading behavior because the term has been such a long standing descriptor of reading difficulty.

Curiously, the term is seldom used in other academic disciplines, even though the concept seems equally applicable.

That such a thing as a "frustrational level" does exist was verified experimentally by Ekwall (1974), who attached measures of respiration and discovered that individuals experienced telltale signs of stress when the reading tasks were beyond their abilities.

While word recognition and comprehension have been at the fore of measures of reading fit, McCracken (1967) and some test developers have traditionally added a rate or fluency criterion. We have emphasized the fluency determination because of its power to determine initially how a student is performing in a given piece of text (Blair, 1980; Guszak, 1985; Hoffman et al, 1984; Salmon, 1990). By counting the number of words a pupil is reading orally in a minute, the teacher has a quick and accurate way to make valid assumptions about reading difficulty.

In our search to establish some minimal performance rates for oral reading, the search took us back to some of the research on silent reading rates (Carver, 1983; Taylor, 1958, 1960, 1965; Tinker, 1965). Taylor (1965) measured reading rates through the study of eye movements of a wide variety of readers reading materials considered suitable for their grade level. His results revealed a steady growth in average rates with comprehension from 80 words per minute for first graders up to 280 words per minute for college students.

While Burmeister (1983) questioned the reliability of word counting because of the varying length of words, Carver (1983) argued the practical nature of counting words rather than syllables. Coleman (1971) supported the use of the word unit for counting by determining that the correlation between average word length measured by words and syllables was .97.

Determining the fit of books seems to be one of those necessary skills that an effective reading teacher must possess. If that teacher can have an easy and reliable means of making such judgments it is all the more likely that such a system will be used. In Chapter 5 you will learn more about how such checks are made.

Reading is Caught When Books That Fit are Read Regularly

Allington's (1977) question in the previous chapter that said "If they don't read much, how they ever gonna get good?" can only be answered with a resounding, **"They won't!"**

A recent survey of how eighth graders in this country spend their time (U.S. Department of Education, 1990) found that they spend 1.8 hours per week out of school on outside reading. When this figure is compared to their 21.7 hours a week of watching the home TV, one has an indication that many won't ever get good. *(A Profile of the American Eighth-Grader,* Superintendent of Documents, U.S. Government Printing Office, Washington, D.C. 20402, 1990, S/N 065-000.00404-6).

Anderson et al. (1985) have documented that out-of-school readers do achieve better than their non reading friends: They found that book reading was the best predictor of reading achievement in grades 2 through 5.

Because it is difficult to control what happens in a pupil's home environment, it seems all the more imperative to turn around the current use of school time that suggests repeatedly that little reading practice occurs in the course of a school day. Recall the studies discussed previously in Chapter 2 that indicated that pupils in the elementary grades spent from eight to fifteen minutes a day engaged in silent reading (Greenwood et al., 1981; Kurth & Kurth, 1987; Ysseldyke & Algozzine 1982-1983).

In their study cited in the previous chapter, Taylor, Frye, and Maruyama (1990) provide clear evidence that time spent on reading at school will contribute significantly to pupil gains in reading achievement. In that study, 195 fifth- and sixth-graders kept daily reading logs from mid-January through mid-May. Using a stepwise multiple regression analysis, the researchers concluded:

> **...the amount of time spent on reading during the reading period contributed significantly to gains in students' reading achievement.**

Since this was the first major study to support the logic of practice, it should provide an important basis for the "regular practice" step.

Regular school practice is where things must begin. Teachers can support their school practice by calling on beginners to take practice readers home for parents or others to listen and sign off on daily. Sometimes the teacher doesn't have to do this because the in-school reading will be such a "turn-on" that the pupils will want to take their books home to keep reading. In any event, we have seen the dramatic effects of home reading practice upon the development of reading in the early grades.

One of the detriments to reading practice in schools is the belief by many administrators and teachers that the separate "skills" are fundamental to reading and that students must spend the bulk of their time in such skills practice. What this "skills practice" translates to is workbook pages, drill sheets, and direct teach lessons on phonics. Although these practices have been widely disparaged (Anderson et al., 1985), the practices continue.

An important part of the skills phenomenon that impedes connected reading is the heavy testing built into the reading series. Many teachers feel compelled to prepare their pupils for the bevy of skill tests that are scrutinized closely as a measure of the teacher's effectiveness in reading instruction. Such tests are the unit tests produced by basal series, state mandated minimum competency tests, and standardized achievement tests. In almost every instance, the subtests on phonic and structural analysis drive a great deal of instruction. An interesting study by Adams (1990) reveals that a pupil's reading ability as measured by a basal series placement test often has little to do with their success on the criterion reference test of the same book. She also found that most of the discrete subtests were not significant predictors of connected reading success.

The calls for increased connected reading practice appear to be the dominant theme of most reading authorities who discuss reading methods (Anderson et al., 1985; Au & Mason, 1990; Clay, 1979; Cunningham et al., 1989; Durkin, 1989; Stoodt, 1989).

Reading Is Caught When Books Are Shared

Some pupils catch reading without this step, but the presence of book and story sharing contributes significantly to the pupil's understanding and appreciation. We have already seen the power of reading aloud to children (Anderson, Hiebert, Scott, & Wilkinson, 1984) as well as the vocabulary acquisition from listening to stories (Elley, 1989; Teale, 1981).

When students can talk with one another about books and stories, the stories take on new dimensions and the students have opportunities to view the perspectives of others.

The most effective sharing sessions are seldom whole-class discussions; rather, they are intimate sharing sessions between a few pupils who have read the same story. In some of our classrooms, four pupils reading the same novel stop periodically and discuss their responses to the plot, characters, and actions. They seem to look forward to the discussions and gain a great deal of insight from each other.

Currently, research on the effects of shared reading is emerging in a literature called "literature circles" or "reading clubs" (Daniels, 1994). Our observations of pupils in second through eighth grades in small novel groups coincides with the findings of these people in that pupils are obtaining the following outcomes from such experiences:

- all pupils are getting opportunities to contribute because of the decreased group size;
- most pupils are taking advantage of the small group size and are contributing;
- the levels of the oral answers are consistently higher than the levels of their written answers;
- the complexity of language is considerably greater in the oral answers than in the written answers.

Beyond the quality of the thinking about books, sharing tends to sell books and authors to children. As pupils verbalize why they like the characters in a Judy Blume book, they generate reasons why they like the author's books. Obviously, this leads them to seek out books by this author so that they can laugh and share with others the neatest experiences.

While the importance of book sharing is hardly a new principle, its importance has become increasingly important as we design programs for special students. The lower reading students, especially, must be afforded with opportunities to share their thoughts and feelings with others who are reading the same stories and books.

Although some might argue that reading is taught rather than caught, they would have little argument with the notion that reading is generated by reading and sharing carefully fitted books every day of the week in school.

PROGRAMS THAT WORK

This section presents example programs that have utilized the preceding four principles about learning to read. These programs have been selected because they essentially represent different populations of readers. It is important to demonstrate that programs such as the one in this book are not limited to a simple population set. It should be pointed out that the following are representative programs.

Included for discussion are the following programs: Fiji Book Flood (Elley & Mangubhai, 1983); Buda Reading Program (Guszak, 1989); Burnet Reading Program (1993); Day Reading Program 1992); Inmate Reading Program (Aaron, 1990): STAR Reading Program (1990), and the Wubbena Reading Program (Wubbena, 1990).

Fiji Book Flood

The Fiji Book Flood (Elley & Mangubhai, 1983) really began as a study of first- and second-language learning for 380 nine- to eleven-year-olds from eight rural Fijian schools with few books available.

Sixteen participating teachers were given directions in two different methods of encouraging the pupils to read 250 high-interest story books in English. One group was taught the Shared Book (Holdaway, 1979) method and the other used a Sustained Silent Reading method (Hunt, 1960; McCracken, 1971). The experimental students replaced the twenty to thirty minutes of formal reading activities each day with Shared Book or Sustained Silent Reading activities. These students were compared with a control group experiencing the normal structured English language program with little emphasis upon reading.

Pre-tests in first and second language as well as reading skill were administered to both groups. After eight months, post-test results showed that the pupils exposed to many stories progressed in reading and listening comprehension at twice the normal rate. It furthermore confirmed the hypothesis that high-interest story reading has an important role to play in second language learning. After 20 months, the gains had increased even further and had spread to related language skills.

When one further considers that the books were bought on average for $2.00 a piece and that the Shared Group teachers had three days of in service training and the Sustained Silent Reading teachers had no training, it's apparent that we're seeing the power of books and connected reading rather than the power of large money and time expenditures.

Buda Reading Program

The Buda Reading Program (Guszak, 1989) has been operational for 19 years in Buda, Texas, a suburb south of Austin, Texas. Operated initially as the training program for the education of pre- service students from The University of Texas at Austin, this program has grown into an exemplary program that has been given various awards for its reading achievement.

The Buda Program is a completely individualized reading program that starts in the first grade, where every student engages in thirty to fifty minutes of connected reading (independent and instructional) and fifteen to twenty minutes of written comprehension (related to books read) as part of the daily routine. That daily routine also includes a writing workshop of one hour's length.

The pupils beyond the first grade initially self-select books from a wide array of reading materials. If they select well they are allowed to continue in the book selected. If not, the teacher offers them a book that will meet the criteria of ease and difficulty. Students in second grade read, on average, 35 minutes a day and 15 pages a day, whereas fifth graders average 40 minutes a day and 20 pages a day in more difficult text.

In the initial years of the university program the Buda teachers operated a traditional reading program. As a part of the relationship with the university program, most teachers voluntarily adopted the techniques of individualization. In time, the school district hired more and more university program graduates. As this book is written, 29 of the 32 teachers in grades 1 through 5 are implementing the program.

The achievement levels for the school have climbed to the point where the program schools are among the highest in Texas on the state mandated criterion reference tests (*Austin American-Statesman,* 1990) and the achievement tests for reading are consistently above the 90th percentile. It should also be pointed out that this is not an affluent school district in terms of money spent on the elementary school pupils. In fact, the elementary school expenditure of $1835 per pupil ranks it among the lowest in the state.

Beyond developing capable, willing readers, the Buda project has produced a large number of reading teachers each year. Approximately fifty new teachers are trained on site every academic year in this program. These trainees go on to become beginning reading teachers in many different school districts in Texas and other states.

Burnet Reading Program (Burnet, Texas)

In the Fall 1993 semester the Burnet supervisors, principals, and teachers made a series of trips to the Buda Elementary and Dahstrom Middle Schools to learn more about starting individualized reading in their schools.

Leading the way was Charles Williams and his staff at the Pierce Street Elementary School. The fifth grade team led by Mrs. Melton and Mrs. Smith gathered a large array of books, procured questions from other schools, wrote questions, and launched their reading program before Christmas. By February, they had instructed other classes and the program was underway.

The staff and parents were so impressed with their initial results that they brought in teachers and staff from other schools in and out of the city and showed off the pupils' on task work and success in both reading and writing. In February 1994, the board of education gave them financial support for implementing the program district wide the following year.

One of the highlights of the program prior to formal testing was a series of letters from the students telling about how much they were reading and how much they were liking to read.

Mr. Williams and his staff were using their funds to buy more and more books for their book hungry pupils.

This program is now located in all of the elementary schools in Burnet as well as in classrooms in the middle school.

Day Reading Program (San Angelo, Texas)

Perplexed by low TAAS (Texas Academic Assessment Skills) in reading, Principal Gloria Weatherman challenged her teachers to find ways to help their children become better readers. Their search led them to Buda, Texas and the Buda Primary and Buda Elementary Schools.

Coming to Buda with Mrs. Weatherman on the Morning of September 28, 1992 was a first grade teacher (Rebecca Amyx), a second grade teacher (Joann Fuchs), a third grade teacher (Judy Knight), and a fourth grade teacher (Kathy Hammons). After visiting classrooms at their grade levels, the teachers and principal gathered in the library to discuss what they had seen. After having their questions answered, all agreed that they wanted to implement.

Back in San Angelo, the four teachers, with the full support of Mrs. Weatherman, initiated their version of what they had seen. When a consultant from Buda was asked to go to San Angelo to see how they were doing, Principal Weatherman brought in the other Day teachers grade by grade to see what the four had started. Each grade level team, the principal, and the consultant visited the guinea pig teachers' reading classes and participated in the reading period. An analysis of what was happening was conducted on the spot.

Within days, most of the Day teachers had implemented individualized reading in their classrooms. Again, the consultant was asked to return to see how they were doing. He was amazed to see a full school implementation with a high level of commitment from the entire faculty.

While the obvious payoff was the pupils' interest and practice in reading, another payoff awaited. In May, when the school received their TAAS Scores, they were astonished. In reading, the school scores averaged 84, second only to a more affluent school which had an average of 86. Most surprising was the fact that Day was one of the lowest SES (social economic status) schools in the district and had climbed beyond all but one of the 14 schools in the district.

Word spread fast and two other schools scheduled wide spread implementation for the following school year. Currently, the following schools are also programming: Bellaire, Goliad, Glenmore, Rio Vista, and San Jacinto.

Inmate Reading

E.B. Aaron (1990), a Curriculum and Instruction professor at Texas Southern University, adds a new dimension to the "reading is caught, not taught" theory in his description of his work with inmates who were taking a Developmental Reading course through a community college so they could improve their reading skills and get college credit at the same time. After having witnessed the shutdown of such programs because the students didn't wish to revisit the SRA boxes of their past schooling, Aaron embarked upon the idea of sharing vital literature with the students. He began by reading to them before engaging them in their own reading.

Aaron describes the excitement of one student who became emotionally involved with the reading:

> The impact of model reading is evidenced by the fact that one of the students became so excited that he started pounding his desk as he read the remainder of the piece with me. "I'm sorry Dr. Aaron," he said after we finished. "I just couldn't help myself."
>
> I knew then that I had struck a nerve, and the rest of the semester would be a joy.

Using a wide variety of pieces that he thought would appeal to adults and depict real life situations with which these people could identify, he provided things for them to read like:

Why I Went to the Woods—Thoreau

The Drum Major Instinct—Martin Luther King

For White Only—Dick Gregory

The Gettysburg Address—Abraham Lincoln

Who Am I?—Felice Holman

I Am—June Jordan

Emphasizing literary reading, discussions of what was, and practice in proper phrasing and intonation, Aaron led the inmate students to use context to discover the word meanings in things like *I Have a Dream* (King).

Aaron printed the positive responses of the five inmates in his initial class and related how the word got out that this was now a class worth taking. The next semester he had 29 students enrolled.

Aaron's report reveals the same kinds of positive reading experiences that Fader (1968, 1971) illustrated when he matched disadvantaged youths with meaningful books.

Like the other programs described, Aaron's program proved to be very inexpensive to operate . As was the case in the other programs, the emphasis was placed on getting the appropriate books for the subjects to read.

Star Reading Program (Lampasas, Texas)

STAR (students targeted at risk) were identified for special help. This resulted in special funding for classes to help these pupils. For their model, the teachers liked what they had seen a first year teacher from our program doing in a Lampasas Elementary School a year or two earlier. Some of the teachers had attempted to follow her pattern of individualized reading whereby the pupils were reading daily from independent and instructional level books and doing special comprehension tasks over the instructional level book.

Seeking special help in the fall of 1992, the STAR teachers asked their superintendent for special help in order that they might refine what they had been attempting to do on their own. With the aid of a consultant from Buda, the teachers decided to observe the implementations in a first grade and second grade room. Armed with seating charts with the books the various pupils were reading, the visiting teachers and consultant went in and observed how well on task the students were, their independent and instructional level reading rates, their written comprehension answers, and the teachers' behavioral management techniques. Emerging from these sessions were further sessions on how to meet the individual needs of pupils.

After the refinements were implemented in all of the STAR program rooms, the teachers observed their pupils' progress and waited for the measures of their success. Those measures indicated that most of the students were reading successfully at grade level by the end of the school year.

Best of all, most of the students developed a love of reading that was demonstrated by voluntary reading of a wide number of chapter books.

Wubbena Reading Program

This program was developed in Weslaco, a small town in the Rio Grande Valley of Texas, eight miles from the border of Mexico. Economically, its citizens are among the lowest wage earners in the United States. Ninety four percent of the population is Hispanic and there is a steady influx from Mexico of pupils who lack formal schooling.

For more than a decade Richard Wubbena (1983, 1990) built and operated a reading program that produced results unlike those of any similar school district in the Rio Grande Valley or the United States. When he started the program in the first grade in 1980, pupil achievement was at the 12th percentile. Since the test had no norm base that compared with his Hispanic students, the idea of giving such a test would have been rejected by many on the grounds that there was no comparable norm group. Still, Wubbena gave the test after his first year of programming and found that achievement had climbed to the 66th percentile in the first year. Results have been maintained over the decade that validate the progress of different cohort groups through their school experience.

Wubbena's program was very much like the one at Buda except that he placed a much greater emphasis on the oral language development of the Spanish-dominant pupils. Like students in the Buda program, Wubbena's students read thirty to sixty minutes a day in connected reading materials (basal). After this, they did a variety of written comprehension work related to the vocabulary and concepts of their story. This "seat work" occupied them most of the morning while the teacher conferred with each pupil individually. In this conference, the student had to read to the teacher, answer questions orally about his reading, and discuss key vocabulary elements.

Wubbena and his staff prepared all the necessary written tasks that went along with the program, and used no commercial workbooks or ditto sheets. Beyond this, a special teacher in each school, designated as a "helper teacher," went into classrooms and actually worked with individual teachers to help them master the program operation.

The Joint Dissemination Review Panel (JDRP) validated this program in 1983 as an exemplary program that had achieved significant results over a period of years. The program continued to produce at the same consistency under Wubbena's direction.

It should be noted that the Wubbena program operated on a cost factor of $25 per pupil per year (Wubbena, 1983). Once again, the reality surfaces that it's more than money that makes for a successful program.

SUMMARY AND COMMENTARY

Basically, the answer for relevant reading instruction is formulated into five critical principles. These principles are:

> ***Reading is caught, not taught.**
>
> **Reading is caught principally from books.**
>
> **Reading is caught from books that fit.**
>
> **Reading is caught when books that fit are read regularly.**
>
> **Reading is caught when books are shared.**

When I argue that reading is caught rather than taught, I don't mean to suggest that there is no role for the teacher to teach. Rather, my concern is that the teaching role is secondary to the teacher's role in creating the reading environment, obtaining the necessary books, developing pupil to pupil support systems, supervising pupil selections, and finally observing the reading process in action and taking whatever actions are necessary to resolve problems.

My view of the teacher is that this person should be a student of the naturally occurring reading process apparent in programs employing the five principles. If teachers are to facilitate that process, they must observe the *pupil + book* equation daily and learn when to stay out of the equation as well as when to enter it.

Programs that illustrate the principles of this book include the following: Buda Reading Program, Burnet Reading Program, Day Reading Program, Inmate Reading Program, STAR ReadingProgram, and the Wubbena Reading.

STUDY SUGGESTIONS

1. Ask your friends to describe how and when they learned to read. Find out if any learned to read prior to entering kindergarten or first grade. For those who remember such early reading, see if they can identify the people who influenced their early reading. For those who learned to read at school, determine who influenced their reading most.
2. Ask your friends about the first books they remember. Have them name these books and describe their experiences with them to you. Make notes to see how many titles were remembered by several of your friends.
3. Ask your friends about any negative experiences they may have had with reading or reading instruction. Try to determine whether any of the negative experiences were associated with difficult books, reading group placements, or whatever.
4. Ask your friends about the kinds of reading materials they read in the early grades. See if they have any memories of oral reading experiences in groups.

4

GATHERING APPROPRIATE BOOKS

Once upon a time, not very long ago, reading instruction was thought of in terms of the following equation:

Reading instruction = Basals + Workbooks + Supplementals

Millions of dollars were pumped into the basal system of reading instruction by school districts that sought to buy the periodic packages, which included the following pieces:

- basal readers
- teacher manuals
- pupil workbooks
- pupil placement tests
- pupil skill battery tests
- ditto master sets

Although basals and basal practices have long been questioned (Chall, 1967; Guszak, 1985; Veatch, 1978), a shift away from the basals began in the 1980s when **The California Initiative** sought to turn reading instruction in the direction of whole language as seen in contemporary children's literature. The movement soon took on the name of "whole language reading" or "literature-based reading programs" (Anderson, Hiebert, Scott, & Wilkinson, 1985; Clyde & Mills, 1990; Goodman, 1986; Hiebert & Colt, 1989; Stephens, 1991) and has continued to grow in strength annually. For many advocates of whole language reading there is no longer a place for basal readers.

As we view the important concept of helping pupils to catch reading from their use of books that fit and that they read extensively, we need to look at the prime forces of both whole language programs and basal reader programs.

Whole Language Programs

Reading people have traditionally embraced new "descriptors" of programs that cross the reading horizon. In the last thirty years, we have experienced a veritable galaxy of new programs. In the 1960s, we saw the introduction of control readers, S.R.A. Reading Laboratories, and various and sundry linguistic programs. The 1970s witnessed multisensory reading, meaning emphasis, code emphasis, as well as management-based programs such as Fountain Valley and Wisconsin Design. Code emphasis programs continued into the 1980s and were joined by "on level" reading programs and a host of "critical thinking" programs.

Unfortunately, these labels failed to communicate discrete sets of materials and practices. Rather, they served only as names for a wide variety of happenings. Because of the problem with labels, it seems prudent to look at what a program "does" rather than what it is called.

Whole language seems to represent a wide array of practices (Stephens, 1991). Because of the prominence of the movement, the Richard C. Owen Publishing Company has been sending out a monthly newsletter called *Teacher Networking—The Whole Language Newsletter.* The newsletter provides support to the Whole Language Umbrella which is a "confederation of whole language teacher support groups and individuals." Goodman, Bird, and Goodman (1991) have published *The Whole Language Catalogue,* which, in the publisher's words, is "packed with nuts and bolts ideas and strategies, hands-on resources, holistic theory and philosophy, language stories, and more."

Presumably, whole language reading practices deal with language in its more complete form, for example, pupil-dictated experience stories, pupils reading a great book and discussing it with a teacher (Junior Great Books, Trevise, 1984), or cooperative learning on a given book (Stevens, Madden, Slavin, & Farnish, 1987). The critical factor appears to be that the student reads a whole piece of text rather than some portion of text, such as a few letters, isolated words, or sentences.

Some whole language programs seem to bring the high school literature classroom to the elementary school through literature study whereby every pupil reads from the same book and participates in a teacher-led literary discussion of the book. Such a move seems to be a step in the direction of producing a younger version of the high school literature course. I have serious problems with such programs.

Basal Reader Programs

Basal readers have been the dominant form of reading instruction in America since the 1840s, when the McGuffey readers came into existence (N. Smith, 1963). Featuring controlled vocabulary, oral reading, and excerpts from the classics, these readers formed the backbone of the reading program for the graded school. At the start of the twentieth century, silent reading and standardized tests became prominent parts of the picture. During the mid 1980s, it was estimated that basal reading materials were used weekly by 90 to 95% of American school children (Flood & Lapp, 1986).

Controlled vocabulary, the feature by which words are introduced gradually through the program, has been the most significant feature of the basals. Vocabulary buildups for the crucial primary grades have included approximately 3,000 words in recent years, which are often structured much like the following example:

First Grade	Readiness Book ——	10 words
	Preprimer 1 ——	35 new words

	Preprimer 2	40	new words
	Preprimer 3	55	new words
	Primer	100	new words
	First Reader	200	new words
Second Grade	Second Reader/1	450	new words
	Second Reader/2	450	new words
Third Grade	Third Reader/1	750	new words
	Third Reader/2	750	new words

Contributing to the dominance of the basal reader has been the "complete program" notion whereby the basal attempts to provide for five days of reading instruction containing activities for every day of the week. The five day basal program as glimpsed in the first chapter of this book presumably contained all the necessary materials as well as the necessary teacher directives to support the following framework:

Day of the Week	Teacher Role with Group	Independent Work
Monday	Build background for story	Workbook pages
	Separate skill lesson	
Tuesday	Introduce new story vocabulary	Workbook pages
	Separate skill lesson	
Wednesday	Guided silent reading	Workbook pages
	Separate skill lesson	
Thursday	Oral rereading (round robin reading)	Workbook pages
	Separate skill lesson	
Friday	Enrichment	

From our vantage point, there is justification for the basal readers without the teachers' manuals and accompanying materials. We believe that some of these readers provide a valuable **vocabulary control** for certain pupils in the beginning stages of reading. They may have advantages over well-selected sets of children's literature.

We find little justification for the five-day basal format, the teacher's manual, the workbooks, and the traditional handling of basal reading instruction in the three reading group structure. Rather, we have used the readers and thrown out the rest of it. Our reasons include the following:

Building Backgrounds. We would argue, for the most part, that the stories placed in a basal series normally draw from student experiences, real or vicarious, and don't require teachers to waste pupils' time by following the guidance of the book. In recent years, the emphasis upon building story webs, meaning maps, and other such things appear to be overdone to the point of delaying pupil interaction with text.

Introducing New Vocabulary. After pupils can read the first few words of their beginning readers, we are reluctant to pre-teach vocabulary because we feel that it defeats the fundamental purpose of reading, which is to use what you know to figure out what you don't know. When this attitude and skill is instilled from the start, pupils look at word forms, word order, and meaning clues in order to generate a prediction that they can immediately test. As students progress, they need to quickly identify words that seem critical to the reading and learn to use things like the glossary to unlock necessary pronunciations and word meanings.

I'm impressed by the research that suggests the limitations of pre-teaching vocabulary and points to the values obtained from extensive reading practice (Fielding, Wilson, & Anderson, 1986; Nagy, Herman, & Anderson, 1985).

Guided Silent Reading. This task has been considered of key importance because the teacher guides the pupils to the most important happenings in a story. The reality is that this is a skill that is quickly learned when pupils are allowed to read at their own speed. The classroom practice of asking pupils to read silently and raise their hand when they have found the answer ensures that fast readers answer all the questions while slower readers quit trying to compete.

Oral Rereading. This practice usually means "**round robin**" reading where each student dutifully waits to read his assigned paragraph or page. Prior to his turn, the next student spends his time polishing up his designated paragraph so that he won't appear foolish in front of the other pupils. The slower reader is prompted until he finishes his agonizing paragraph. Besides being a boring waste of time for most pupils concerned, there are serious questions about the negative effects of such practice (Austin & Morrison, 1963; Durkin 1983; Goodman, 1976; Guszak 1985). If teachers want pupils to maximize practice, they will turn the round-robin reading into a situation whereby each pupil reads on his own and the teacher moves about and monitors individual pupils. Those pupils who need to reread text can do so on their own as often as is needed without the worry of what the person nearby will think.

Workbooks Workbooks fit under the title of "extended skills", which include the daily teacher skills lessons detailed by the teacher's manual and those same skills, embodied in accompanying workbook and duplicator pages. Planned so that the teacher can have a full compliment of busy work for most of the children, these materials are very expensive in terms of the cost package and keep pupils away from the most important aspect of reading, the connected reading of text (Anderson, Hiebert, Scott, & Wilkinson, 1985). Another rap on the materials is that the so-called "independent work" materials are rarely independent in nature (Fitzgerald, 1979) and force pupils to deal with materials that are frequently too difficult.

At the outset of the 1990s, the basal reader publishers became more sensitive to their critics from the whole language movement and moved toward the development of a stronger literature base.

Since basal readers moved totally away from the idea of controlled vocabulary and word order, some teachers will want to search for old basals for those pupils unable to prosper from the newer books without vocabulary control features. In our experience, the old 1960's Scott, Foresman basal readers are the best materials we can give certain slow readers. Because of the careful vocabulary control and redundancy, we are able to move pupils quickly through these readers to a point where they can pick up and read other materials in a short time. We feel that such would not be possible without the vocabulary control.

Curiously, basal readers have responded to criticisms by increasing the rapidity of word introduction. The number of words introduced in the first grade over four decades:

Publishers	1960s	1970s	1980s	1990s
Houghton Mifflin -	315	510	463	1875
Macmillan -	335	675	593	2238

As illustrated, vocabulary increased slightly every decade until the 1990s when the "whole language" movement virtually ended vocabulary control. Curiously, in addition to more difficult vocabulary, each new decade also saw sharp increases in the amount of space given to illustrations. This meant that pupils had less textual reading opportunities with more vocabulary challenges than they had in each previous adoption. In other words, the pupils had a smaller amount of connected reading material in which to read a much larger number of new vocabulary.

In noting the increasing vocabulary and the diminished practice opportunities in the newer reading materials, I feel that there is a major need for beginning reading materials with controlled vocabulary. To help teachers manage this problem, we are encouraging them to identify the vocabulary of certain beginning reading materials and construct buildup readers (discussed later in this chapter) that provide some vocabulary redundancy.

Whole Language and Basal Programs Blend Together

With the replacement of basal reading by whole language literacy based programs in the nineties, one might expect to find a radically different structure. The truth is that the structure of the basal reading program has simply been transposed to the new literary readers. Consequently, you have the old and the new looking something like this:

Basal Reader Lesson Format	**Literature Based Reading Program**
Build background for **story** Separate skill lesson (workbook)	Build background for **book** Separate skill lesson (journal)
Introduce new **story** vocabulary Separate skill lesson (workbook)	Introduce new **book** vocabulary Separate skill lesson (journal)
Guided **silent** reading Separate skills lesson (workbook)	Guided **oral** reading (teacher reads as pupils follow along in their books) Separate skills lesson (journal)
Oral **rereading** (each pupils takes a turn and reads a paragraph or page) Separate skills lesson (workbook)	Oral **shared reading** (teacher and pupils choral read story read by teacher) Separate skills lesson (journal)
Enrichment	Pupils read story individually (extra help provided for those with difficulty)

Rather than placing students in three reading groups, reading instruction is done with the whole class. Whereas the teacher previously built the background for the new story, she now introduces the new book. Skills practice is very much the same as in the past except the skills materials are no longer called workbooks but rather carry the title of something like "journal."

New vocabulary is introduced for the book rather than the story since the focus is not on reading whole books. Initially, the books are very short. This stage of the lesson is followed by the obligatory journal pages of skills.

Previously, the children's first reading of the story was silent. Now, the first reading is usually done by the teacher with the pupils following along in their text. This is intended to give them a model of how the reading should sound in order that the students will be better prepared to read it on their own later.

On the day after the pupils have followed along as the teacher read, they are provided with the experience of reading in unison with the teacher and the other pupils. After another round of journal pages or some other skills activity, they are asked to read the story on their own. Those who have trouble are supposed to be helped by more able readers in the class. Very slow readers are sometimes provided with tape assists to help them read the story on their own.

Separate skills lessons in word recognition and comprehension are still found in the teacher's manual. The accompanying pages for the skills practice is now placed in the journals as well as separate ditto sheets.

WHOLE LANGUAGE FOR LISTENING AND READING

In light of the previous discussion, it seems important at this point in the book to make a distinction between those **1) books that should be read to the pupils** and those **2) books that should be read by the pupils.** While pupils may subsequently read some of the books that are read to them, it seems important to establish a dual curriculum of books. On the one hand, we have books that the teacher will read to the pupils to motivate interest as well as those books which will stimulate deeper thinking. At the same time, pupils must have access to books that they can read on their own with as little help as possible.

LISTENING

For those children who have been read to as toddlers, the book-experience of listening to the teacher is always a highlight. For some of those children who lack such backgrounds, the listening experience has to be acquired over time.

Children's books are coming fast and furiously and number in excess of 40,000 (Huck, Helper, & Hickman, 1987). No longer do these books limit themselves to the nostalgia of happiness and innocence but rather chronicle the realities of the day such as death, child abuse, drug abuse, and other contemporary problems. Although Huck, Helper, and Hickman have developed lists of the 100 books children should have read to them at different ages, many other authorities argue that situational concerns mandate the books chosen for any particular child or group of children.

There are numerous studies that support the values of reading aloud to children. Irwin (1960) found that the systematic reading of stories to infants over an 18-month period increased spontaneous vocalizations. Cazden (1965) found that parent reading stimulated parent-child bonding as well as the conversations about pictures. Chomsky (1972) found a high positive correlation between children's linguistic stages of development and their previous exposure to literature. Elley (1989) further documented the values of reading aloud to children.

One of the more popular contemporary books about children's listening was written by Trelease (1985). *The Read Aloud Handbook, Revised Edition* is targeted primarily at parents and provides tips on how to read to children of various ages. The author breaks down significant age groups and provides annotated bibliographies of books for each level.

Big Books

Some of you may recall that the old basal series had a "big book" as a part of its materials as early as the 1940s. These big books were simply oversized blowups of the first preprimer that were placed on a chalk tray or easel by the teacher as she modeled and practiced early reading with children.

In recent years "big books" have been more closely associated with the "shared book" experience coming from New Zealand (Holdaway, 1979) that described how books were enlarged for reading and sharing with young children. In the New Zealand program, the books were not basal readers but rather simple books for children. After reading the books with the children, the New Zealand teacher would do such things as dramatize the story, reread parts, invite children to read pages or lines, and invite children to write about what they had read. Careful procedures were outlined for using the "big book" in a shared learning experience by Holdaway.

From a few expensive "big books", the "big book" market in the United States has blossomed to the point that big books are becoming increasingly affordable.

The following publishers are among those selling "big books":

Source: DLM TEACHING RESOURCES
P.O.BOX 4000
ALLEN, TX 75002

Allafred the Anteater *Argyle* *Turkey Goes to Sea*
Captain Tom Cat *Don't Be a Thief*
There's a Mouse in the Caboose *Word Song*

Source: RESOURCES
DEPARTMENT R
SALEM, OR 97309-0399

I Can Read Colors *I've Got A Cat*
Oh, A Hunting We Will Go *Down By the Bay*
Teddy Bear, Teddy Bear

Source: SCHOLASTIC
P.O.BOX 7501
JEFFERSON CITY, MO 65102

Caps For Sale
Clifford's Family
Madeline
Rosie's Walk
What Do You Do With a Kangaroo?
Chicken Soup and Rice
The Little Red Hen
The Owl and The Pussycat
The Three Billy Goats Gruff

Picture Books

Picture books are those books that are characterized by a predominance of pictures with rather limited amounts of text. Most of these books can be read in 10 minutes or less and appeal especially to younger readers.

Alexander and the Terrible, Horrible, No Good, Very Bad Day. (Judith Viorst: Atheneum, 1972)

Amelia Bedelia. (Peggy Parrish: Scholastic, 1970)

Benjie. (Joan Lexau: Dial, 1964)

Blueberries for Sal. (Robert McCloskey: Puffin, 1976)

Corduroy. (Don Freeman: Puffin, 1976)

East of the Sun, West of the Moon. (Mercer Mayer: Four Winds, 1980)

Frederick. (Leo Lionni: Pantheon, 1966)

Frog and Toad Are Friends. (Arnold Lobel: Harper, 1979)

The Giving Tree. (Shel Silverstsein: Harper, 1964)

Tikki Tikki Tembo. (Arlene Mosel: Scholastic, 1972)

The Very Hungry Caterpillar. (Eric Carle: Collins, 1969)

Where The Wild Things Are. (Maurice Sendak: Scholastic, 1969)

Short Novels

Call It Courage. (Armstrong Sperry: Macmillan, 1971)

Freckle Juice. (Judy Blume: Dell, 1971) This is but one of many fine books by this outstanding children's author.

Peanut Butter Pilgrims. (Patricia Reilly Giff: Dell, 1988)

Sunny-Side Up. (Patricia Reilly Giff: Dell, 1986) This is one of a large number of books by the same author that are written around the second grade level. Children like the short books very much.

The Best Christmas Pageant Ever. (Barbara Robinson: Avon, 1973)

The Secret At The Polk Street School. (Patricia Reilly Giff: Dell, 1987)

Poetry

Alligator Pie. (D. Lee: Houghton-Mifflin, 1974)

And So My Garden Grows. (P. Spier: Doubleday, 1969)

A New Treasury of Children's Poetry: Old Favorites and New Discoveries. (J. Cole: Doubleday, 1984)
In The Trail of The Wind: American Indian Poems and Ritual Orations. (J. Bierhorst, Ed.: Farrar, Straus, & Giroux, 1971)
My Black Me: A Beginning Book of Black Poetry. (A. Adoff, Ed.: E.P. Dutton, 1974)
My Daddy Is A Cool Dude. (K. Fufuka: Dial, 1975)
Quentin Blake's Nursery Rhyme Boo. (Q. Blake: Harper & Row, 1983)
The Dream Keeper. (L. Hughes: Knopf, 1932)
The New Kid On The Block. (J. Prelutsky: Greenwillow, 1984)
Where The Sidewalk Ends. (S. Silverstein: Harper & Row, 1974)

READING

Although pupils will undoubtedly choose to read many of the preceding books that may or may not have been read to them, it is important for them to have a wide variety of books in their school reading diet. These books are discussed under the categories of wordless books, predictables, basal readers, buildup readers, play books, supplementary readers, and trade books.

Wordless Books

Although the students don't technically read these books, they interact with the pictures and generate plots, story lines, characterizations, and the other necessary components of narrative reading. Consequently, their inclusion allows pupils to author their own books. Some fine wordless books are:

Apples. (N. Hogrogian: Macmillan, 1972)
Bubble, Bubble! (M. Mayer: Parents Magazine Press, 1973)
Frog Goes To Dinner. (M. Mayer: Dial, 1971)
Paddy Finds A Job. (J. Goodall: Atheneum, 1981)
Sebastian and the Mushroom. (F. Krahn: Delacorte Press, 1968)
The Grey Lady and the Strawberry Snatcher. (M. Bang: Four Winds Press, 1980)
The Hunter and the Animals. (T. dePaolo: Holiday House, 1981)
Up And Up. (S. Hughes: Prentice-Hall, 1979)

Predictables

Predictables come from the larger category of "picture books" as indicated in the listening section. The following books are called "predictable" because the books use repetitive phrases such as Martin's *Brown Bear Brown Bear, What Do You See?* The book repeats the same pattern throughout the book, inserting the various animals, for example, "Yellow duck, yellow duck what do you see? I see a blue horse looking at me."

A Bug In A Jug. (G. Patrick: Scholastic Press, 1970)
Animals Should Definitely Not Wear Clothes . (J. Barrett: Atheneum, 1970)
Chicken Soup with Rice. (M. Sendak: Scholastic Press, 1962)

Do You Want To Be My Friend? (E. Carle: Crowell, 1971)
Drummer Hoff. (B. Emberly: Prentice Hall, 1967)
Eighteen Cousins. (C. Hogan: Parents Magazine Press, 1968)
Go, Dog, Go. (Dr. Seuss: Random House, 1960)
Green Eggs and Ham. (Dr. Seuss: Random House, 1960)
Hailstones and Halibut Bones. (M. O'Neill: Doubleday, 1961)
Henny Penny. (P. Galdone: Houghton-Mifflin, 1975)
I Know an Old Lady Who Swallowed a Fly. (N. Westcott: Little, Brown, 1980)
Never Talk to Stranger. (I. Joyce: Golden Press, 1967)
One Fish, Two Fish, Red Fish, Blue Fish. (Dr. Seuss: Random House, 1960)
Over in the Meadow. (E. Keats: Scholastic Press, 1971)
Pancakes for Breakfast. (T. dePaolo: Harcourt Brace Jovanovich, 1978)
Rosie's Walk. (P. Hutchins: Macmillan, 1968)
Spoiled Tomatoes. (B. Martin: Bowmar, 1967)
The Friendly Book. (M.W. Brown: Golden Press, 1954)
The Important Book. (M.W. Brown: Harper and Row, 1949)
Three Billy Goats Gruff. (P. Galdone, Houghton Mifflin, 1973)

Basal Readers

The case has been made previously that some slower readers need "controlled vocabulary." In our experience, slower readers have used older preprimers, primers, and early readers to move quickly and happily through text.

At Buda, we often have entering second graders from other schools with preprimer reading skills at the beginning of the year. Normally, we put them in the highly controlled Scott, Foresman series from the 1960s and they progress through preprimers, primer, first reader, and end up reading paper backs for independent reading and on-level basals for their challenge reading.

We have older students who come to us with preprimer reading skills and we, too, place them in some of the older basal materials. Often, we have to cover the books so that no one else can see what they are reading because they are super sensitive to the fact that they are reading so-called "baby" books. Yet when they see that they are moving, they are willing to stay with the program. While many teachers suggest that such pupils will not stay with such materials, we have found that they will if they are successful. Success has previously eluded these students and most of them believe that they can not learn to read. When they are matched up with something that they can read they begin to think that there is some hope after all. When they can move through text with some rapidity their motivation grows.

Unfortunately, many of the better controlled basals have become extinct. One of the best sources for such books are book rooms at elementary schools where some of the older books have been laid up for years. Sometimes, older schools have old texts that they are happy to get rid of in order to clear their shelves for newer books.

For those interested in pursuing some of the older basals, I would suggest the following series produced in the late 1980s by Houghton Mifflin Publishing and Harcourt Brace Jovanovich Publishing companies. **Wilcox and Follett, 1000 West Washington Boulevard, Chicago 60607** deals in older reading books such as these that are purchased from private schools.

Houghton Mifflin Reading Series 1986

PP1	(Bells)
PP2	(Drums)
PP3	(Trumpets
P	(Parades)
1/2	(Carousels)
2/1	(Adventures)
2/2	(Discoveries)

Harcourt Brace Jovanovich Reading Series 1986

PP1	(New Friends)
PP2	(Mortimer Frog)
PP3	(Mr. Fig)
P	(Wishes)
1/2	(Smiles)
2/1	(Streamers)
2/2	(Stairways)

Buildup Readers

Buildup readers is a term that we gave to teacher-made books that feature the vocabulary, syntax, and story characters from a basal reader (such as the preceding books). These books are produced to allow slower readers with extended opportunities to practice the reading matter of beginning preprimers.

The readers are called buildup readers because they start with a few words and then build up by adding only one new word per page. This type of material was done to some extent in some of the commercial readiness programs of certain reading series in the 1980s. They built consumable readers of the first ten to fifteen words that could be clipped out and read by the pupils. Unfortunately, these publishers no longer continue this practice but assume that the task will be accomplished by some of the predictable books in their array of literary readers.

Juel (1991) found the buildup readers to be very successful when her college student athletes used them with at-risk pupils in a special tutoring program at The University of Texas at Austin. Juel's buildups began with the word *run* and added one word each day.

The practice of using pattern vocabulary books has parallels in the New Zealand reading programs (Adams, 1990; Clay, 1979, 1985), where the students are introduced to colorful, easy books with repeated patterns. It should be noted that the New Zealand books do not follow the same type of patterning as shown here but rather repeat phrases and sentences about the illustrations in the books. The idea seems to be that students will transfer their reading knowledge from the predictable books to new books that incorporate similar elements.

The example shown on the following pages is the **first readiness buildup reader** for the Houghton Mifflin Reading Series (1986). The book was designed and constructed by the first grade teachers in the Buda Primary School. You can note how each word and sentence pattern is repeated so that the pupil will have many opportunities to learn the vocabulary and the syntactical patterns.

Similar books have been prepared by these same teachers for the three preprimers of this reading series. The other books are far too long to illustrate in this book. With the increasing amount of vocabulary and word order, these later books take on a great deal more meaning than the first book illustrated here.

It should be noted that some slower readers may need to go through the buildup of a given book prior to going through the book itself. Thus, *Drums* can be read easily after reading the *Drums* buildup reader. Other children, however, may read these books alternately with their basal readers. Faster readers, though, don't require the use of the buildups and should be allowed to move through the preprimers without the use of buildups because an over reliance on the buildups will harm their emerging reading skill.

It is this author's view that the buildup readers are of most value for the first two preprimers and have a diminished return after that. Continued use after this can cause pupils to lose interest in the many other factors of reading that are found in real books.

Some slower readers, though, have needs for more practice than the buildup readers and basal readers can provide. For these pupils, we shall discuss "play readers," multiple oral rereadings, and tape assists.

While "whole language" purists will take exception to the vocabulary control exercised in the development of buildup readers and the lack of colorful pictures, we have found that neither poses a big problem. Vocabulary control is not only desirable but essential for some pupils. We find that it is necessary to introduce only one new word per page and practice all the previous words so that certain pupils can rehearse the previously learned words. As for the necessity of pictures, we find that many pupils take great pleasure in reading the words and focus most directly on them when pictures are not around.

Contrary to some popular opinion, many children love their buildup readers as a starting place for reading and relish every page that they learn to read independently. Furthermore, they quickly develop confidence that they can read subsequent pages by figuring out the single new word on the page.

HOUGHTON MIFFLIN

READINESS READER

BUILD-UP

1. Go, go

Go. ________________.

________________ go.

Go. ________________ go

Go. go. ________________.

Go. ________________ go.

________________ go. go. go

Go. ________________ go.

2. Can, can

________________ can go.

Can ________________ go?

________________ can go.

Can ________________ go, go, go?

________________ can go, go, go.

Go, ________________ go.

3. I

I go.

I can go.

I can go, go, go.

Can I go?

I can go.

________________ can go.

I can go, go, go.

4. Not, not

________ can not go.

I can not go.

Can ________ go?

Can I go?

I can not go.

________ can not go.

5. Help, help

Help, ________, help!

________ can not help.

I can help.

I can help ________.

Can I help?

I can help.

Can ________ help?

________ can not help.

6. We, we

Can we go?

We can go.

Can we help?

We can not help.

Can we help ________?

We can not help ________.

We can go.

We can not help.

7. You, you

You can go.

You can go, go, go.

You can help.

You can help, help, help.

Can I help you?

I can help you.

Can ________ help you?

________ can help you.

Some special students may require even more practice than the buildup reader can provide. Consequently, vocabulary and syntax needs to be carried into "play books," which can provide even more connected reading and practice than the buildup reader.

Play Books

Play books operate on the same principle as do the buildup readers. That principle simply suggests that connected reading practice in varied forms can help build the desired word recognition. When a pupil cannot find sufficient reading mastery by rehearsing the buildup readers, we take the same vocabulary and produce a play book that features a two part dialogue so that the reader can experience the vocabulary and syntax in a play format.

Max:	Can you come in, Boo?
Boo Bear:	No, I can not come in.
Max:	It is fun.
Boo Bear:	I do not want to come in.

The human interaction of two pupils reading the parts from the play book adds a dimension of excitement to the reading task that previously has been done individually. It's a neat motivator to have pupils of similar abilities sharing the play but it's alright to use other combinations of pupils. Strong and weak readers in pairs provide valuable peer teaching experiences when the pairs are carefully matched. The main thing is that those involved are having satisfying reading experiences. Later, individuals will want to learn to voice both parts and do the play books as a single.

In some instances, we have found that it is desirable to put the illustrations and text on facing pages. This causes some pupils to focus upon the pictures and connected reading parts separately. Exciting computer programs are developing now so that pupils will be able to write their own plays and illustrate them with computerized graphics.

Playbooks, like buildup readers, don't have to have pictures. At best, though, the books should have a story line that will permit the pupils to identify with what's happening to the point where they can get excited and provide some expression as they read their parts in the play. Illustrative of such a play book is the one on the preceding page with simple line drawings. It is based on the characters Max and Boo Bear from the first preprimer *Bells* of the Houghton Mifflin reading series.

Supplementary Readers

In the early 1900s, the supplementary reader arrived and played an important part in the early reading programs. According to Smith (1963), pupils read alternately between their basals and supplemental readers. That practice, though, has seemingly been changing as supplemental readers are used variously in the classrooms around the country. At one extreme, they are rarely used because the teachers spend all of their time simply trying to do most of what is called for in the comprehensive basal program. At the other end of the practice pattern, the supplementals are used very frequently so as to provide more reading than that of the basal. The key to how frequently the supplementals are used seems to be linked directly to the teacher's feelings about the importance of extensive reading in school. As indicated in the earlier chapters, connected reading seldom exceeds ten to fifteen minutes a day.

Because many states have a supplemental reader adoption, there is still a large market for these books. In recent years, the supplemental readers have looked very much like basal readers with the exception that they don't generally come with an extensive teacher manual package or skills package (workbook, ditto).

Trade Books

Trade books or children's literature books are simply those books that have been written to be purchased by school libraries and sold in book stores. Because of the burgeoning market in children's books (Huck, Helper, & Hickman, 1987), it seems very important to have some guidelines for the purchase of these books. At this point, rather than listing the thousands of books, it seems more reasonable to provide some fairly accessible guides to children's books. Among the guides for the selection of pupil books are children's literature anthologies, children's book awards, and recommended reading lists.

Children's Literature Anthologies

Because there are so many books available, we have to be careful about our purchases. Our experiences with the large collections provided by some publishers have not been completely happy. We find some very good selections but some that aren't interesting to our children. If you haven't done so, it would be wise to refer to the following treatments of children's literature. The Trelease book is included because of its unique contribution to the area of reading to children.

Bettelheim, B. *The Uses of Enchantment.* New York: Knopf, 1976.

Cullinan, B. *Literature and the child* (2nd ed.). San Diego: Harcourt Brace Jovanovich, 1989.

Huck, C., Helper, & Hickman, *Children's Literature in the Elementary School* (5th Ed.). Fort Worth, TX: Holt, Rinehart, and Winston, 1993.

Trelease, J. *The Read Aloud Handbook, Revised Edition.* New York: Penguin Books, 1985.

Children's Book Awards

Although there are many children's book awards, I have chosen to use the IRA's Children's Choices and the list of recent winners of the Caldecott and Newbery Awards as a starting point for this selection guide to children's literature.

Children's Choices is a joint project of the International Reading Association and the Children's Book Council that each year involves over 10,000 children in the selection of 100 most widely chosen books. An annotated list is available by sending a self-addressed 9"x12" envelope stamped with sufficient postage for 4 ounces to:

IRA Public Information Office
Dept. A
800 Barksdale Road
P.O. Box 8139
Newark, DE 19714-8139

Caldecott Medal Winners (Age 4 and up)

As a tribute to Randolph Caldecott (1846-1886), an outstanding English illustrator, Frederic C. Melcher named and donated the Caldecott Medal. Since 1938 the medal has been awarded every January by the Children's Service Division of the American Library Association to the illustrator of the most distinguished picture book for children published in the United States during the previous year.

The following is a list (title and illustrator, and publisher) of the winners since 1963:

1997 *Golem*. Wisniewski (Clarion)

1996 *Officer Buckle and Gloria*. Rathmann (Putnam)

1995 *Smoky Night*. Bunting (Harcourt)

1994 *Grandfather's Journey.* Say (Houghton Mifflin)

1993 *Mirette on The High Wire.* McCully (Clarion)

1992 *Tuesday.* Weisner (Claron)

1991 *Black and White.* Macaulay (Houghton Mifflin)

1990 *Lon Po Po.* Young (Putnam)

1989 *Song and Dance Man.* Ackerman (Alfred A. Knopf)

1988 *Owl Moon.* Yolen (Philomet Books)

1987 *Hey ! Al!* Yorinks (Farrar, Straus, & Giroux)

1986 *The Polar Express.* Van Allsburg (Houghton Mifflin)

1985 *Saint George and the Dragon.* Hyman (Little Brown)

1984 *The Glorious Flight: Across the Channel with Louis Bleriot.* Provenson and Provenson (Viking)

1983 *Shadow.* Brown (Scribner)

1982 *Jumanji.* Van Allsburg (Houghton Mifflin)
1981 *Fables.* Lobel (Harper and Row)
1980 *Ox-Cart Man.* Cooney (Viking)
1979 *The Girl Who Loved Wild Horses.* Goble (Bradbury)
1978 *Noah's Ark.* Spier (Doubleday)
1977 *Ashanti to Zulu:African Traditions.* Dillon (Dial)
1976 *Why Mosquitoes Buzz in People's Ears.* Dillon (Dial)
1975 *Arrow to the Sun.* McDermott (Viking)
1974 *Duffy and the Devil.* Zemach (Farrar, Straus, & Giroux)
1973 *The Funny Little Woman.* Lent (Dutton)
1972 *One Fine Day.* Hogrogian (Macmillan)
1971 *A Story—A Story.* Haley (Atheneum)
1970 *Sylvester and the Magic Pebble.* Steig (Windmill/Simon & Schuster)
1969 *The Fool of the World and the Flying Ship.* Shulevitz (Farrar, Straus, & Giroux)
1968 *Drummer Hoff.* Emberly (Prentice-Hall)
1967 *Sam, Bangs, and Moonshine.* Ness (Holt, Rinehart, and Winston)
1966 *Always Room for One More.* Hogrogian (Holt, Rinehart, and Winston)
1965 *May I Bring a Friend?* Montresor (Atheneum)
1964 *Where the Wild Things Are.* Sendak (Harper & Row)
1963 *The Snowy Day.* Keats (Viking)

Newbery Medal Winners

Frederic G. Melcher, the originator of the Caldecott Medal, also started the Newbery Medal in honor of John Newbery (1713-1767), the first publisher of books for children. Since 1922 the Newbery Awards have been awarded by the Children's Service Division of the American Library Association to the author of the most distinguished contribution to the literature for children published in the United States during the preceding year. Like the Caldecott, the award, presented each January, is restricted to United States citizens or residents.

The following is a list (title, author, and publisher) since 1963.

1997 *The View From Saturday* (Konigsberg) Simon & Schuster
1996 *The Midwife's Apprentice* (Cushman) Clarion
1995 *Walk Two Moons* (Creech) Harper Collins
1994 *The Giver.* Lowry (Houghton Mifflin))
1993 *Missing May.* Rylant (Orchard)
1992 Shiloh. Naylor (Antheneum)
1991 *Maniac Magee.* Spinelli (Little, Brown)
1990 *Number the Stars.* Lowry (Houghton Mifflin)
1989 *Joyful Noise: Poems for Two Voices.* Fleischman (Harper & Row)

1988 *Lincoln: A Photobiography.* Freedman (Houghton Mifflin)
1987 *The Whipping Boy.* Fleischman (Greenwillow)
1986 *Sarah, Plain and Tall.* McLachlan (Harper)
1985 *The Hero and The Crown.* McKinley (Greenwillow)
1984 *Dear Mr. Henshaw.* Cleary (Morrow)
1983 *Dicey's Song.* Voigt (Atheneum)
1982 *A Visit to William Blake's Inn: Poems for Innocent and Experienced Travelers.* Willard (Harcourt)
1981 *Jacob Have I Loved.* Patterson (Crowell)
1980 *A Gathering of Days.* Blos (Scribner)
1979 *The Westing Game.* Raskin (Dutton)
1978 *Bridge to Terabithia.* Paterson (Crowell)
1977 *Roll of Thunder, Hear My Cry.* Taylor (Dial)
1976 *The Grey King.* Cooper (Atheneum)
1975 *M.C. Higgins, The Great.* Hamilton (Macmillan)
1974 *The Slave Dancer.* Fox (Bradbury)
1973 *Julie of the Wolves.* George (Harper and Row)
1972 *Mrs. Frisby and the Rats of N.I.M.H.* O'Brien (Atheneum)
1971 *Summer of the Swans.* Byars (Viking)
1970 *Sounder* Armstrong. (Harper & Row)
1969 *The High King.* Alexander (Holt, Rinehart, & Winston)
1968 *From the Mixed-Up Files of Mrs. Basil E. Frankweiler.* Konigsburg (Atheneum)
1967 *Up a Road Slowly.* Hunt (Follett)
1966 *I, Juan de Pareja.* de Trevino (Farrar, Straus & Giroux)
1965 *Shadow of a Bull.* Wojciechowska (Atheneum)
1964 *It's Like This Cat.* Neville (Harper and Row)
1963 *A Wrinkle in Time.* L'Engle (Farrar, Straus, & Giroux)

Recommended Reading Lists

Experts in children's literature have identified lists of outstanding books that should be read to children in the various age groups. One of the most widely recognized sets of books to be read to children is that of Huck, Helper, and Hickman (1987). They have a list of 100 books that is broken down by age levels: 1 to 3, 3 to 5, 5 to 7, 7 to 9, 9 to 11, and 11 to 13. In each level, there are ten uniquely valuable books. Such a list can provide you with a good start in your search for books to read to pupils. This same book also provides valuable information about selecting books for children to read.

SUMMARY

Although basal reading programs previously dominated the reading landscape, they have been replaced by literature based programs. Curiously, the literature based programs perpetuate most of the methodology of their predecessors in that pupils are prepped to read good literature books rather than stories. The process includes teacher instruction from a teacher's manual and accompanying workbook type materials that are now called journals. The current emphasis puts the focus upon teaching the class as a whole whereby the pupils listen to the teacher read the story, read the story in unison, and finally read the story on their own.

While many decry any use of the old basal readers, we believe that their vocabulary control can play a significant part in helping some pupils to learn to read.

In viewing reading, we emphasize reading good books to children as well as allowing them daily time for reading certain books on their own or with help. Books suggested for reading to pupils include big books, picture books, short novels, and poetry. Books for pupil reading include wordless books, predictables, basal readers, buildup readers, play books, supplementary readers, and trade books.

Sources for identifying quality books include children's literature anthologies and children's book awards.

STUDY SUGGESTIONS

1. Start building your knowledge of children's books by studying various sets at your local bookstores and libraries. If possible, try to start building your own school room library of Caldecott and Newbery Award books as well as other quality children's paperbacks by shopping for inexpensive books at second-hand stores or garage sales.
2. Get a good picture type book like those suggested in this chapter and read it to a young child. Note the child's interest in the story. Watch the child's expression as much as possible. Ask him how he liked the story and if he would like for you to read him another book. If possible, read several stories and see which ones are liked best. If time permits, read the same set of books to children at three different age levels and observe their responses to the books. Note whether you have increased in your reading skills with a given book after you have read it several times. Start to build the set of books that you like most to read aloud to children.
3. Find an old basal reading series and read the stories in the first preprimer through the second reader. Observe how the sentence length and vocabulary becomes increasingly difficult in each new reader. You might want to take a page at the middle of each reader and determine the average sentence length by counting the total words in ten sentences and then dividing by the number ten.
4. Study the first preprimer of a basal series and try writing a buildup reader for the first ten new words in the book. Recall that each page adds a new word to those already practiced. Type your stories on a computer in a type style similar to the book and then try your story out on a beginning reader.
5. Try to write a play book similar to the page illustrated in the book. Use two characters and a small vocabulary and see if you teach it to a beginning reader.
6. Find a good children's literature anthology at your library and spend some time getting acquainted with some of the literature you will be using in your classroom.

5

CORRECTLY PLACING STUDENTS IN THE BOOKS

In Chapter 4, we viewed a wide variety of books for children to hear and read. Now we are at the point of providing for the all important match between each pupil and his or her appropriate book. The equation suggests:

Pupil + appropriate book = Reading

Although simplistic, this equation is the basis for everything that will follow. If the book fits, the child will most likely continue to receive satisfaction from reading. Conversely, if the book doesn't fit, that child is most likely to find reading unduly challenging and seek to avoid it.

SELF-SELECTION

The tenets of individualized reading were first stated by Willard Olson (1952) as **seeking, self-selection**, and **self-pacing**. These concepts were popularized in the writings of Jeannette Veatch (1966, 1978) who argued that children could and would make appropriate choices if given the opportunity. In support of the Veatch's argument, we have operated programs for over twenty years that have featured pupil self-selection of their reading materials (Guszak, 1978, 1985).

In considering self-selection experience for children, the teacher must plan carefully for the following three things: 1) the array of books from which the pupils will select an appropriate book, 2) the teacher directions for selection, and 3) the verification of placements.

The Array of Books

Because successful self-selection depends upon the availability of appropriate reading materials for every selector, it is important to look back at the preceding chapter. All of the book types listed for reading should be included so that the pupil may choose from predictable books, buildup readers, basals, and trade books (library).

Predictables/Buildups. Initially, we must consider the easiest end of the reading spectrum. If a non-reading student finds no book within his skill level, he is likely to be frustrated about his chances of reading. To reduce such a possibility, it is necessary to provide predictable books and buildup readers in the array.

Predictable books (see Chapter 4), such as the following may have been read to the child so that he may feel comfortable in selecting one as a starting book:

Brown Bear, Brown Bear, What Do You See? (1983) Martin, New York: Henry Holt.

Green Eggs and Ham. (1960) Seuss, New York: Random House.

Henny Penny. (1975) Galdone, Boston: Houghton Mifflin.

For pupils who don't have success with these, it's useful to try buildup readers such as the one on pages 58 and 59.

Mary, our disabled reader from the third grade class at the beginning of the book, might choose one of the buildup readers with ten words in it and read the early pages with great ease. Often, children who have experienced no success with the available books like to read from controlled books such as these because they can manage the text.

Basal Readers. Along with the predictable books and buildup readers, it's wise to have a collection of basal reader materials that will reach the expanded range of readers (e.g., 2/3 of the average age of the readers) which would include very high readers. The chart on the following page indicates basals that might be needed for any given grade. It's always possible that you may have a gifted reader who will read beyond what is listed here. Still, that pupil can usually find satisfaction in the fact that they are allowed to choose something obviously above their grade placement level.

The same pattern could be extrapolated even farther, to the point that there is always simple material as well as material that is at least four grade levels beyond the indicated grade level.

Range of Reading Materials Needed for Self-selection

Grade	Low Readers	Middle Readers	High Readers
1st	PR, BR, PPs	PPs, P, 1	2, 3, 4
2nd	PR, BR, PPs, P	1, 2	3, 4, 5
3rd	PR, BR, PPs, P, 1	2, 3	4, 5, 6
4th	PR, BR, PPs, P, 1, 2	3, 4	5, 6, 7
5th	PR, BR, PPs, P, 1, 2, 3	4, 5	6, 7, 8

Note. The codes for the above abbreviations are: PR = predictable readers; BR = buildup readers; PP = preprimers; P = primers; 1 = first reader; 2 = second reader, and so on.

At this point, one may ask why basal readers are suggested. The answer resides in the fact that a teacher can quickly note the progression of reading difficulty in a basal series that she has studied closely. This knowledge is especially important if a low level reader selects a book that is too difficult. Whereas some pupils may go back and get another book, some pupils will sit and suffer with an inappropriate text. If the teacher sees this, that teacher can offer the pupil a lower level book based upon what the teacher notes from the pupil's efforts with the first chosen book.

Trade Books. Paperback and hardback children's novels should be available for those pupils who are capable of reading them. Many teachers hit the garage sales and arrange projects so that the pupils gather used paperbacks from their neighborhoods. For a few coins it's possible to buy used copies of great books from well known authors like Judy Blume, Roald Dahl, Beverly Cleary, Patricia Reilly Giff, E.B. White, Betsy Byars, and Barbara Parks.

Once all the books are obtained, they may be placed in their order of difficulty (lowest to highest) or in random order. An advantage of putting the lowest books at one side of the room in ascending order is that it provides the teacher with a quick visual check of what level of difficulty each pupil is selecting. That can also be a disadvantage, in that all the other children see who is at the easy end and who is at the hard end. When the books are randomly distributed throughout the room, there is not as much attention focused on the level of difficulty.

Teacher Directions for Self-selection

Clear directions can communicate to them what self-selection means. Consequently, we encourage teachers to use either of the two versions of instructions for self-selection that are shown on the following page.

Instructions for Self-selection: Short Version

* I have many books here today on the tables for your selection. I want you to choose a book you can read **easily.** That means that you must know all the words on the first page of the story. (Teacher demonstrates what is and is not the first page of a story).

* Once you've decided that you have an easy book for yourself, read it aloud in a low voice so I can hear you. This means that all of you will be reading at once.

* Continue reading for the next thirty minutes or until I tell you to stop.

Instructions for Self-selection: Longer Version

Teacher: Girls and boys, I have a lot of books up here (motioning to the books on the classroom tables). You may recognize some of them as books that you have already read. The main thing about these books is that they are different, just as we are different. Some books (pointing to preprimers) are easier, while others (pointing at difficult books) are very difficult. What I want you to do when you come up here is to find a book that's easy for you to read. Please try not to worry about what anyone else is selecting or what they will think about what you have selected.

Teacher: In a few minutes, I'm going to call upon small groups of you to come up to select books. When you come, I want you to look at the first story in the book. Try it out to see if you can read it easily. Now, let me say that again. I want you to look at the first story in the book. Try it out to see if you can read it easily. Read it in a low voice. I'm going to be listening to see how well you followed my instruction.

(At this point the teacher models how to choose a book and read the first page of the first story to see if it is easy enough for her.)

Teacher: Now, Joan, what kind of book are you going to choose?

Joan: An easy one.

Teacher: Good, Joan! You listened well! (The teacher then asks several other pupils what kinds of books they are going to choose.) When you come to choose your book, please open it to the first story and read it to test it. Read the first page of the story to decide if the book is easy for you. If it is, take it to your desk and continue reading aloud. If it isn't easy, search until you find one or ask me for help.

Teacher: (as pupils select) I want to hear everybody's low voice as they read.

Special emphasis was provided by the teacher to the directive, "I want to hear everybody's low voice as they read," because this is a signal to the pupils that the teacher will be checking to see if they are really reading their chosen book. Consequently, some who might choose difficult books may revise their strategy.

The Verification of Placements

Once the pupils have begun to select books, the teacher must observe the selection process, the simultaneous oral reading, and the reading behaviors of individual pupils.

Because the idea of selecting an easy book to read is somewhat different from the self-selection tasks employed previously on trips to the library, the pupils may not be certain of the teacher's expectations. Some pupils may spend time flipping through the pages of the various books without making a selection. Others may quickly choose a book without looking at the first page of the first story and bring it to their desk. When it's apparent that a student is not reading aloud, it's important to intervene quickly and say, "Please read this page aloud." This permits you to see if the text is too difficult.

Because the pupils are making selections and returning to their seats to read, the teacher's attention is quickly divided between those pupils selecting and those pupils reading at their desks. It's imperative to stand back and observe both sets of pupils so that you can create a climate where every single one is reading.

With **simultaneous oral reading** happening, teachers have to support this novel phenomenon. There will be a few pupils who will complain of being unable to concentrate and others who will read only when the teacher sits by them. To avoid getting trapped by dependent pupils, the teacher should issue positive statements about hearing everyone's voice as well as the neat sound of so many readers. Unless necessary, it's important to avoid individual praise. Once the teacher feels that simultaneous reading is underway, the observations can be turned toward monitoring the behaviors of individual readers.

By facing all the students, the teacher can quickly see if a pupil raises his or her head to look around. Similarly, other off-task behaviors are instantly visible and can generally be solved by simply looking directly at the student involved.

The teacher should not move from the observational spot during the first part of self-selection. If the teacher moves out to monitor prematurely, it may transmit the unwanted message, "Read only when the teacher is listening to you." Once again, the quick glance by the teacher is often sufficient to pull an off task pupil back on task.

With all the pupils reading, the teacher begins the process of sizing up the readers in greatest need. These pupils will be apparent almost instantly through the following behaviors:

looking around.

looking at the teacher.

rapid page turning.

inaudible mumbling.

holding book in front of face.

hunching over a book in lap.

When nearly every pupil is at least attempting to read, the teacher can take the first tentative steps away from the "watch station" to make some confidential assessments of individual behaviors. At this point the teacher is ready to start informal monitoring procedures.

The following criteria for reading ease and difficulty give the teacher a means for making up close judgments of whether a pupil is reading material which is independent, instructional, or frustrational.

You will note that the initial assessment is usually fluency because it is the easiest and quickest assessment to make. Teachers with many children must make quick assessments if they are going to keep pupils on task.

CRITERIA FOR READING EASE AND DIFFICULTY

INDEPENDENT LEVEL

Fluency (Rate)		Word Recognition	Comprehension
Book Levels	**Minimums**	97% and better, as based on definite miscues that can alter the meaning of text, such as bad substitutions, words told, and omissions. Indefinite miscues that don't alter the meaning of text are not counted.	80% and better
First	80 wpm		
Second reader	90 wpm		
Third reader	100 wpm		
Fourth and up	110 wpm		

INSTRUCTIONAL LEVEL

Fluency (Rate)		Word Recognition	Comprehension
Book Levels	**Minimums**	92% to 96%, as based on the definite miscues listed above.	60% to 79%
First	60 wpm		
Second reader	70 wpm		
Third reader	80 wpm		
Fourth and up	90 wpm		

FRUSTRATIONAL LEVEL

Fluency (Rate)	Word Recognition	Comprehension
Rates are below the minimums above. When a pupil drops below the minimum rate, he is considered frustrational despite his word recognition and comprehension scores.	91% and less, as based on the previous definite miscues.	59% and less.

Independent reading: To be considered independent in reading materials, the reader must meet or exceed the minimums in rate, word recognition, and comprehension. **Instructional** reading: If the pupil can work within these criteria, it is assumed that he or she can work at this level with some assistance from the teacher, another pupil, or a tape assist. **Frustrational** reading is the usual outcome when pupils read materials that are too difficult. If the pupil falls below any one of the three criteria, that pupil should be placed in easier materials within the instructional criteria.

INFORMAL MONITORING PROCEDURES (IMP)

The **informal reading inventory (IRI)** discussed previously has suffered many limitations because it is often viewed as an end in itself. In the traditional informal inventory, the teacher finds a reading level in some graded materials. Unfortunately, that level may not transfer to the reading materials available for that pupil in the classroom. The whole concept of matching pupils with appropriate books is based on the **continuing appropriateness** of such matches. Consequently, we prefer to call the process whereby we measure book fit as the **informal monitoring process** (**IMP** for short). The practice utilizes the basic concepts of the informal reading inventory (independent, instructional, and frustrational levels of word recognition and comprehension) but goes further by adding fluency as the initial determinant. Rather than determining whether a pupil can read an isolated set of materials, the teacher uses the IMP to determine how well a pupil is performing in his self selected book. Such determinations don't end on the first day, but continue for as many days as that pupil reads from that book.

Note that the **criteria for reading ease and difficulty** is the same thing as the informal monitoring process. You simply use the criteria in the monitoring process. Fluency is always the initial determination because it tells how much difficulty the pupil is having with the text. From that decision, subsequent decisions can be made as to whether the pupil understands or has specific word recognition problems.

In applying the criteria in a busy classroom, the initial considerations are those of rate and comprehension. Word recognition is considered subsequently as the teacher wants to get a better grasp of the pupil's word recognition needs.

Fluency (Rate)

Because rate is such a useful indicator of word recognition and comprehension, it is the first screen that a teacher should apply as he observes a pupil reading self-selected text. Such verification can provide support as to whether the pupil is prospering or suffering in that text. If the rate is fast and fluent the student is obviously doing well. If, however, the rate is near or below the minimums, there is strong reason to question why that pupil is reading so slowly.

To make a rate check, you must initially locate where the pupil is reading. With a child who points, such is not difficult. Once this is accomplished, you must catch the first word that the pupil reads in the text as the second hand passes a handy reference point on your watch or clock, like the 3,6,9, or 12. For example, if the child is reading the text on the following page, you note the first word that the child reads ("Grandmother"), and put a slash mark in front of it. At the same moment, you must catch a good starting place on your watch, like the 15 second mark. Then keep track of the reading and time, making a second slash mark after the last word read in the 15 seconds. Your next step is simply to count up the number of words that were read in the 15-second segment and multiply by 4 (the number of 15-second segments in a minute). The selection on page 73 shows one example of tracking a student's fluency.

/"Grandmother," said Pablo.

"Now that the tamales are ready,

can I go out? Tomas and/ I have to

help Mr. Black."

"You can," said Grandmother. "And

Maria, you and Alicia can go out too."

Maria and Alicia went to Mr. John's

store to look for a surprise for Pablo.

Normally, I recommend a **15-second time check** for measuring rate because it allows the teacher to sample a lot of readers. It also allows the teacher some easy mathematics because the teacher can count the number of words in the segment and double that number twice, as shown below:

16 words doubled = 32, doubled again = 64 (64 words per minute)

(Note that compound words like *grandmother* count as two words.)

After a teacher practices a few rate checks, he will discover that the time segment to be used is dependent upon the speed of the pupil's reading. A 15-second time check on a fast reader will produce a great number of words to be counted whereas the 15-second count on the slow reader will produce very few. Consequently, with greater experience, the teacher may choose to use a **10-second time check** with the faster reader and multiply the words in the brackets by 6. When listening to the slower reader, the same teacher may allow a **30-second time check** in order to get a more reliable measure of the pupil's skill. If time will permit, I'll get a **one-minute time check** on a very slow reader.

The only way to develop the skill of rate checking is to do it. As you do it, you will discover that it's important to remember the following things:

Oral Rate Checking Procedures

1) Try not to interrupt the pupil's reading. You can get a time check without stopping the pupil.
2) Try to catch the first word in an early paragraph or sentence so that you can easily recall where you started your timing. It's good to pick up where the child is reading in the text before you catch the second hand on your watch.
3) Learn to look quickly between your watch and the text.
4) Be sure to teach the pupils how to hold the book so that they won't obscure your view with their hands.

5) After you have caught the first word and time, concentrate on trying to see the last word read in the time frame. Count backwards from the last word to the first word while the pupil is continuing to read.

6) Develop the habit of jotting down the page and the rate like this so that you will know where the rate was taken. This can pinpoint particularly easy or difficult pages and/or words.

In the preprimer 1 that he selected, **Robbie** was reading page 16 with a comfortable rate of 80 words per minute:

Page/Rate

16/80 wpm

Rate checking is primarily a quick determination to see whether the pupil can handle his text so it's important to be as unobtrusive as possible. Pupils will soon learn to pay little attention to you and continue their reading if you are able to perform this task with a minimum of fanfare.

In many instances, the rate check will verify that the pupil can read the words with sufficient speed. Therefore, the more detailed rate checks will focus on those students who are having apparent difficulty in meeting the rate minimum. These students need to be timed at different points in the story and may need to reread the story to determine the benefits of repeated reading on their performance. For students repeating a page, we like to add an additional code that indicates the number of the reading, as in the example below:

Robbie 16/62 1 (The 1 indicates 1st reading.)
16/80 2 (The 2 indicates 2nd reading.)

When able readers like **Stan** exceed the minimum oral rate figures by a great number of words, it is good to obtain silent reading rates. This is done by asking the pupil to read silently as follows:

Silent Rate Checking Procedures

1) Tell the student that you are going to uncover the page with your hand and ask him to read as fast as possible with understanding.

2) Explain to him that you will give him the **go** signal and the **stop** signal.

3) Explain that when he hears the stop signal, he should immediately touch the last word read and retell you what he has read.

4) Do these procedures and have the pupil touch the last word read in 30 seconds.

5) Ask the student to retell the story as you look at the text. Evaluate his retelling and provide stimulus questions as needed.

6) If you're satisfied with the pupil's comprehension, count the words and double them to come up with the silent reading rate. If you're dissatisfied with any part of the procedure, repeat at another time.

Some pupils retain oral reading patterns too long and consequently fail to develop properly in silent reading. Consequently, oral and silent rate checks over similar materials can help in the determination of this. The following is illustrative of such a student.

Tom	25/85 **o** (oral)
	25/80 **s** (silent)

We would hope that practice in silent reading for specific purposes and tellback would result in a pattern like the following where the silent rate would far exceed the oral one.

Tom	45/ 85 **o** (oral)
	45/105 **s** (silent)

Under the Informal Monitoring Process (IMP), the teacher is taking periodic rate checks that can support the pupil's book selection, reveal rate growth over time, reveal the differences between subsequent readings of a passage, and chronicle the growth of silent reading skill.

Stan, our gifted reader should be timed exclusively in the silent mode as his rate exceeds 200 words per minute in narrative materials. Currently, he is reading approximately 140 words per minute in the oral checks performed by his teacher.

Comprehension

Rate checks were the first screen in the informal monitoring process. Once you are satisfied that the pupil can deal with the fluency, it is critical to determine how much that student knows about what he is reading.

Comprehension assessment is difficult because of the criteria employed and the subjective nature with which we use those criteria.

In the criteria of reading difficulty, we suggest that 80% plus comprehension is independent, 60 to 79% percent is instructional, and 59% or less is frustrational. These determinations are certainly argumentative. The point is that we probably can't get total agreement on any set of percentages even though many people like the idea of a 70% minimum. The important thing is that we have some approximate benchmarks for making determinations.

With the benchmarks in place, the big trouble comes when we listen to the pupil's tellback of the story. If we have the book in our hand we may demand that his retelling be too exact. Such an expectancy would be unreal as we would surely find out if the child held the book and we answered the questions. For this reason, I suggest that we grant some leeway in terms of what we expect.

With the foregoing discussion in mind, we like to ask pupils for brief tellbacks of their story in the hopes that they know what is happening to whom and where in their story. If we are satisfied with what they say (they understand a majority of the material), we move on. If we are not satisfied, we may probe with leading questions or simply ask them to reread the story in a fashion so that they can retell it to us.

It may seem apparent but it's absolutely essential for a teacher to know the stories that they are questioning about. It doesn't mean that every detail must be possessed because such is difficult when you're working with long, detailed stories. Nevertheless, it's important to be conversant with your pupils over the various stories they are reading.

For the recording of comprehension checks, we usually use a simplified system that tells us the following:

+	comprehension appears to be good.
√	comprehension appears to be satisfactory
–	comprehension appears to be obviously flawed

By simply recording such marks, it becomes evident whether students are succeeding or failing in their comprehension tasks during reading. A series of minus signs should suggest some type of intervention.

Tanya, the pupil reading below third grade level in the first chapter, appears to be functioning below her capability because of her attention problems. More specifically, the teacher determines by comprehension tellbacks that Tanya fails to set purposes for reading and thus has less than a complete tellback. This can be remedied as we shall see later.

Word Recognition

As previously indicated, word recognition in the informal monitoring procedure is secondary to rate and comprehension. When rates are consistently slow, it is good to take another book or a photocopy of what the pupil is reading and mark that copy to see where the problems are occurring. In marking the pupil text, we try to mark **more definite miscues** and **less definite miscues.** A tape recording of the pupil's reading is a good help for practicing in the early stages.

More definite miscues include the following: poor substitutions, words told, and omissions.

Poor substitutions. Any substitution of a word, word part, or phrase is circled and the substituted portions are written above:

	house
word	He got on his (horse) and rode away.
	i
word part	He got (o)n his horse and rode away.
	house and got away
phrase	He got on his (horse and rode away)

These substitutions alter the meanings of the sentences in significant ways.

Words told. Words told are those words that are given to a pupil after a 5- to 10-second wait reveals that the child is unlikely to say the word. A line is drawn though each word told so that the teacher may subsequently count up and qualify the nature of the words told.

The ~~pretty~~ dog ran. He tried to ~~reach~~ the fence.

In some error noting systems, proper names are not counted as words told because they are presumed to be beyond the attack capability of the pupil. We will count words told as miscues if it is reasonable that a child has similar words and syllable patterns within his command. Thus, this is purely a judgment call.

Omissions. Omissions are those words, phrases, and sentences that are omitted as the pupil reads the text. Some omissions may not change the meaning significantly so should be treated as indefinite miscues. If, however, the omission substantially changes the meaning, it should be counted as a definite miscue.

indefinite

The pretty dog ran to the fence. He tried to jump over
the fence. As soon as he would try to jump, he would
definite
barely leave the ground. His legs were apparently
injured.

Less definite miscues include insertions and repetitions.

Insertions. Insertions are seen with able readers who occasionally make adjustments in tense to accommodate their fluent reading as well as with less able readers who insert because they have made other miscues. It is important to determine which kind of insertion is operant. For the most part, the designation of this behavior to the less definite miscue category suggests that it is the behavior of the better reader more often than the poorer reader. The following illustrates embellishments by an able reader.

He had powerful eyes that would allow him to
could see
see farther than most people. He used his eyes to scan
over
headlines on a newspaper a block away.

Repetitions. Repetitions refers to the repeating of words, word parts, phrases, or sentences. Any repeated element (letter group, word, phrase, sentence) is underlined with a wavy line and counted as a single repetition. Because repetitions are often the mark of a child's use of contextual clues, we see such behaviors as desirable and try to note that as a developmental reading behavior. At times, though, the repetitions may become constant as a struggling reader attempts to solve unknown words or word meanings in his path. In this case, the repetition behavior will undoubtedly be reflected in the reading rate. Consequently, we see little value in counting repetitions but rather wish to note them in order to see how the student is using them.

Mr. Jones, the dogcatcher, had his work cut out for him
this Friday. There on the street corner stood a pack of

dogs that seemed to include big dogs, small dogs, nice
dogs, and some not so nice dogs.

Strategies for dealing with these word recognition problems are illustrated in Chapter 7.

APPLYING RATE, WORD RECOGNITION, AND COMPREHENSION

Before going further, it seems important for you to apply the concepts of rate, word recognition, and comprehension that you have been reading about. Thus, Tanya's reading from a self-selected reader is presented in order that you might determine her 1) rate, 2) word recognition, and 3) comprehension. From those three judgments, you are to determine if this story is independent, instructional, or frustrational.

Tanya read this 69-word second reader selection aloud. The two 15-second rate checks are numbered 1 and 2 and marked with slash marks, e.g. 1/ /. Please note that compound words *another, everyone* and *something* are counted as two words each for word recognition and rate analysis purposes.

1/The bright spring days were almost gone. April and May had come to an end. The fruit / blossoms and tulips were gone for another year, and summer was very near.

2/Out in the Jones School on First Street, there was a strange feeling around. Everyone was waiting for something to / happen. It was the last day of school and school would soon be closed for summer.

Question: What was this story part mainly about?

Pupil's Answer: Spring was almost gone.

At this point, please carry out the following computations relative to the preceding selection:

1) average your rate from the two fifteen second samples;
2) divide the total number of words read into the total number of words read correctly for the word recognition percentage;
3) determine the comprehension percentage by judging the value of the answer in terms of your holistic assessment.

Then pencil your three sets of findings into the blocks on the next page for **rate, word recognition**, and **comprehension** and make a decision as to whether this selection is **independent, instructional,** or **frustrational** for Tanya.

Rate___________ READING LEVEL OF TEXT IS:

W.R___________ INDEPENDENT________

COMPR.________ INSTRUCTIONAL______

FRUSTRATIONAL______

Discussion of the Sample

What, if any, **rate problems** are evident in this sample? Counting each compound word as two words, it's apparent that Tanya read the first 17 words at a pace of 68 words per minute (no. of words read in 15 seconds x 4 = 68) while she read the second 22 word sample at a pace of 88 words per minute (compound words *everyone* and *something* count as two words each). While the first sample is less than the minimum of 70 words per minute, the second exceeds that easily. Although this averages around 78 wpm, the fluctuating rate is a cause for concern and bears watching. How might the teacher assist the pupil with these problems? The strategy of having the pupil reread the selection would probably be sufficient for this pupil. If, however, the pupil failed to inflect properly, the teacher might wish to model reading, segment the material, or mark punctuation marks.

What, if any, **word recognition problems** are evident? The only word recognition problem that is apparent is the substitution of the sound associated with *b-* for the *br-* sound in bright and the *bl-* sound in blossoms. How might the teacher assist the pupil with these problems? Since the pupil had no trouble with the normally difficult later parts of the words, the teacher might simply want to take a known sight word like *right* and add some *bl-* blends to the *-ight* pattern to see if the student has problems with others. If so, the teacher could take a known word like *blue* and isolate the beginning sounds and letters for substitution on *-ight, -ack, -and,* etc. With regard to the word recognition percentage, the total words in the story are divided into the number of words read correctly to produce a score like the following:

.98 or 98% accurate

$\frac{68}{69}$ = 68 words recognized out of 69 possible

$$69 \overline{)68.000} = .985$$

What type of **comprehension** questions did the teacher ask? The teacher asked only an organizing question about what the segment was mainly about. How adequate was the student's answer? The student's answer was not adequate because the student seemed to have picked up on the topic sentence notion about spring being almost gone. What might be done to assist the pupil toward a more adequate answer? The most obvious strategy would be to ask the pupil to tell back to see if she had more information. If there was no more information, the student should be asked to read the segment carefully in order that he might tell it back to the teacher. This should produce a longer understanding segment. Later, the teacher might want to take the segment and go through it with the student and mark out the extraneous information to get at the main idea that school was about over and summer beginning.

Because the pupil's comprehension is suspect, I would classify this selection as **frustrational** until I could get a better sample of understanding. Remember, if the selection satisfies *any one* of the three criteria for being frustrational, then the selection is considered to be frustrational, regardless of its ranking on the other two criteria. The mere fact that a pupil understands a selection does not necessarily mean that he can read that selection comfortably. Such readers are frequently called **context readers** because, through an inordinate amount of effort, they can derive comprehension.

Through the use of the informal monitoring procedures of rate, comprehension, and word recognition, we are able to make determinations about pupil self-selections. If the pupils have self-selected beyond their capabilities, it is the teacher's job to quickly place readable text in front of that student in order that he might read material with a minimum of difficulty in terms of the previously stated criteria.

SUMMARY

The following equation illustrates where effective reading must begin:

Pupil + appropriate book = Reading

Teachers need to provide sufficient books and then carefully study each pupil's interaction with the self-chosen book.

Self-selection requires: 1) a wide array of books, from buildup readers and predictable books to higher level reading books; 2) explicit teacher directions on how to self-select; and 3) careful teacher verifications of each child's placement in a book.

One of the greatest challenges of self-selection is providing things for non-readers and beginning readers to read. Buildups and predictable books provide such possibilities.

Nearly every pupil can manage the self-selection process if the appropriate books are present and the children are presented with clear expectancies as to how to choose an appropriate book—a book that fits.

After pupils have chosen books, teachers have very clear roles to play so that the pupils don't misunderstand the process. Consequently, teachers are provided with directions for observing the whole class as well as making the subsequent determinations of rate, comprehension, and word recognition that are so crucial for correct placement.

STUDY SUGGESTIONS

1. For each level from Preprimer 1 through Fifth Reader, photocopy the first page of a story at the middle of the reader. Beginning with the first selection, ask a school-age child to read it to you and then tell you what he has just read. Record the pupil's

reading with a tape recorder so that you later listen mark the copy for rate, word recognition, and comprehension. Stop when the pupil becomes **frustrated**, and then determine his appropriate **independent** and **instructional** levels.

2. Try the preceding things with other pupils to further refine your emerging skills as a teacher. Attempt to find a pupil in the first grade as well as one in a higher grade.

6

THE FITTING ROOM

To better understand the role of the pupils self-selection and the teacher's subsequent intervention in the process, we shall follow our original group of special students into the fitting room. The "fitting room" simply suggests that the students arrive in a classroom where the teacher fits books to individual pupil reading needs.

Under each child's name and head picture, you will see the descriptive information from the first chapter relative to the following variables:

Grade level and whether the child has been retained.

Chronological age in years and months.

Reading achievement test percentile information.

Math achievement test information.

I.Q information .

Family information about parent(s) and siblings.

After noting the above information, you will see the level of reading material self-selected by each of our six students. This is represented by the letters SS.

While observing the level selected by each student, you can see what the teacher's assessment was. As you will discover, some pupils picked too low while others picked too high. If the pupil choices are not widely different from the teacher's, this suggests that the pupil did a good job of choosing. It's important to realize that good pupil self-selection is not always a sure thing.

Later, after each pupil's independent reading level is verified, you will see how the teacher places each pupil into a challenge (instructional) level reading book. Again, this latter fitting process is usually directed by the teacher who matches pupil reading skill with book demands. Of course, it's always helpful if a teacher knows the increasing difficulty of the books available in the classroom.

STAN	MARY	ROBBIE	TANYA	GREG	SAM
Third Grade	Third Grade (retained)	Third Grade (retained)	Third Grade	Third Grade (retained)	Third Grade (retained)
8yrs,3mos.	9yrs,6mos.	9yrs,1mo.	8yrs,8 mos.	10yrs,2mos.	9yrs,7mos.
Rd.90% ile Ma.85% ile IQ 120 Family- both parents and two siblings	Rd. 7%ile Ma. 40%ile IQ 100 Family- both parents	Rd.20%ile Ma.60%ile IQ 110 Family - single parent, one brother	Rd.40%ile Ma.30%ile IQ 95 Family- single parent, three sisters	Rd.20t%ile Ma.30%ile IQ 75 Family- both parents and two siblings	Rd.40%ile Ma.50%ile IQ 95 Family- single parent, three siblings
S.S 4	**S.S. P**	**S.S.PP1**	**S.S. 3**	**S.S. 3**	**S.S. 3**
R.L. 5	**R.L PP1**	**R.L. P**	**R.L 2**	**R.L P**	**R.L. 3**

The Pupils Select Independent Reading Books

Stan, our very able reader, chooses a trade book to read and immediately begins to read. It's apparent from a glance that he and other able readers are engaged with their books. Because of their engagement, there is seldom any need to give them immediate attention. As you may suspect, there will be ample need for the teacher's attention elsewhere in the classroom. Verifications of the higher readers can be made after the lower readers are accurately placed.

Stan's choice of *Charlie and the Chocolate Factory* for independent reading is a good choice although some may be concerned by the fact that he has the capability to read a more challenging book. Really, the levels marked on trade books are not valid indicators of whether some kids can or should read these books. The primary tests are 1) whether the pupils want to read the books and 2) whether they can read the books at an independent level in terms of fluency, comprehension, and word recognition.

While Stan is an avid reader, there are students with high reading skills who are not avid readers. We call these folks **alliterate** readers. They possess the skill but not the desire to read extensively. To build reading habits, it is often necessary for them to begin with small novels and gradually build the kind of reading muscle that will help them to take on more hefty volumes and become truly **literate**.

Mary, our most needy reader, initially selects a primer book and attempts to read it. As she flips through pages, it's apparent to the teacher that Mary is not reading the book. Consequently, the teacher approaches her with a handful of buildup readers (homemade readers featuring the first words of the preprimers). To hopefully start a successful reading experience, the teacher hands Mary the first buildup reader (BR1 - a reader composed of ten words) and says in a low voice "Please read this!"

When Mary successfully completes the page, the teacher asks her to continue reading until she gets to hard words. In this way, Mary can read the books that add one new word per page until she reaches an instructional level.

Essentially, the teacher is trying to start Mary at a success level in the hope that Mary will stay with it. With success, most reluctant students see that there is hope for improvement.

Robbie, unlike Mary, takes the teacher's words to heart about selecting a book where he can read every word on the first page of the first story. Thus, he selects a preprimer one and reads it carefully. His attention is fully occupied. Because he reads in a low voice, his teacher can tell that he has made a good choice that will sustain him until she can see him. Some pupils want to play it "safe" during self-selection by getting a book that is easy. This usually isn't a great problem as they will quickly finish such books and move up to more appropriate levels. It's certainly better to err in the direction of choosing an easy book than in the direction of choosing one that's too difficult.

Sometimes, pupils like Robbie have never been given an opportunity to choose something that they can read in a classroom. Their choices, when they have them, are usually predetermined by the grade level and represent a choice between difficult or impossible books. With books present that lower level readers can actually read, many will choose books they can read.

When the teacher heard Robbie's fluent reading in the first preprimer, she recognized instantly that he had greater reading capability than the first preprimer. Consequently, she asked him to read a preprimer two story and found that he could read too well. After trying a preprimer three story and finding success, she found that he could read fairly fluently at the beginning of the primer level. Thus, the teacher made the modification to start him at the beginning of the primer for independent reading. It should be pointed out that the teacher had him read only a page in each book so the time expended in getting this placement was less than four minutes.

Tanya, classified previously as having ADD (attention deficit disorder), has the capability to read on grade level. Still, her reading skill seems to be below tha, as was witnessed in the first chapter when she was frustrational because of comprehension in a second reader.

Tanya selects a third grade book but obviously struggles with it. The teacher tries her in a second reader and finds that the oral fluency is fine although there are questions about her understanding of what she is reading.

As previously indicated, Tanya's problem in comprehension might be the effect of her failure to set purposes for understanding text. Consequently, the teacher decides to subsequently set purposes before stories, pages, etc. in an effort to make Tanya accountable of what she has read. Hopefully, Tanya will internalize the process and establish and confirm her own goals for the various things that she reads.

In reflecting about Tanya's off task behavior that was eventually diagnosed as attention deficit disorder, it is important to note that such disorders can often be overcome in reading when these pupils get interested in their reading.

Greg, a ten year old pupil with Downs Syndrome in third grade, has been quite successful in reading despite his understanding limitations. Perhaps because of his uncertainty about the self-selection process, he chose a thick third grade reader and attempted to read it. As previously indicated, it takes an alert teacher only a few minutes to see when a student can't read a chosen book. This was especially clear when the teacher requested that all read in a low voice after they made their selection. In Greg's case, the tip-off was his halting reading.

The teacher quickly moved to Greg and repeated the procedure of trying him in one of her lowest readers. In a few minutes, the teacher discovered that Greg could operate independently in the primer level. This would allow him to progress toward the point whereby the book will become challenging or instructional.

Sam, the pupil who had been mistakenly placed in a special education program because of the failure to diagnose a correctable visual problem, chose a third grade reader that he could read fairly successfully, although his fluency was not good. Since his visual correction, Sam has responded positively to books and is seemingly making up for lost reading opportunities.

The Teacher Makes Independent and Instructional Reading Assignments

Building on the constructs of Chapter 5, it is important for pupils to read both independent level material and instructional level material. The independent material builds confidence and the love of reading while the instructional or challenge level teaches them that reading is a problem solving process that requires their development of new skills.

To help the reader to understand some of the differences between independent and instructional level reading for our targeted six pupils, their independent and instructional level reading assignments are listed and discussed below. The code for book difficulty is as follows:

PP1,2,3(preprimers 1,2,3), P (primer), 1/2 (first reader), 2/1 (second reader-one) 2/2 (second reader two) 3/1 (third reader - one), 3/2 (third reader two), 4 (fourth), 5 (fifth), and 6 (sixth).

STAN	MARY	ROBBIE	TANYA	GREG	SAM
IND. 5	IND. BR1	IIND. P	IIND. 2	IIND. P	IIND. 2
INSTR 6	INSTR. BR1	INSTR. P	INSTR. 2	INSTR P	INSTR. 3

Stan's independent reading of *Charlie and the Chocolate Factory* is extended by his placement in a more challenging sixth grade basal reader. The teacher has done this so that he might have the opportunity to read narratives for his independent level and then do more **content type** reading in the fifth grade basals and reference books.

As a part of his instructional basal reading, Stan is being directed to use other content sources such as encyclopedias to find things related to the basal stories and articles.

Mary, a true **beginning reader**, appears to be in the same place for independent and instructional reading. She is, except that her progress is now measured in terms of pages. After the teacher placed her in the first page of the first buildup reader for preprimer 1 (BR1), Mary read pages 1 - 6 successfully (a vocabulary of 6 of the reader's 10 words). Consequently, her instructional level assignment will be the next two pages each day, providing she is successful in learning the new words. With continued success, she moves into the second buildup reader (BR2) on Wednesday. Most of the words are repeated in the upcoming buildup reader pages.

To ensure that Mary doesn't forget what she's already learned, she reads the independent pages for the twenty minutes of independent reading each day. The next twenty minutes will be spent on reading those old words along with the new words of the new pages. If she has a good day, the teacher may speed up her pace. If she has difficulty, the teacher may ask her to repeat of back up until the minimum fluency of sixty words per minute is maintained. Her weekly reading schedule would look like this:

Monday	Tuesday	Wednesday	Thursday	Friday
IND BR1 pp1-6	IND BR1 pp1-8	IND BR1 pp1-10	IND BR2 pp1-2	IND BR2 pp1-4
INST.BR1 pp 7,8	INST. BR1pp9,10	INST. BR2 pp1,2	INST. BR2pp 3,4	INST. BR2 pp 5,6

As Mary progresses further, she will stop reading the earliest pages of the book.

Robbie's primer level reading assignment of independent and instructional reading reflects the same pattern as Mary. The main difference is that because Robbie is further advanced in reading than Mary, his assignments will be larger each day. Instead of reading two pages, he will read a **complete story each day** at his independent and instructional levels. The new story read at the instructional level of reading will become the independent level story the next day if he can meet the minimum criteria of eighty words per minute. If he can't meet the minimum rate requirements for a given story, he will continue to practice the story until he has achieved a minimum rate of eighty words per minute. Thus, if things go well, his progress might look like the following as he progresses through the primer.

Progressing at the rate illustrated, Robbie can read nearly fifty pages a week. If he is able to maintain this pace with success, he can finish this book in a matter of three or four weeks.

Monday	Tuesday	Wednesday	Thursday	Friday
IND. pp16-24	IND. pp25-29	IND. pp30-36	IND. pp37-43	IND. pp44-50
INSTR. pp25-29	INSTR. pp30 -36	INSTR.pp37--43	INSTR. pp 44-50	INSTR. pp51-60

We find students who are correctly placed and paced like this can often move incredibly fast. One summer we had a pupil advance from preprimer two through the second reader in the course of four weeks, improving his rate from forty words a minute to over a hundred words a minute. It's not uncommon to see pupils progress through two years of reading in a few weeks or months. Of course, it should be noted and understood that some can't achieve so much.

Because Robbie's success is contingent upon a steady buildup of the same vocabulary, we insist that he stays within the same reading series (vocabulary controlled). Unfortunately, many teachers make the mistake of taking pupils like Robbie into what they call **"lateral reading."** That is, they assign him to another primer when he has finished the first one. Because the vocabulary of the new primer is very different, the student often suffers and regresses if he has not developed a great deal of word attack skill.

Lateral moves in reading, I believe, should come after pupils reach a strong second grade reading level and possess enough sight vocabulary and word attack skill to figure things out. If lateral moves are made prematurely, the student loses the familiar words and often regresses. This is particularly damaging to pupils who have built a sight word vocabulary of a hundred words or more. It can be just as devastating for a pupil who has mastered most of the words in a preprimer with forty words.

Tanya's second grade reading skill level is such that she is approaching the needed skills to read from a greater variety of material. It is not so great, though, that she can range far from her sight vocabulary and word analysis skill. Thus, **she reads from two second reader books of the same series**. She reads from a second reader-one (2/1) for her independent reading and a second reader -two (2/2) for her challenge level. This means that she is beyond the rehearsal stage of her classmates Mary and Robbie who have to rehearse their instructional assignment the next day as independent reading.

Like Robbie, Tanya's normal goal is to read a story per day in both independent and instructional level books. This can be seen in her reading schedule.

When looking at Tanya's independent level reading, it appears as though page information has been left off. She has only the starting page of the second reader - one (2/1) book. This pattern is because Tanya is to read as far as she can each day in that book. We call this **unrestricted independent reading**. Because it is fairly easy, she should have few problems. Consequently, she doesn't need to repeat the stories like Robbie did. Children, like Tanya, can progress more rapidly at this stage by extensive reading, so she is encouraged to read ahead.

Monday	Tuesday	Wednesday	Thursday	Friday
IND. pp. 4-	IND. pp	IND. pp	IND. pp	IND. pp
INSTR pp5-10	INSTR. pp.11-17	INSTR. pp.18-24	INSTR. pp.25-34	INSTR. pp.35-42

It should be noted, though, that the teacher needs to take periodic samplings of Tanya's reading to be sure that she is proceeding well in the independent reading as well as the instructional reading. If she has major slowdowns, she will need to repeat stories until she works out the problems.

Greg's reading situation is very similar to Robbie's in that he needs to read at the primer level for both independent and instructional level reading. Both boys are reading from the same book, *Parades* (Houghton Mifflin).

Monday	Tuesday	Wednesday	Thursday	Friday
IND. pp. 16-20	IND. pp.20-24	IND. pp.25-27	IND. pp.27-29	IND. pp.30-32
INSTR. pp.20-24	INSTR. pp.25-27	INSTR. pp.27-29	INSTR. pp.30-32	INSTR. pp.33-36

While some would see this as an opportunity to group these boys together for reading, the teacher does not feel that such a grouping would help the boys at this time. While they might share a play from the reader that both have read, they each need to move at their own pace.

It's apparent by looking back at Robbie's pace that he is doing a story per day. That pace is too rapid for Greg who **needs to repeat each instructional level story page twice as he reads** in order to deal with the words and meanings. Essentially, Greg operates at half the pace that Robbie does. Pupils have differing practice needs and the teacher must gauge these by taking periodic checks to see how they are doing.

Greg's obvious mental retardation requires that the teacher mediate a great deal of the comprehension to be sure that he has sufficient understanding for continuing each story.

Sam reads instructionally at third grade level. He is instructional because he does not possess good fluency in his word attack and tends to over- rely on context. To help him read with greater fluency, the teacher has chosen to place him in a second reader one (2/1) for easier reading that will allow him to operate at a more fluent level.

Monday	Tuesday	Wednesday	Thursday	Friday
IND. pp. 16-	IND. pp.	IND.. pp.	IND. pp.	IND. pp.
INSTR. pp.20-30	INSTR. pp.30-38	INSTR. pp.39-48	INSTR. pp.49-60	INSTR. pp.61-73

Like Tanya, Sam's independent reading is not restricted. Because of his previous visual problems, he didn't do a lot of reading. Consequently, he simly needs to read a great deal in order to accomplish greater fluency. Because he understands what he reads rather well, there is little need for monitoring his comprehension of independent reading. Rather, the teacher is more interested in monitoring his improved speed in silent reading and his better prosody in oral reading.

We find that reading a great deal of relatively independent level material can build both skill and habit. As we have seen in Sam's case and a lot of other students, their needs for reading volume is very great. As we have seen, research clearly supports extensive reading as one of the most powerful means of improving reading skill.

Sam's instructional level reading in the third reader-one (3/1) requires some second readings when his prosody or word attack needs become apparent as he is unable to break down multisyllabic words.

This chapter has spelled out the means by which reading can be caught by daily, extensive reading of appropriately sized books. For some children, there may be little need for anything other than reading every day. Yet, there are other considerations that are important, such as comprehension, fluency, and word analysis.

When some of these pupils appear to be reading far below what we might expect, we may seek to explore reading potential determination.

READING POTENTIAL DETERMINATION

The **reading potential** concept focuses on the realization that hearing people initially develop vocabulary and comprehension by speaking and listening. Reading comes later and allows them to read what they have previously said and heard. Consequently, the gap between what a person can understand from listening and reading is greatest before they can read. This gap is subsequently narrowed as they become fluent readers. Presumably, in time there should be a match between what can be processed by listening and reading.

Because some high ability pupils fail to develop word analysis skills and there is some uncertainty about their basic understanding skills, it is possible to get a quick contrast of their reading and listening skills by reading stories to them and asking them questions. If the listening level is significantly higher than the pupil's reading level we refer to the listening level as the "reading potential." The "potential," of course, depends upon his ability to gain the necessary word attack skills.

While most students with special needs have undergone a comprehensive understanding assessment, some will not have undergone such assessment. It is these latter students this section addresses. More specifically, these are the students who are reading far below that of most of their peers at their age level.

When a student has gone through the preceding self-selection procedures and has been found to be reading at a level below what might be expected for his age, we may seek to measure what he is capable of understanding by reading him a series of graded passages from a basal reader. If he can understand the majority of the material (60% or more), we would argue that he has a basic comprehension of the material, and with the necessary reading skills could manage this material.

To illustrate, we test **Mary,** our learning-disabled third grader who is not reading at all. Although she has been tested and it's apparent that she has the necessary understanding skills, it's still worthwhile to see specifically how well she can understand the book language of graded reading selections. Consequently, short stories are read to her from a graded reading series.

The following illustrates the stories from the Houghton Miffline Readers that are read to Mary and her apparent comprehension of those stories as determined by tellbacks immediately after each story was read.

> **Primer Selection** (PARADES) Houghton Mifflin, 1986. *Tooley.* Mary tells that it was about two boys trying to find a dog named Tooley for a reward. The one boy finds a lot of dogs that aren't Tooley while the other boy finds Tooley. The two boys decide to share the reward money after they return the dogs that aren't Tooley. This is determined to be a high-quality tell back.
>
> **First Reader Selection** (CAROUSELS) Houghton Mifflin, 1986. *What Mary Jo Shares—Part 1.* Mary says it's about this shy little girl who couldn't think of anything to share at Sharing Time. She was going to share an umbrella one day but saw a whole lot of them. She was going to share a grasshopper her brother caught another day but another boy caught three himself. She still hadn't shared. One day she brought her dad and shared him with the class. They liked what she shared. Once again, this is a very well-detailed tellback.
>
> **Second Reader Selection** (ADVENTURES) Houghton-Mifflin, 1986. *Penelope Gets Wheels.* Mary recounts the story of the girl who got ten dollars for her birthday

and discovered that she couldn't buy a bike with so little money. She buys some skates instead and finds out that she can get places on her skates that other people can't get to on bikes. She beats her dad and a friend to the ball game. Once again, the tellback is complete.

Third Reader Selection (CARAVANS) Houghton-Mifflin, 1986. *Benny's Flag.* Mary knows that Benny won the contest to design the flag for Alaska but is very uncertain about the significance of the star arrangement on the flag and many of the facts in Benny's life. The teacher felt that this story might be beyond her.

While "Benny's Flag" may be beyond Mary, it's apparent that she understood everything up to that story. Possibly, she would understand other stories from the same third grade reader. What is important, though, is that she has an understanding level far in advance of her nonexistent reading level. Such testing for her and other non-achievers can quickly rule out any questions about the absence of language or understanding.

Graphically, Mary's performance on the reading potential testing is as follows:

Primer (PARADES)	Good tellback
First Reader (CAROUSELS)	Good tellback
Second Reader (ADVENTURES)	Good tellback
Third Reader (CARAVANS)	Uncertain tellback

This suggests that although Mary has no reading skill she has the potential to read at least second grade books with good understanding. The emphasis in her instruction will be upon recognizing simple sentence patterns that can be expanded.

SUMMARY

This chapter extends the concepts of Chapter Five by allowing the reader to observe how different level pupils function when given the opportunity to select independent level books to read. It further illustrates the accuracy of the pupils' choices by revealing how the pupil choices correspond with the placements made by the monitoring teacher.

After pupils are placed in independent levels, the teacher must decide what kind of instructional level reading assignment will allow each pupil to further develop in terms of his or her needs. This is illustrated along with such concepts as page per day, story per day, unrestricted independent reading, repeated readings, and lateral reading.

For some students with limited reading abilities, reading potential assessment is a simple process whereby the teacher reads stories beyond the pupils' current reading levels to determine if they understand these higher level stories. If the students understand the stories read to them from these higher level readers, they obviously have the understanding skills with which to read the books.

STUDY SUGGESTIONS

1. Ask a pupil to self-select from a series of graded books. Check the pupil's rate, word recognition, and comprehension to see if s/he chose a book that could be easily read. If the

student did not choose an appropriate level book, try placing the pupil in a book of appropriate difficulty. If time permits, attempt to have the pupil read far enough to find his/her instructional level.

2. On another day when the pupil you have tested is fresh, try the reading potential task. Begin with a story at the pupil's frustrational level and ask the pupil to tell back what he hears you read. Continue reading higher level selections until you read a point where the student no longer understands the majority of the text. Determine how much, if any, the pupil's understanding level may be than his/her instructional reading level.

7

DEVELOPING FLUENCY

Fluency represents a quick view of many factors relevant to the reading process. Poor fluency can reveal areas of word recognition and comprehension difficulty.

Initially, we think of fluency as the smoothness of reading, whether it be oral or silent. In the earliest phases of reading, it is useful to think of fluency as the rapidity with which a reader covers text. I like to measure this early oral reading fluency in terms of the reader's **oral rate.** As you will discover, this can be computed by a simple words per minute determination.

Along with the reader's oral rate progress, we are very interested in his/her fluency in terms of **prosody.** Prosody includes the various means by which we describe intonation, such as pitch, stress, and juncture. Without proper inflections it's difficult to understand what is being said, especially when characters are dialoging.

As the reader progresses, oral fluency in terms of rapidity and prosody gives way to **silent fluency.** Silent fluency is an important necessity to becoming a skillful reader who is not dependent on the limitations of his/her voice. Most pupils have the capability of going much faster and understanding a great deal more as silent readers.

Oral Fluency

Oral fluency is considered first from the one-to-one perspective in terms of the ease or difficulty of the text being read. The teacher moves quickly to see if the pupil's rate is independent, instructional, or frustrational.

Minimum Fluency Levels

Independent Reading Materials		**Instructional Reading Materials**	
First Grade	80 words per minute	First Grade	60 words per minute
Second Grade	90 words per minute	Second Grade	70 words per minute
Third Grade	100 words per minute	Third Grade	80 words per minute

When the teacher notes a specific rate or prosody deficiency, the teacher may wish to employ one or more interventions. In the text which follows, some of the most common oral fluency problems are outlined along with teacher interventions designed to help the pupil solve the problems.

Oral Fluency Interventions

Problems	**Teacher Interventions**
Pupil loses place	Tracking
Pupil reads slowly	Rereading
Pupil reads very slowly	Tape Assist
Pupil neglects punctuation	Punctuation marking
Pupil neglects dialogue	Dialogue marking
Pupil fails to phrase	Segmented discourse

Pupil loses place

Tracking is suggested so that the pupil can track each word with his finger as he reads. The use of line markers should be avoided as markers cause pupils to cover important text above or below the marker. Barr and Johnson (1991) support finger-pointing.

Pupil reads slowly

Rereading is the simplest means of improving fluency. The pattern may be one of reading a story twice or more, rereading each page multiple times, or rereading segments of a page until the material meets the minimum rate (words per minute). Much research supports this practice.

Pupil reads very slowly

Tape assists are simply teacher made recordings of the story. The recordings should be slow enough that the student can carefully track the print as he listens to the tape. Tape assists have been very successful with slower readers (Carbo, 1978; Dowhower, 1987).

Pupil neglects punctuation

Punctuation marking refers to the process whereby the teacher lays a clear piece of plastic over pupil text and marks punctuation marks with a colored marker so that the student can have secondary cues for inflection.

Pupil neglects dialogue

Dialogue marking is the same process as punctuation marking except the teacher now marks the speaker markers and speaker parts in color. For example, the speaker marker could be colored green while the speaker part (the spoken part) could be marked in red:

Speaker Marker	Speaker Part
John said,	"Get out of here!"

Pupil fails to phrase

Segmented discourse refers to the process of breaking up text into meaning chunks (Cromer, 1970; O'Shea & Sindelar, 1985). The following illustrates such a clustering.

One hot afternoon • Lucky Masters and his dog Duke • had started their trip • to the base of the mountain. • On the way • they saw a large bird • hovering in the sky.

Although each of the above interventions can be used to help pupils to obtain improved fluency in their reading, teachers should start with the repeated reading procedure because it seems to be the most effective strategy for a large number of pupils.

It's important to note, though, that if tracking, rereading, and tape assists fail to produce the minimum rates, it's probably best to move to another form of materials. These other materials might be easier basal materials or predictable book materials.

Some pupils have **speech problems** while others have **oral encoding problems** that cause them to struggle with oral reading. Whenever a pupil repeatedly has difficulty reading aloud, the teacher should check the student's silent rate as well as the oral reading rate. If this comparison reveals a consistently slower pattern in the oral mode, the student should be exempted from oral reading as much as possible. We see such pupils in summer reading programs because they are referred by teachers who are unaware that the students have problems that will never allow them to be fluent oral readers. Yet, when these students are allowed to read silently, they can often function quite well. For lack of a better term, I refer to these pupils as the **non oral readers.** This is a short way of saying that we shouldn't ask them to read orally but should emphasize their silent reading.

Silent Fluency

As pupils become skillful readers, their eyes move considerably ahead of what their voices can read. This pattern is referred to as the **eye-voice span**, which is the number of words between the last word read aloud and the last word read beyond that by the eye. Because the eye can move so much faster than the voice, it is imperative that such pupils move into silent reading as soon as possible.

Because silent reading emerges naturally in most individuals, it is best not to make a big deal about it in the first grade. **By second grade, though, there is a danger that a total concentration on oral reading may impede silent reading. Therefore, I feel strongly that second graders should be encouraged to read silently more often than they read orally.**

When students are doing quite well with their oral reading and achieving "rapid" rates, it is a good idea to ask them to read silently. **Nothing should be said about "speed" or "speed reading," lest they get the notion that we want them to speed through their reading.** Remember, you only count the words read in a time segment *after* the pupil has satisfactorily retold the content of the passage just read. For details on how to administer the silent rate check, refer back to Chapter 5.

Some students may be so locked into oral reading that they have difficulty in not verbalizing what they are reading. For them, a one-to-one intervention like the following may be necessary on a number of occasions.

A Silent Fluency Intervention

1) Select a story the child has not read in his book and mark off some major event chunks (around 50 words in length).
2) Using the child's book, ask him to look at a given chunk (or group of chunks) to find out a specific event. Warn him that you are going to allow only a few seconds for him to find it.
3) Uncover the page so that he may search the material in a brief time frame, usually 10 to 20 seconds.
4) Ask the child to tell you the answer contained in the chunk.
5) If the child can satisfactorily tell the answer, proceed to more chunks, cutting down the reading time slightly on each new chunk. If the child cannot perform the task, move on to the next step.
6) Ask the child to find a specific piece of information in the chunk to be read. Repeat the same procedures. You are now setting a purpose in advance that the child can use to direct his search of the chunk.
7) Determine if the child can find the answer. Continue until the child can skillfully read larger and larger chunks with adequate comprehension.

In time, the pupil should be cutting away from verbalization of text to the task of attempting to process print rapidly in an effort to find information and then to organize it.

By the time pupils reach the third grade level of reading, their silent rates should be at least 20 words per minute faster than their oral rates; some students' silent rates will even be double their oral rates. This difference should further widen as they go on.

DIRECT TEACHING FLUENCY

While we have discussed specific interventions for fluency at the one to one level, we have not yet addressed how such interventions might be conducted with small groups.

The first two lessons that follow deal with oral fluency while the third lesson concerns silent fluency.

LESSON 1 (Oral Fluency)—Inflecting for terminal markers, periods, and question marks:

Behavioral Objective: After the lesson, the pupil will correctly inflect fade/fall and fade/rise intonations for periods and question marks in their oral reading.

Anticipatory Set: From the overhead screen, the teacher will read the following sentences without intonation for periods and question marks:

> Jane said I am having my party this afternoon can you come you don't have to bring a present Mary said I can come if my mother will let me I will ask her and tell you when can I call you

The teacher asks the group what is wrong. The group notes that there are no stops and everything is run together. The teacher accepts their analysis.

Instructional Input: The teacher rewrites the original message below the unpunctuated message, reading aloud with the correct intonation as she writes:

> Jane said, "I am having my party this afternoon. Can you come? You don't have to bring a present."
>
> Mary said, "I can come if my mother will let me. I will ask her and tell you. When can I call you?"

The teacher carefully puts red dots over the periods and blue marks over each question marker and explains that she must see the marks in advance of reading each sentence in order to correctly inflect the words in the sentence.

After marking the rewritten text, the teacher carefully reads it again, indicating the appropriate intonation for each sentence.

Guided Practice: For guided practice, the teacher has the pupils read with her. Next, half of the group reads Jane's part while the other half responds with Mary's part.

Independent Practice: At this point, the teacher reveals more of the dialogue and asks the pupils to read the dialogue in pairs at their desks.

Jane said, "O.K., you call me as soon as you get home. I will wait by my telephone."

Mary said, "You do that. I'll call you as soon as I can."

Closing: The teacher asks the pupils to summarize what they have learned about reading sentences with periods and question marks. The pupils state that they must pause briefly for each. They show how to inflect their voices accordingly.

This same basic lesson format can be used for teaching pupils to read other punctuation markers as well as the protocols of reading dialogue that allow the speaker designation to be placed at the front of the paragraph, at the end of the paragraph, or in the middle of the paragraph:

> <u>Front</u>
>
> Jane said, "I want to go to the store."

Mother said, "Not now, Jane."

End

"I want to go to the store," said Jane.

"Not now," said Mother.

Middle

"I want to go to the store," said Jane, "to get a hat."

"Not now." said Mother. "We have to fix the car."

LESSON 2 (Oral Fluency)—Phrasing:

Behavioral Objective: After this lesson, the pupils will orally phrase as they read their materials.

Anticipatory Set: From the overhead screen, the teacher reads in a word-by-word fashion as the students observe.

> One/ hot/ afternoon/ Lucky/ Masters/ and/ his/ dog/ Duke/ had/ started/ their/ trip/ to/ the/ base/ of/ the/ mountain./ On/ the/ way/ they/ saw/ a/ large/ bird/ hovering/ in/ the/ sky.

After completing the reading, the teacher asks for an analysis of her oral reading. Pupils explain that it was not natural, unlike reading and speaking. The teacher agrees and points out that the marks between words were put there to show what reading is like without smoothness.

Instructional Input: The teacher reveals the same material written on the bottom of the transparency in the following phrased fashion:

> One hot afternoon / Lucky Masters and his dog Duke / had started their trip/to the base of the mountain./ On the way / they saw a large bird / hovering in the sky.

The teacher reads the material, hesitating slightly at each break between groups of words, as the pupils observe. The teacher then explains that she has broken up the text into more meaningful phrases to show what we do when we read with greater expression. She carefully explains that our mind does the breaking and that we don't really need to have spaces like this when we become fluent.

Guided Practice: For guided practice, the pupils read the phrased text from the transparency. For further practice, the teacher reveals more of the story for pupils to practice in pairs.

Independent Practice: Pupils practice reading on their own from the transparency, using first the broken up (phrased) material and then the regular material with which they can do their own phrasing.

Closing: The teacher asks different pupils to summarize the importance of phrasing for getting the proper meaning of text.

LESSON 3 (Silent Fluency)—Silent reading for purpose in a limited exposure:

(As indicated previously, an over-reliance on oral reading can retard the development of efficient silent reading. Consequently, by third grade level, teachers may wish to emphasize some direct teach lessons geared at speeding up silent reading.)

Behavioral Objective: After the lesson, the reader will silently read and answer previously stated questions about the text.

Anticipatory Set: The teacher asks the students whether they can read faster orally or silently. There is some debate and the teacher tells them that they should read most things faster silently.

Instructional Input: The teacher begins by explaining that reading is most often driven by **purpose**. She explains that if her purpose was to find out where the monthly meeting of the Sierra Club was to be held, she would quickly scan the club meetings section of the paper until she found the date and time of the Sierra Club meeting. Continuing, the teacher says that she has been given two tickets to the Friday night football game and wants to know when and where it will be. Consequently, her purpose for reading the upcoming text will be to find out the **game time and place**. She explains that she's going to display the article about the game and spend only as much time as it takes **to find the game time and place**. Students are invited to do so also, but without calling out the answer. The teacher puts up the following for 3 seconds:

> The LBJ Jaguars and the Reagan Raiders are set to square off this Friday night at 7:30 p.m. at Nelson Field to see who will get to represent the district in the state play-offs. Both teams bring in winning records and both schools have been caught up in the excitement of the week.

The teacher then tells that she found that the game was to be at 7:30 p.m. at Nelson Field. She asks who else found the fact quickly. She then proceeds to read the piece in a normal oral reading voice and has one pupil time how many seconds it took her to read orally until the information was found. The difference between the two times is discussed.

Guided Practice: For guided practice, the teacher has prepared a series of paragraphs with specific purpose questions in advance of them so that the pupils may read the purpose and try to accomplish it within the limited amount of time by a quick visual search of the material. An example of such paragraphs would be the following:

Purpose: To find out how the boys are going to get to the lake.

> The big picnic is set for Lake Travis Sunday afternoon. On tap will be soft drinks, grilled hamburgers, chips, cakes, pies, and watermelons. Free boating, swimming, running races, volleyball, and softball will be available for all those attending. Everyone going needs to be at the church before 2:30 because that's when the bus will be leaving.

Independent Practice: After extensive practice in this format, the teacher passes out paragraphs for the pupils to do on their own in order that they might practice trying to get information as rapidly as possible. The information will shift from specific purpose to broader purpose, where the students have to tell back the whole paragraph.

Closing: The teacher will emphasize how purpose can drive rapid reading and will encourage the pupils to provide actual experiences in their lives wherein they have to get information rapidly. Such things as the following should be offered: finding a bus route, locating the score of a favorite team, getting the time of a favorite program on TV.

SUMMARY

Fluency refers to the rapidity with which a reader covers text. In the earliest phases of reading, that rapidity is normally described by the reader's **oral rate** (words per minute) and **prosody** (intonation). As the reader progresses, silent fluency becomes increasingly important and efforts are made to gauge **silent rate** and **comprehension** in different types of text.

Teacher Interventions for oral fluency include: tracking, rereading, tape assist, punctuation marking, dialogue marking, and segmented discourse.

As pupils become skillful readers, their eyes grasp text much more quickly than they can orally encode words. This pattern, the **eye-voice span**, refers to the number of words between the last word read aloud and the last word read beyond that by the eye. Because the eye can move so much faster than the voice, it is imperative that such pupils move into silent reading as soon as possible. A silent reading intervention is illustrated to help those pupils who do not read more rapidly silently than orally.

Direct teach lessons are included for teaching oral and silent fluency.

STUDY SUGGESTIONS

1. If you can find a pupil who reads with a fair degree of accuracy but with little **prosody** (intonation), it would be helpful to get a clear piece of plastic and lay it over a book page that the pupil can read independently. Start by marking periods in red and question marks in blue with your washable colored markers. Model how to inflect in a sentence or two and then ask the pupil to follow your lead. Practice until the pupil is skillful in inflecting for these marks. If the pupil catches on quickly, try marking the quotations of different speakers to see if the pupil can get the idea of voicing differently for the different characters in a dialogue. Refer back to the chapter for details about how to do this.

2. Find a pupil whose oral and silent rates are about the same. Get some easy reading material and ask the pupil to read silently to find a given piece of information in a segment of text. Allow the pupil only a few seconds to find the specific piece of information so that he will be forced to visually search the passage for the desired information. Reread the instructions for this intervention and see if you can assist pupils to read more efficiently silently.

8
DEVELOPING WORD RECOGNITION

Word recognition usually refers to the skills of recognizing and understanding the meaning of text through the use of **context analysis** (closure), **sight word analysis**, **structural analysis**, and **phonic analysis**. Consequently, the initial focus of this section will be upon the components of phonic word recognition that may not be discovered efficiently by some pupils. Subsequently, interventions will be illustrated.

It is my conviction that every teacher needs to have some notion of the components of phonic word recognition for two very critical reasons. First, it is important to have some rudimentary knowledge of the components of phonic analysis in order that you can make clear judgments about the myriad of such programs you will see. Second, it is important to use your knowledge of phonic components to make valid assessments about pupil needs in these areas. Consequently, this section is intended to provide such knowledge in terms of (1) the components of word recognition and (2) an overall plan for assessing and teaching word recognition in an **inductive** fashion.

It should be noted that phonics can be approached inductively as well as deductively. The desired goal of both is a reader who analyzes words and word parts efficiently. That efficiency can be enhanced with careful instruction that utilizes effective blending of consonants and vowels from the start.

Inductive instruction builds from the known to the unknown. Thus, pupils in the program described are led to use what they know about words and word parts to solve what they don't know. The clever teacher quickly learns what pupils know and don't know and works to engineer the use of the known. An alternative would be that the teacher would decide that the students should be deductively taught a short vowel sound and a few consonants that could be blended together quickly to read the simple sentences shown in the examples which follow, e.g. Dan can fan. Richard Wubbena has an excellent deductive phonics program called ***Figeritowt*** (Twenty First Century Blueprint, Round Rock, Texas).

The components of phonic word recognition are broken down into the consonant and vowel sectors along with their components. Try to get a working knowledge of the various descriptors of consonants (single, blend, digraph, silent) and vowels (single—long, short or variant), adjacent pairs, and diphthongs. This knowledge will help you when you're discussing phonics with your colleagues and friends. It will also be a help when you arrive at the application section.

It should be noted that adjacent vowel pairs carry a wide array of sounds. Consequently, you will not see the adjacent vowel pairs treated in the application section. Because so many studies of the behavior of vowel pairs have indicated their instability, it is believed that the pupils are best served by dealing with the more regular cvc patterns that you will be seeing in the application section. I believe that if pupils can manage the high frequency patterns, there is a great likelihood that their analysis by analogy behaviors will allow them to deal with the differences. I would like to avoid teaching pupils things that they will not actually use in their reading.

Quick, one-to-one interventions for closure and compound word analysis will be discussed at the end of the chapter. Although structural analysis typically contains the skills of affixes, compounds, endings, and contractions, I feel that instruction in these elements is seldom productive because pupils learn those elements independently or with a few teacher prompts.

THE COMPONENTS OF WORD RECOGNITION

Consonants				Vowels	
Single	**Blend**	**Digraph**	**Silent**	**Single**	**Adjacent pairs**
b	bl	sh	-ight	**Short (unglided) in VC,**	**Digraphs**
d	cl	ch	write	**CVC patterns**	(Sound of one of
f	fl	th[6]	know	a (at, can)	the vowels or
h	gl	wh	chick	i (in, fin)	another vowel is
j	sl	ph	bomb	e (bet)	heard)
k	br			o (oz, top)	ai (hail, again)
l	cr	-nk		u (up, tug)[7]	ay (say, says)
m	dr	-ng			ea (each, great)
n	gr	-ck			ei (believe, lie)
p	pr			**Long (glided) in CVCe, CV**	**Diphthongs**
r	tr			**patterns**	(Sound of both
t	sc			a (rate, vapor)	vowels is heard)
v	sk			i (hide, bicycle)	oi (boil)
w	sm			e (fete, he)	ou (out)
y	sn			o (hope, motel)	au (audio)
z	sp			y (by)	
c[1]	scr				
g[2]	spr			**Variant sounds in various**	
s[3]	str			**patterns**	
q[4]				a (bär, båll, fâre, åkin)	
x[5]				e (hêr)	
				i (fîr)	
				o (wön, fôr)	
				u (tûrn)	

[1]The letter *c* tends to be associated with a hard sound when it precedes the letters *a, o,* or *u* and a soft sound when preceding *i, e,* and *y: cake, city.*

[2]The letter *g* tends to be associated with a hard sound when it precedes the letters *a, o,* or *u* and a soft sound when preceding *e* and *i: go, gem.*

[3]The letter *s* is associated with three different sounds: *s* as in *so, z* as in *his,* and *sh* as in *sugar.*

[4]The letter *q* is normally associated with the sound of *kw* when it occurs (followed by *u*) at the beginning of a word.

[5]The letter *x* is normally associated with the sound of *z* when it occurs at the beginning of a word.

[6]The letters *th* are represented by two different sounds: *th*in, *th*en.

[7]The short or unglided sound associated with *u* is also produced by other letters occurring in unaccented syllables: hast*e*n, char*i*ty. This is called the *schwa* sound and is represented by the symbol ə in dictionaries and glossaries.

Assessing and Teaching Word Recognition

The table shown above provides a listing of the components of word recognition, but there is no indication of how those elements might be sequenced and taught systematically. In order that the teacher might have some idea of how to assess and deal with specific word recognition deficits, the following word recognition progression is provided.

You will note that the prerequisites of auditory and visual discrimination must be apparent before proceeding with the first step, sound to symbol. Assessments of auditory and visual discrimination involve asking pupils to repeat sound pairs such as *bat-cat* for auditory discrimination and asking pupils to match letters for visual discrimination. When pupils can't repeat different phoneme pairs, they may have difficulty with auditory discrimination. Likewise, pupils who confuse letter pairs might suffer from inadequate visual discrimination capabilities.

WORD RECOGNITION PROGRESSION

PREREQUISITES: AUDITORY DISCRIMINATION AND VISUAL DISCRIMINATION

STEP 1	**SOUND TO SYMBOL**
STEP 2	**INITIAL CONSONANT SUBSTITUTION**
STEP 3	**FINAL CONSONANT SUBSTITUTION**
STEP 4	**MEDIAL VOWEL SUBSTITUTION**
STEP 5	**CVCE PATTERN SUBSTITUTION**
STEP 6	**MULTISYLLABIC ATTACK PLAN**

In order for the Word Recognition Progression described below to be useful, the student must first be capable of auditory discrimination (able to distinguish significant speech sounds from each other) and of visual discrimination (able to distinguish different letters by their forms).

STEP 1: SOUND-TO-SYMBOL

Behavioral Objective: When asked for the consonant letters that begin one syllable regular words, the pupil will accurately write the letters or point to the letters on a letter card:

b, c, d, f, g, h, j, k, l, m, n, p, r, t, v, w, z.

It is important that pupils have sound-to-symbol knowledge for most of these letters before initiating a second step. Thus, the teacher is urged to give all the students in a kindergarten or first grade a piece of paper and ask them to write the letter that begins each word that she says:

Teacher says:	*boy*	Pupil writes on paper: *b*
Teacher says:	*cap*	Pupil writes on paper: *c*

Teacher says: *dog* Pupil makes an X if he doesn't know

Teacher says: *girl* Pupil writes on paper: *g*

On the basis of the each student's written responses, a teacher can prepare a grid, like the one that follows, that will indicate which pupil lacks which sound-to-symbol elements. The teacher is then aware of what sound-to-symbol instruction each pupil needs and is prepared to develop a plan whereby she may teach individuals or small groups.

Pupil Sound-to-Symbol Needs*

Pupis	b	c	d	f	g	h	j	k	l	m	n	p	r	s	t	v	w	z
Al																		
Tara																		
Carl	x						x											
Tom	x	x																
Eve		x			x													

*An *x* indicates that the student lacks sound-to-symbol knowledge of that letter.

Although most children pick up sound-to-symbol on their own or outside the classroom, some will not have caught it. If a pupil has no sound-to-symbol matches, then it is best to start with one of the easier hookups. If the child's name begins with a consonant, that is often a good starting place. If not, the letter *f* is a good starting place because it has a distinctive sound and a distinctive letter form. The dialogue for teaching the first sound-to-symbol connection goes like this:

Teacher: (Showing a large letter *f)* This is the letter *f*, and we hear its sound at the beginning of the word *fish*.

(The teacher then places the letter on a paper fish, perhaps as shown below.)

(insert sketch of fish here) f

Listen carefully. *Fish* (with some exaggeration of the first letter sound).

*F*ish. Can you hear the sound I'm making at the start of the word *f*ish?

Pupils: (Respond) No!

Teacher: Now, listen as I say some other words that start with this same *f-* sound. *Fun, five, four, finger, father...* now, please say these words after me. (Repeats each word, and waits for students to respond.) What letter sound begins each of these words?

Pupils: They don't sound alike. (This is a typical response because many pupils have dealt with rhyming sounds and they are not attuned to listening for alliteration.)

The teacher must calmly repeat the above dialogue, continuing to try for the breakthrough of getting the pupils to hear what sound begins a word. For some pupils, the task may not occur after several lessons so the teacher must be patient and not seek to develop the skill quickly with these pupils.

Sessions should be no longer than 5 minutes so that it's not a struggle. When the pupils do get the idea, the teacher will then pronounce words and ask pupils to hold up a small *f* card each time the teacher says a word beginning with *f*. Distracter words are thrown in so that the teacher can be sure that the pupils are attending. Avoid asking pupils for words that begin with *f* because it is not a rapid process and tends to waste time.

When pupils have a sound-to-symbol match, others are added in the preceding manner. If, for example, the pupil has *f* and *m* and the teacher is adding *p*, the teacher should review them over the previously learned elements by having the children raise cards with those elements on them. When they have a lot of letters, the teacher can ask them to touch a given letter on a card such as the following:

f m s p d c

STEP 2: INITIAL CONSONANT SUBSTITUTION

Behavioral Objective: When a pupil sees a new CVC pattern that is like a known pattern except for the first consonant, the pupil will use his knowledge of initial consonants and word forms to correctly read the new pattern.

Initial consonant substitution is the process whereby the student uses his knowledge of consonants along with his knowledge of CVC words to open up a wide array of CVC words and syllables.

We generally don't like to bring overt attention to this process until the pupil is reading over a hundred sight words because we think the natural process of **analysis by analogy** (Smith, 1978) will allow him to do it on his own and because there is a danger that early word mediation may slow down reading. Some pupils develop a form of tunnel vision whereby they look so hard at individual letters and words that they fail to see the larger meaning of the passage.

Research support for the use of initial substitution is provided by Adams (1990) in *Beginning to Read: Thinking and Learning About Print.* Parts of syllables called **onsets** and **rines** have been found to be very effective in teaching written language. Such phonograms (syllable patterns that can be altered with initial consonants) avoid the dubi ous phonic rules often associated with vowel patterns and provide a stable set of patterns for children to learn. Research by Lieberman, Rubin, Duques, and Carlisle (1985) indicates the ease with which pupils can manage specific rines.

Rines or **phonograms** (as we shall call them) allow pupils to manage the variant vowel sounds with minimal difficulty. One study found that of 286 phonograms in primary text, 95% were pronounced the same way in every word in which they were found (Read, Yun-Fei, Hong-Yin, & Bao-Qing, 1986).

While I see little need to teach pupils 286 phonograms, I think that some teachers may wish to use rines or phonograms with some pupils who have difficulty with vowel elements. Therefore, the following list of phonograms seems to be particularly useful because they can produce a vocabulary of approximately 500 words (Blachman, 1984). The pupils might be able to play some word making games whereby they attempt to blend consonant elements with the phonograms.

-ack	-ank	-eat	-ill	-ock	-uck
-all	-ap	-ell	-in	-oke	-ug
-ain	-ash	-est	-ine	-op	-ump
-ake	-at		-ice	-ore	-unk
-ale	-ate		-ick	-or	
-ame	-aw		-ide		
-an	-ay		-ight		
			-ing		
			-ink		
			-ip		
			-ir		

Some teachers may wish to take a few consonants and assess a pupil's ability to deal with the preceding patterns in a left to right progression, a, e, i, o, u.

For pupils who appear to have no knowledge of initial consonant substitution, we like to start with a known sight word or rine. If the child's name is amenable, it's a good idea to start with something like Jan, Jack, or Sam. Because the word ***cat*** seems to be such a fundamental word, we like to start with that, or possibly ***can,*** which is usually learned rather quickly by beginning readers. *Can* permits you to use the word in connected patterns for practice.

Starting with the underlined known word *can,* the teacher produces a short list of words as follows and seeks to have the pupil read the first word and attempt to read either the second word or any other recognized word on the list.

can

fan

man

ran

tan

If the pupil cues off the first consonant and says a word like *for,* attention should be given to covering all the initial consonants except the one in *can* and telling the pupil that all the words end like *can.* Then, you reveal the word *fan* under *can,* and attempt to get the pupil to generalize the sound.

For pupils who continue to have difficulty with the concept, it is sometimes useful to have them pick out the word *tan* from your list. This type of help should be given on a few words in the hopes that they can make the generalization.

When the generalization is made, it is important to have the pupil apply the concept to another known word or phonogram and to practice the patterns in a connected reading application.

Short stories can be constructed or obtained from linguistic readers such as *A Pig Can Jig* from the Basic Reading Series (Science Research Associates, 1976). While too much practice in this format may have negative effects (Badderly & Lewis, 1981A; Perfetti & McCutcheon, 1982), I believe that a certain amount can be desirable so that the child has opportunities to deal with the new skill of initial substitution in significant depth.

Dan has a van.

Dan has a tan van.

Dan ran the van.

When pupils reveal confusions in reading these stories or similar words in their reading books, it is well to have them practice the vertical ladders in order that they can rehearse the skill of initial substitution.

STEP 3: FINAL CONSONANT SUBSTITUTION

Behavioral Objective: When a pupil sees a CVC pattern that is unknown because of the **final** consonant, the pupil will use his knowledge of consonants to correctly blend the CV_ pattern to the consonant.

Final consonant substitution can be initiated with a constant CV_ pattern such as the following where the pupil is asked to read each word as the teacher writes in the final consonant.

ca**n**	
ca_	ca**p**
ca_	ca**t**
ca_	ca**m**
ca_	ca**b**
ca_	ca**s**
ca_	ca**d**

After the pupil is skillful with the single pattern, it is wise to put up a different set of words so that the student can apply the substitutive principle to such words:

bu**g**	ra**n**	do**g**
bu_	ra_	do_
bu_	ra_	do_
bu_	ra_	do_

Next, the pupil should read text with a lot of final consonant pattern substitutions. The text can be made up by the teacher or something like *A Pig Can Jig* (Science Research Associates, 1976) can be used.

Dan ran to tag Pat.

Dan can tag Pat.

Dan had the bat.

When pupils show continuing problems in reading the stories, they should be sent to the ladder patterns for additional practice.

STEP 4: MEDIAL VOWEL SUBSTITUTION

Behavioral Objective: When a pupil notes a CVC pattern (in a word or syllable), the pupil will instantly blend the short medial vowel sounds to the surrounding consonants.

During their connected reading, pupils will reveal difficulties with medial vowels. This is a good lead for doing a follow-up assessment where they are asked to read either pattern sentences or a medial vowel assessment chart.

The following pattern sentences allow a pupil to demonstrate their knowledge of medial vowels. An absence of such knowledge can be easily noted by the teacher who listens carefully and notes any delays or substitutions.

A tan bug sat by his cobweb.

"If lots of bugs get in my web," said the tan bug, "I can get fed."

From *A Hen In A Fox's Den* (Science Research Associations, 1976)

A medial vowel assessment chart is used to see which, if any, medial vowels or vowel pairs cause the pupil any problems. The easiest way to use the chart is to simply begin at the left and move across. If you wish to assess several students at once, you can have them put five lines at the top of the page and then write in the five words as you dictate them aloud–perhaps *bat, bit, bet, bot,* and *but.* If the pupil has difficulty writing in one of the medial vowels there is a good likelihood that he has trouble with it in reading. After the pupils have written in the five words, you can pronounce words from the various medial vowel patterns and observe the pupils' skills as they seek to determine by the medial vowel both where to write their words and how they write their words.

Medial Vowel Assessment

bat	**bit**	**bet**	**bot**	**but**
cat	hit	set	hot	cut
tap	fib	red	top	fun
ram	hip	leg	rob	tub
sad	win	Ted	sob	wup
spam	twist	best	chop	crust

Typically, the problems occur between the medial *-i-* and *-e-* pairs. When this occurs, isolate the attention on these two pairs and work down the list from two known words:

pit	pet
lit	let
nit	net
sit	set
bit	bet
fit	fet

Practice for the medial vowel substitutions can be provided with teacher made materials or commercial materials like *A Pig Can Jig, A Hen In A Foxs' Den*, (Science Research Associates, 1976). An example of such material is as follows:

"It's a dog—a pet dog.
It's a dog I can hug and pet."
Max ran to his mom and said,
"I got a pet dog.
I am six and I am big."

Pupils having difficulty with this passage should be taken back to the basic patterns where their problems exist. By practicing the appropriate ladders, they can develop instant recognition of the needed patterns.

STEP 5: CVCE PATTERN SUBSTITUTION

Behavioral Objective: When the student sees CVCE (consonant-vowel-consonant-*e)* patterns, the pupil will instantly read the patterns correctly.

Generally called the "silent e" rule, this step involves practice with those CVC patterns that experience a change in the vowel sound when the letter *-e* is added to the pattern.

For assessment, a simple contrastive pattern can be setup for the pupils to read:

CVC	CVCE
fat	fate
bit	bite
pet	pete
hop	hope
cut	cute

Materials for practice can be created so that the pupils can read sentences such as the following:

His fate is to be fat.
He can bite the bit.
Pete had a pet rat.

Hop on and hope we don't fall.

Cut the cute rope and I'm free.

STEP 6: MULTISYLLABIC ATTACK PLAN

Behavioral Objective: When a pupil has no clues for breaking apart a multisyllabic word, the pupil with divide the word in front of the second vowel and every vowel thereafter, sound out each part, and blend the parts together.

This attack plan (Wubbena, 1983) is only for pupils who are not using their own attack plans effectively. The plans that pupils develop inductively are far more sophisticated and shouldn't be tampered with if they're effective. This simple plan is designed for that student with no system, so he can approximate a word closely enough to recognize it.

The rules are as follows:

1) Number each vowel.

1 2 3

macadam

2) Put a mark in front of the second vowel and each vowel thereafter.

1 2 3

mac/ad/am

3) Sound out each part, e.g.

1 2 3

mac/ad/am

4) Blend the parts together and repeat.

Blending has to be practiced so that the parts can be put together rapidly. What often happens is that the pupil will get close enough to the word through this process so that the real word can be unlocked. In order to get fluency in the process, pupils need to practice on a lot of words to speed up their processing time as they sound out and blend the parts of words. The following words may be decoded with short vowel patterns.

a	**e**	**i**	**o**	**u**
aback				
abaft	abbess	fabric	modest	bumpkin
abash	abed	fabricant	monastic	bunting
backlash	absent	fanatic	mongolism	button
badland	accent	fantastic	mongrel	buttstock
bagman	accept	fascist	monolithic	custom
ballast	access	festival	moppet	fundamental
bantam	addend	finish	nepotism	fungo
bathmat	advent	fistic	nominal	fungus
calabash	affect	frigid	noneffect	funnel
canal	amend	frisket	nonmetal	husting
canvass	bedlam	galvanic	novel	hunting
damask	bedpan	gambit	podzol	mullet
fantasm	Bengal	gastric	polish	multiplex

fastback
gallant
gasplant
jackshaft
landsman
macadam
madam
mammal
Manhattan
rampant
rascal
rattan
salad

bethel
bevel
camlet
Campbell
cancel
caslet
cement
crenel
cresset
decadent
dextral
flaxen
velvet
venal

gaslit
gelatin
genetic
habit
hagridden
hamstring
happening
hematic
hemstitch
hesitant
Hispanic
kitchen
lacrimal
magnetic

political
pollen
pollute
pontifex
poplin
pragmatic
rocket
rollicking
rosin
rotten
sodden
solemn
venison
venom

nutmeg
nuthatch
studding
subabtomic
subcontact
subject
subplot
subsist
subtract
tunnel
unihibited
unintelligent
unlash
vulcanism

WORD RECOGNITION INTERVENTIONS

As indicated previously, word recognition is reflected in fluency. Pupils who are displaying problems with fluency are often revealing specific word recognition needs. By noting the following word recognition miscues, the teacher can exercise the interventions suggested. After this, the teacher can determine whether the interventions have assisted the word recognition and fluency.

Because fluency interventions (Chapater 7) can solve so many word recognition problems, I recommend that teachers use those interventions first. Then, the teacher should try the following word recognition interventions.

Word Recognition Interventions

Problems	Teacher Interventions
Knows very few sight words	Give words
Doesn't attempt new words	Closure
Confuses similar sight words	Sight word contrasts
Doesn't solve compound words	Compound word breaking
Doesn't substitute consonants	Initial/final substitution
Doesn't substitute medial vowels	Medial vowel substitution

Knows very few sight words Teachers should give words readily to beginning readers in order that they may see the meaning of the whole. This complements the tape assist and predictable text programs previously discussed.

Doesn't attempt new words When pupils possess 80 to 90% of the words in a selection, they should no longer be given the words but should be encouraged to read through the materials, inserting a place holder like "huh" for the missing word until they get it. If they have read the page twice and still don't get it, the word should be given by the teacher or someone else.

Confuses similar sight words Contrasting sight words in similar sentences allows the pupils to study the similarities and differences in the words and the ways that they are used in sentences. Paste contrasting sentences such as the following on the pupil's desk and ask the pupils to check them as they come upon the words in their connected reading.

What dog can run?

That dog can run.

The boy **and** girl can go.

The boy **said**, "I can go."

Compound word breaking When beginners hit compound words for the first few times they may have difficulty. Because of this, the teacher needs to watch carefully for compound words as beginners read. When the pupils have difficulty, the teacher simply covers the front or back half of the compound and helps the pupil to view the word as a combination of two words.

Doesn't substitute consonants When beginners hit variants of known words, it is reasonable to jot the known words quickly on a piece of paper and ask them to read it. Then, you reveal the unknown word below and they can often read it:

not

It is too **hot** to eat.

The teacher may jot down the following words to see if the pupil can unlock the word:

not

pot

hot

For students with other major problems in this area, give them a pattern text like *A Pig Can Jig* (Science Research Associates, 1976). The pupil can practice reading at the points of difficulty for a few minutes each day at the independent reading time.

Doesn't substitute medial vowels The teacher may use contrasting vowel ladders so that the pupil can discover the unknown medial, as the *-e-* in p**e**t. The pupil reads both ladders at a convenient stopping place in his story:

bet	bit
set	sit
net	nit
pet	pit
set	sit

Recall, that inductive instruction builds from the known to the unknown. Thus, pupils will be led to use what they know about words and word parts to solve what they don't know. The clever teacher quickly learns what pupils know and don't know and works to engineer the use of the known.

The components of word recognition are broken down into the consonant and vowel sectors along with their components. Try to get a working knowledge of the various descriptors of consonants (single, blend, digraph, silent) and vowels (single—long, short or variant), adjacent pairs, and diphthongs. This knowledge will help you when you're discussing phonics with your colleagues and friends. It will also be a help when you arrive at the application section.

It should be noted that adjacent vowel pairs carry a wide array of sounds. Consequently, you will not see the adjacent vowel pairs treated in the application section. Because so many studies of the behavior of vowel pairs have indicated their instability, it is believed that the pupils are best served by dealing with the more regular cvc patterns that you will be seeing in the application section. I believe that if pupils can manage the high frequency patterns, there is a great likelihood that their analysis by analogy behaviors will allow them to deal with the differences. I would like to avoid teaching pupils things that they will not actually use in their reading.

SUMMARY

The content of word recognition as well as word recognition mediations were presented in this chapter. Phonic word recognition was presented in terms of the following steps: Step 1: Sound-To-Symbol; Step 2: Initial Consonant Substitution; Step 3: Final Consonant Substitution; Step 4: Medial Vowel Substitution; Step 5: CVCE Pattern Substitution; and Step 6: Multisyllabic Attack Plan. Other interventions were suggested for sight word, closure, and compound words.

STUDY SUGGESTIONS

1. Find and assess a pupil reading between primer and third reader on the **word recognition progression**. See if you can determine how well the pupil manages initial consonant substitution, final consonant substitution, medial vowel substitution, and CVCE substitution.

2. If you discover a third grade and above reader who is reluctant to attack long words, try the **multisyllabic attack plan** with that pupil and see if you can assist him in breaking and attacking words.

9

DEVELOPING READING COMPREHENSION

When teachers are discussing pupil reading problems, this statement is often heard:

"She reads well, but she doesn't comprehend."

Such a statement suggests that reading is something other than comprehension. Presumably, it is a matter of attaching sounds to letters and approximating accurately the words of sentences and stories. By definition, I consider that **reading is comprehension** and that there can be no satisfactory performance of reading without comprehension.

Because reading is comprehension, I particularly like Kenneth Goodman's conceptualization of a distinction between **process** and **product** comprehension. **Process comprehension refers to the comprehending processes that are underway as a reader reads text, whereas product comprehension is the understanding that remains after the text has been closed.**

In one-to-one sessions, teachers have unique opportunities to monitor both process and product comprehension to discover voids and needs.

Process Comprehension

In order to get at the process understandings, our teachers try to make such assessments as soon as they are satisfied that the fluency is satisfactory. After the most tentative rate verifications, the teachers move about and ask pupils to tell what their stories are about.

While the thought of moving around the room and asking pupils about their reading may sound exceedingly difficult to some and very easy to others, I would submit that it's quite difficult. Not only must the teacher be well versed in a wide variety of books, that teacher must become very skillful at teaching the pupils the nature of the responses that she needs to hear. That is, she must hear tight summary responses rather than long, rambling narratives.

Beyond knowing the books and training the pupils in short response techniques, the teacher must have a system for determining which readers are to be monitored on which days. Certainly, the teacher will be unable to make the process comprehension rounds of every pupil every school day. The means for prioritizing will be discussed subsequently.

In the initial one-to-one session, I think the teacher is simply trying to place the students into one of the three broad categories below:

> **Processors** are those who can tell a great deal about what they are reading. They have no apparent comprehension problems. Most pupils will be "processors" when they are reading at the appropriate levels and they will be quickly checked on the teacher's roster as "processors". The teacher needs to re-check the reading level of a processor no more than once a week.
>
> **Dubious Processors** are those who can tell something about what they are reading but are obviously confused due to limited background and vocabulary. The suggestions and interventions described below are designed for the benefit of these students.
>
> **Non Processors** are those who routinely don't have much of an idea about what they are reading. When students fall into this category, the teacher must try to determine whether the failure to process is the result of **limited language**, **limited experience**, or **limited understanding**. If the problem is one of deficiencies in the new language, providing numerous opportunities for oral and written language development can help. For students with appropriate language skills but limited experience, reading provides one of the best means of filling voids. Students with severe cognitive limitations (often labeled Mentally Retarded) have basic limitations that the teacher must understand in order to prepare appropriate comprehension challenges.

"Dubious processors" will be those students that will be placed on the everyday check list so that the teacher can find out if the dubious processing is a unique function of a given book or story or whether it is a continuing way of life with the student. If the processing difficulty is contingent upon the given story, the best intervention will be one that allows the teacher to explain and direct the pupil's thinking toward the conceptual voids. Often, extensive reading will tend to fill those voids faster than anything else. Extensive reading builds concepts and understandings rapidly.

For those "dubious processors" who seem to operate in this fashion routinely, it is often a question of their lack of any directional signals for reading. In other words, they read without "purpose" or a realization of how text is constructed. **These dubious processors need to be given purposes for both narrative and expository reading that will help them to identify the important story structures.**

Product Comprehension

Product comprehension is the understanding that remains after the reading act. Consequently, the teacher must have a basic understanding of the stories and books that students are reading. That knowledge doesn't have to be detailed, but the teacher must be able to stop and ask pupils about the major events in stories and sample orally their recall of important detail, their knowledge of the sequence, and their awareness of where things happened in the story.

Product comprehension is sampled primarily in the students' PLORE assignments. You will recall that the students answer one or more of the questions regularly. It is during this work time that the active teacher moves around and samples the written responses that the pupils are producing. It is important to be able to move efficiently so that a few pupils do not receive all of the attention. I have counted some of our teachers making something like fifteen contacts during a twenty-minute period. While there will be situations in which some students need longer feedback sessions with the teacher, there is a danger that the teacher may focus too selectively and be unaware of other problems in the room. Teachers need to develop quick response techniques that serve as a sort of shorthand for cueing pupils to problems in their answers.

PLORE is further detailed into its component parts for the following discussion. Teachers will want to sample the various forms of PLORE on a one-to-one basis as often as they can. Some teachers like to take a given PLORE category each day of the week so that they manage to see how all the pupils are doing on a given skill. Thus Mondays would be for predicting, Tuesday for locating, Wednesday for organizing, Thursday for remembering, and Friday for various forms of evaluation.

Written Comprehension

When the pupils have completed their instructional level reading, they normally answer written questions over the last story read. In order to stimulate the pupils to a wide variety of reading-thinking skills about reading, the teacher will utilize different types of comprehension questions for this aspect of the program. The teacher questions are organized around the concept of PLORE (Guszak, 1985). PLORE is the acronym for predicting, locating, organizing, remembering, and evaluating. It is deemed important that pupils are able to manage an extensive set of skills under each of the five headings. PLORE is considered to be a set of organizers that will include any comprehension skill. Consequently, the learning of PLORE is a never ending process that all of us will carry out through our lives.

PLORE COMPREHENSION SKILLS

Predicting | **Locating** | **Organizing** | **Remembering** | **Evaluating**

PLORE is more than a set of questions. It is a way of viewing thinking about reading. PREDICTING is the first listed skill because it is the initiating factor in almost everything we read. After predicting, we verify what we want to know. Verifying is simply LOCATING. If we want to remember information or do something with it after reading, we must organize it. Thus, the skill of ORGANIZING comes into the mental picture. Of course, to organize something, you have to remember significant pieces of information and/or their temporal sequences. This means that REMEMBERING makes ORGANIZING possible. Finally, EVALUATING is a skill that stands alone. It may or may not be utilized by readers, but the chances are very great that most readers will be puzzled if an author disagrees with himself in the same piece of text. Also, as we read we are most likely to judge the material on the basis of our values, politics, and viewpoints.

In greater detail, the five basic types of comprehension are as follows:

PREDICTING (PR) Predicting is the driving force that makes us want to read to answer the questions in our mind. As such, it drives the reading process from the selection of a piece of reading material right on through the acquisition of sufficient information to satisfy our curiosity. Our predictions can be **convergent** (toward likely conclusions) or **divergent** (toward the unlikely possibilities). Convergent predictions are dominant because we are usually trying to use information to make sense of the text. Divergent prediction is the kind that drives humor, invention, and creativity. It is the novel or unexpected response.

LOCATING (LO) Locating refers to a set of never-ending skills that we shall be acquiring with each new day of life. Specifically, we perform the following three types of location: 1) **We locate specific information in embedded text**, for example, the sentence that tells how to record on the VCR; 2) **We locate specific information holders** like sentences, paragraphs, sections; 3) **We locate information with book parts such as an index, contents, bibliography**; and 4) **We locate information in a wide variety of reference sources such as dictionaries, encyclopedias, bus schedules, directions sheets, etc.** Efficient locating skills assist all of us to do tasks more quickly with greater satisfaction.

ORGANIZING (OR) Organizing refers to the process whereby a student is asked to take information that he has read and reorganize it into other forms such as a summary, synopsis, outline, main idea, conclusion, graphic representation, sequence, etc. Such organizations of text are very difficult skills for those who have not learned how to read with purpose for the organizing task that is to be performed. Organizing questions are the most dominant form of response called for in state mandated criterion tests as well as standardized achievement tests.

REMEMBERING (RE) Remembering is the basis for organizing. Because of this, students must be assisted toward the remembering of the pertinent. Unfortunately, there is ample research that suggests that children have been taught to remember the trivial at the expense of the important (Guszak, 1968). Consequently, the focus of remembering instruction is to teach pupils to recognize and remember big ideas and patterns rather than names and dates.

EVALUATING (EV) Evaluating refers to the need for teaching students to make judgments about what they have read by using **internal** and **external** factors. Internal judgments are those which determine whether the text is consistent from the first to the last. Pupils in command of their reading can determine whether the characters are consistent or not as well as whether the facts stay the same from the first to the last. Whereas internal evaluation deals with the internal consistency of a piece of text, external evaluation goes outside the given text to compare it with other similar pieces of text. For example, does the British author treat the "Battle of Bunker Hill" in the same way as a patriot author?

PLORE In the Curriculum

PLORE instruction is usually initiated with a direct teach session where the teacher models how questions are supposed to be answered. In the **kindergarten** or **first grade**, the teacher reads a story that would tell on the first page that Mary can play. Modeling both the question and the answer, the teacher would arrive at the answer - **Mary can play.** Then, the pupils would have an opportunity to read a second page which would have for its answer: **John can play.** The pupils would then follow the model of the teacher and reorganize the scrambled word cards into a complete sentence answer. As an added clue for the pupil, the period is placed behind the last word that will occur in the answer. Thus, the pupil can use capitalized first words and punctuated last words as clues to the boundaries of the sentence that they will unscramble.

The print for the question and answer should be as close to that of the text as possible to maximize transfer:

Who can play?

John	play.	can

As their handwriting skills develop, the pupils answer such questions on their tablets or primary paper. They are taught to reorganize the words of the question into the answer via an edit process whereby they change the question statement into an answer statement. After the questions statement is converted to the answer statement, the pupils are taught to copy the answer statement down on the writing paper below the question statement. Beginning with simple questions like the following, the pupils advance to more difficult questions that require extensive editing of the question text.

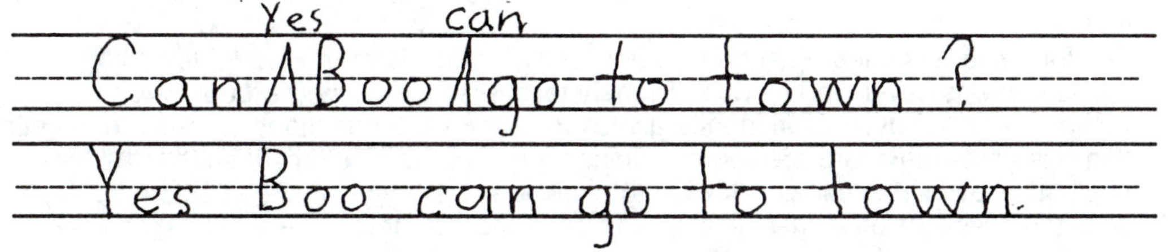

These first graders subsequently add location questions, organization questions (sequence), and prediction questions.

By the **second grade**, pupils are experiencing the full range of PLORE at lower levels of difficulty. The levels of difficulty within each question type will become increasingly complex over the following years so that the students have to deal with complex thinking skills about reading.

Whenever possible, teachers should try to formulate PLORE questions for each of the stories in their reading materials. In preparing the questions, the teacher should read the stories, close the book, and attempt to write most of the questions from memory. This is the way that the students are expected to do the task, so teachers should write the questions in the same manner. This avoids the tendency to pick out small pieces of information and a host of names that are seldom memorable to readers, adult or child.

The teacher made PLORE questions can be put in folders and used over the years by the pupils reading those books. Our PLORE sheets contain multiple questions for each comprehension type but the teacher makes the determination as to how many each pupil will answer. These means that some pupils may answer a few questions while others will answer many.

Building on the pattern started in the first grade, pupils are taught to use the question statements in the formulation of their answers. Also, they are taught to check their spellings against the words in the written questions. Heavy penalties are assessed when the pupils don't spell the words in the question correctly. For words not present in the question, some students will not be penalized if they lightly underline such words in their written answers.

Teachers construct reminder charts such as the following to help students edit.

PROOFREADING FOR MECHANICS

CS (COMPLETE SENTENCE) 5 points off for every PR,RE,EV sentence that does not restate the question in a complete sentence answer, e.g.

BAD - To make him tired.
GOOD- Una wanted Tim to split the rocks so that he would get too tired to fight.

CA (CAPITALIZATION) 5 points off for every sentence that does not begin with a capital and 5 points off for every proper name that doesn't begin with a capital.

PUNC (PUNCTUATION) 5 points off for every missing period.

SP (SPELLING) 5 points off for every question word that is misspelled in the answer.

The following illustrates a second grade PLORE sheet from the Houghton Mifflin reading series that was developed by Buda Primary teachers. Note how the book, story, and page numbers are displayed prominently across the top of the questions for ease of identification. Also note that there are two questions for each PLORE element so that the teacher or pupil may have some choices in what to respond to on any given day. Seldom do pupils do all of the questions on a sheet in a given day. Teachers determine which skills need to be emphasized with which pupils as well as how much quality written work can be expected from different pupils.

PLORE 1
CARAVANS "Finn McCool" pp.62-77

PR 1. If Cuhullin found out who Finn was and decided to fight him, what do you think would have happened to him ?

PR 2. What do you think would have happened if Mrs. O'Malley and Mrs. Shane had not come to visit Una and Finn?

LO 3. Read the information about the author. Write the sentence that tells what May Lynch does besides writing.

LO 4. Use the encyclopedia to see if you can find the country where Finn lived. Try to locate the place on a map of that country. CONTENT READING QUESTION

OR 5. List the major events in this story.

OR. 6. Write these sentences in the correct order.

a. Cuhullin turns the house around.
b. Granny, Mrs. O'Malley, and Mrs. Shane visit the McCools.
c. Finn dresses like a baby.
d. Cuhullin breaks his tooth on the bread.

RE 7. Why did Una want Tim to split the rocks?
RE 8. What did Cuhullin think the cheese was ?

EV 9. Tell why Una was very smart or not smart?
EV 10. Tell why or why not Finn McCool would be a friend.

To make PLORE work, it's helpful if a teacher has a set of questions for much of what is being read. If such questions are not available, it's possible for the teacher to use what we call **generic questions** with the pupils. Generic question sets such as the following, allow the students opportunities to demonstrate various comprehension skills. The teacher then has the opportunity to make some judgments about the quality of the students' understanding.
There is nothing sacred about the ordering of these generic questions and other types of patterns might be used.

Monday/ Summarize your story.

Tuesday/Write a brief paragraph to tell the following:
Who or what was the story was about?
When did the story take place?
Where did the story take place?
What was the story problem?
How was the problem resolved?

Wednesday/Outline your story.

Thursday/ Prepare a story grammar about your story.

Friday/Prepare five good questions over your story.

With questions and some direct instruction on how to write answers, pupils learn quickly how to produce complete sentence answers to the questions. If these answers can be done in a **comprehension spiral**, the teacher has a ready means for gauging progress in comprehension and writing skills. This progress can be readily communicated to the pupils, parents, other teachers, and administrators. Progress in written comprehension is something that is verifiable when teachers systematically assist pupils and keep records of those improvements.

Because students are working daily on different written comprehension answers, teachers are often fearful that they will not be able to manage such a large undertaking. To ease this fear, I like to suggest the following thoughts relative to management:

1) Limit the students to a few questions and answers each day so that the pupil can concentrate on quality and so that you can readily evaluate their answers.

2) Try to move about the classroom and grade as many as possible in process because this is your best opportunity to clarify and improve the pupil product.

3) Attempt to leave the highest quality work for your after-class checking because this material is usually the easiest to check.

4) Provide the pupils with models and protocols for your scoring. For example, tell them the point losses for incomplete sentences, missing capitalization, missing

punctuation, and misspellings of words that appear in the question. These things can provide the pupils with self-proofing checks or peer-proofing checks.

5) Enlist able pupils to check certain questions of their peers' papers. Pupils can check remembering, locating, and organizing questions quite well.

PLORE SKILLS AND TEACHER INTERVENTIONS

The following illustrates a range of PLORE skills along with specific interventions that can be used by a teacher.

PREDICTING (PR)

SKILLS	TEACHER INTERVENTIONS
Predicting new words	Ask the student to read past an unknown word in the passage until the context provides enough meaning information to allow him to figure out what the word is.
Predicting other titles	As a pupil completes his story, ask him to name or describe the main characters and to tell what happened. After that, encourage him to predict a title without looking at the book.
* **Predicting convergent endings**	Before a student finishes a story, get him to summarize for you and predict the ending. Have him jot it down on scratch paper and tell you later how accurate he was. Also, ask pupils to predict from pictures, titles, and subheadings.
* **Predicting divergent endings**	After the child has finished a story, the teacher can insert a small *What if...?* question that suggests the possibility of a different ending for the story. The goal is that the student should generate different endings.
Predicting unknown meanings	Cue the child to read past unknown words so as to obtain information that will help him to figure it out. You can teach him to put a place holder like "huh" for the unknown word.

LOCATING (LO) SKILLS	TEACHER INTERVENTIONS
Locating specific information	Ask the pupil to scan material to locate specific facts. Start with a simple fact and then build up to more information.
Locating specific information holders	The following location tasks illustrate some of the three main types of information holders.
specific sentences	Limit the student to the first page of a story with limited text. Ask the pupil to locate a given piece of information or a specific sentence. Have the student use his thumb to indicate the answer.
specific paragraphs	Show the student the dimensions of indented and blocked paragraphs. Guide them during PLORE to what the question is calling for and how to use recall to narrow the search to where the paragraph can be found.
specific pages	Show the students how to extend what they have learned about the structure of paragraphs by asking them to search through whole pages for the answer to a simple question. Once they have mastered individual pages, extend the search to a group of pages, and ask the pupils to narrow the search to a single page.
Locating with book parts: **title** **preface** **introduction** **contents** **publication information** **lists of illustrations** **bibliographies** **indexes** **glossaries** **appendices** **lists footnotes**	These things can be taught by a quick modeling with the following book parts. Direct teaches should be provided when students don't catch it quickly. These skills should be taught as they become important to a pupil's reading and research.

Locating with references:

dictionaries
encyclopedias
atlases, maps, or globes
telephone books
newspapers
magazines
schedules

Because some students need these skills before others, it is important to develop these as needed, generally by modeling with the pupil in need.

ORGANIZING (OR) SKILLS
<u>Narrative</u>

TEACHER INTERVENTIONS

Discovering schema

As the pupils work with generalized schema, ask them to identify the critical elements of a story (setting, theme, resolution). Apply the same type of activity to other stories through the *who, what, why, when,* and *where* format. Schema, according to Rummelhart (1981), is a design whereby the reader interprets and evaluates each sentence to discover the interpretation that best fits the clues in the passage. Schema are the building blocks of understanding.

Recalling temporal events

Teachers who know the temporal events of a story can call upon the pupil to identify such events (time, progression, recipe, etc.). If the child has not internalized such progressions, he is directed to reread and to be able to reconstruct a temporal (time) sequence. Because of memory problems and distractions, some pupils are asked to note the temporal events along with their page and paragraph numbers, as in the example below:

First stop—bakery, 34,
para 3.
Second stop—grocery, 36, para 2.
Third stop—drug store, 38, para 4.

Making story maps

The teacher helps the pupil to map out events (much like the previous skill of recalling temporal events). In a story where the disposition of baby kittens is the main theme, the teacher helps the pupil to create a story map such as the following to illustrate the placement of the new kittens:

The New Kittens

Kitten 1 to Aunt Carrie

Kitten 2 to Grandma

Kitten 3 to the paper boy

Kitten 4 stays

Summarizing

The teacher builds upon the previous notion of temporal order and asks pupils to use the following structure for summarizing the story.

Who (and/or) what—

When—

Where—

What happened—

Expository

Identifying the main ideas

This topic will be treated at length in Chapter 10 as something that will be a prominent part of direct teach lessons in organizing. Suffice it to say, the teacher may wish to point out how some content books feature stated main ideas in the initial or final sentence of paragraphs while others call for implied main ideas.

1. **stated**
2. **implied**
3. **no main ideal**

Teachers can illustrate how some paragraphs contain stated main ideas, whereas others contain main ideas that are only implied. The teacher should also guide the pupils to the realization that some paragraphs have no main idea.

1. **Descriptive paragraphs**
2. **Sequence paragraphs**
3. **Cause/effect paragraphs**
4. **Comparison/contrast paragraphs**
5. **Problem/solution paragraphs**

Teachers subsequently move to helping pupils to identify Piccolo's (1987) five types of paragraphs. Each of the paragraph types can be described by graphic means. When such occurs, these are called **graphic organizers** (Piccolo, 1987).

Building frames

A **frame** (Armbruster, 1989) is a concrete, visible representation of the organization of ideas in a selection. It is applied to the preceding paragraph types. In a problem/solution paragraph, a frame would indicate **the problem**, **the action**, and **the results of the action**.

REMEMBERING (RE) SKILLS

TEACHER INTERVENTIONS

Setting purposes

The teacher has the student review the fact questions before reading so that the student will have specific purposes generated in advance of the actual reading. In time, the student should have a **set** for the nature of the questions to be asked. This strategy is applicable to narrative reading as well.

Monitoring your remembering

At the lowest extreme, the teacher asks the pupil to tell back a sentence in his own words. When a pupil can do this, he can be asked to tell back increasing amounts of text. This incremental buildup should progress to the point that the student can recall entire stories.

For individual work, the pupils can answer questions or write short summaries at the end of each page so that the teacher can subsequently check their remembering.

Monitoring your understanding

Ask pupils to explain in their own words what has happened in the course of a paragraph, page, or group of pages. Cue the pupils to do this themselves.

EVALUATING (EV) SKILLS	TEACHER INTERVENTIONS
Narrative	
Judging desirability	The teacher asks a student to tell why he did or did not like a given character, story, or ending. The teacher simply tries to get him to apply his value system to a problem.
Judging realism	The teacher tries to get the pupil to apply his knowledge of the real world to story situations so that the pupil will be able to state whether something in a story is likely or not.
Expository	
Finding contradictions	This skill has the following two dimensions:
internal contradictions	The teacher clues the child to find places where an author contradicts himself within a given passage. For example, a news article about an athlete might contain conflicting statements about the athlete's weight. The teacher can point out one such difference and ask the pupils to look for more examples.
external disagreements	The teacher guides pupils to discover differences between fact and opinion on the same topic. Usually, the pupil must use multiple sources in order to make comparisons of information. This can be done by comparing different political views on a given piece of legislation.
Identifying propaganda devices	The teacher helps pupils identify the following propaganda devices (as well as others) by pointing them out in text and advertising (including the media of print, radio and television).

plain folks

The teacher locates advertising examples that illustrate the idea that the people in the ads are "plain folks"—just like the rest of us.

beautiful people

The teacher shows the students other advertisements that suggest that glamorous people use the products in the ads—and that we, too, can become "beautiful people" if we use those products.

glittering generalities

The teacher shows examples of ads that use vague words and claims in such a way as to make their product more glamorous than it really is. Pupils are asked whether the products advertised effect them as positively as they effect the people in the advertisements.

Independence Day

While the teacher works constantly with individuals on PLORE in the early weeks of instruction, there is a point when the pupils must be taught to rely on their own judgments and instincts through the range of questions and answers. To help bring this about, we developed what we called **"Independence Day."** This was to be a day on which the teacher would help no one and that each student would do his own work without help from anyone. We talked up the day for a week or two in advance to indicate how important this day would be.

When the important day arrived to be on their own, the teacher sketched the flag of the U.S.A. on the board, wrote **INDEPENDENCE DAY** in bold letters above the flag, and started the process. To our surprise, everything went exceedingly well and the pupils turned out some of their finest products of the year. We felt that the pupils took a special pride in being able to do their answers without assistance from the teacher or anybody else on this day.

Independence day taught us that pupils not only needed independence but that they longed for it. The time arrives when they must be self-sufficient in most tasks. For them, this self-sufficiency time was provided at PLORE time. Because of the success of this special day, some teachers moved to a format in which the pupils would have two days a week of Independence Day.

It's important to note that the development of Independence Day is *not* a repudiation of the idea of collaborative learning. Collaborative learning should be the operational format, but there should be times when pupils need to learn to do things without help. Most of them will have such experiences at the various testing times that are becoming regular parts of the school program.

Sharing Day

In keeping with the realization of collaborative learning, we felt that it was important to have special days where certain pupils could collaborate on their PLORE and produce joint efforts which represented the best thinking of two pupils. The way it worked was to have two pupils work on the same story and share the same answers.

Two pupils would meet after reading their story and discuss their answers to the PLORE questions for that story. Usually, they would decide which one would write out their joint answer or whether or not they would take turns writing down answers. In this fashion, they would continue through the questions until they had a completed set of answers that both would sign and take credit for as a pair.

Special emphasis was placed upon the answers to the predicting and evaluating questions, because careful thinking was the exception rather than the rule on these questions. With two minds working on these difficult questions, we generally found a greater elaboration than normally seen when the pupil did his or her own questions.

Because sharing days involved collaborative learning, there was a collaborative grade given to each individual for the group project. This seemed to help the focus of each group as they realized that they had to have a quality product for their effort. It also indicated that they had to make time allocations for each question.

Sharing day became a weekly event in some classrooms. To ensure that all pupils were involved, the teacher would change some of the students' assignments on this day. For example, a better reader might move down a book level in order to share with a lower reader.

Sharing groups appeared to greatly enhance the capabilities of children who had learned English as a second language. The interaction between a native English speaker and a student learning English as a second language proved beneficial to both pupils. The native English speaker had a unique opportunity to explain and clarify, thus enhancing her understanding skills. The pupil receiving this help had the opportunity to learn new vocabulary as well as to pick up other subtleties of language and understanding.

SUMMARY

Written comprehension over the instructional level story becomes a regular part of the program and pupils learn to answer five kinds of PLORE (predicting, locating, organizing, remembering, evaluating) in accurate, neat, and complete sentences. The pupils learn to work independently as well as in small groups to formulate quality answers.

Comprehension interventions focus on **process** (while pupils are reading) and **product** (after the pupils have finished reading). Process interventions are designed to help students do specific things with narrative and expository reading selections while they are actually reading. Product interventions usually take place after the pupil has already read and include the following: prediction, location, organization, remembering, and evaluating.

PLORE involved Independence Days and Sharing Days. On the Independence Days the pupils would seek to do their written comprehension questions without any assistance from the teacher or classmates. On Sharing Days, pupils would be paired up to answer the questions over a common story.

STUDY SUGGESTIONS

1. After you have established a pupil's instructional level take a story from that level and write a set of **PLORE** questions for it. Have the student look at the questions, read the story, and then try to answer the questions in complete sentence answers.

2. Try one or more of the **comprehension interventions**. If you haven't had an opportunity to attempt a process intervention, ask the pupil to read a page and then ask him to tell you what he has read. If he is unable to do this, repeat the process. Some pupils do not realize that they are to tell back the happenings of the story, and so they rush through it as they read. Remember, you are not to calculate the pupil's rate if his comprehension does not reveal that he understands a majority of the material.

3. Try one or more of the product comprehension interventions to see how well a pupil can **organize** materials that he has read before. Determine whether the student can provide you with a **summary** that tells the *who, what, why, when,* and *where* of a narrative or identifies the main ideas of expository material (content books, news articles, etc.).

10

DIRECT TEACHING COMPREHENSION

Direct teach and comprehension have become synonymous in the minds of some teachers during the past decade because of the direct teach studies previously reported. Adding more impetus to the discussion has been Durkin's (1978-1979; 1987) research, which has indicated that basal readers and teachers have traditionally done little to develop comprehension.

While the message of this book has been that reading is caught rather than taught, I believe that specific comprehension skills may not be caught readily unless the teacher draws the student's attention to them. In the previous chapters you have read about PLORE and how the students systematically interact with text across many thinking fronts. You have also read about how teachers can make one-to-one interactions with the pupils during reading (**process** comprehension) as well as after reading (**product** comprehension). Now you will read about how the teacher direct teaches comprehension.

It should be noted that direct teach lessons should be directed toward those who need the given skills. In some of the sequences, the term **diagnostic check** will be used to indicate that the lesson starts with a diagnosis of the individual pupil attainments of the skill to be taught. Ideally, a group would not be gathered unless there is strong need for the lesson.

The PLORE lessons described in this chapter have been organized with the same format that was used for the lessons described in Chapter 8. Each contains these features:

Behavioral Objective: A statement of what the learner will do;

Anticipatory Set: A focusing statement provided by the teacher;

Instructional Input: The teacher actually teaches the skill or concept;

Guided Practice: The class practices the new skill, guided by the teacher;

Independent Practice: Each pupil practices the new skill (or concept);

Closing: The closing or summary of the new skill learned.

Direct teach lessons are provided for the predicting, locating, organizing, remembering, organizing, and evaluating categories. Some lessons are initiated with a diagnostic task so that the teacher can make determinations of whether or not certain students can profit from participating in those lesson.

DIRECT TEACH LESSONS—COMPREHENSION

Predicting Lessons
1. Predicting new words
2. Predicting other titles
3. Predicting convergent endings
4. Predicting divergent endings
5. Predicting unknown word meanings

Locating Lessons:
1. Locating specific information
2. Locating specific information holders
3. Locating in a table of contents
4. Locating information with reference

Organizing Lessons:
1. Finding Main Characters
2. Finding Main Characters and Settings
3. Finding Main Characters, Settings, and Problems
4. Finding Schema in a Simple Story
5. Finding Schema in a Multi Problem Story
6. Finding Schema on a Page by Page Basis
7. Recalling temporal events
8. Summarizing narratives
9. Identifying expository main ideas
10. Outlining (data chart skills)

Remembering Lessons:
1. Setting purposes
2. Monitoring your remembering
3. Monitoring your understanding

Evaluating Lessons:
1. (Narrative) Judging desirability
2. (Narrative) Judging realism
3. (Expository) Finding internal contradictions
4. (Expository) Finding external disagreements
5. (Expository) Identifying propaganda devices

PREDICTING

Predicting lessons include predicting new words, predicting other titles, predicting convergent endings, predicting divergent endings, and predicting unknown word meanings.

Lesson 1: Predicting new words

Behavioral Objective: When a pupil meets a new word in the context of his instructional level reading material, he will insert a place-holding "hmmm" and continue reading past the word until he obtains sufficient information to generate a logical prediction for the word.

Anticipatory Set: On a large chart or transparency, the teacher prepares a story using known vocabulary words for all the pupils who will be participating in the lesson. New words have been covered with a flip tab. It is easy to prepare transparencies of book pages and then tape small closure tabs over the words to be closed.

Diagnostic Check: The teacher asks those who think they can read the passage to raise their hands. The teacher then quickly has them whisper the passage in her ear. Those who are successful are exempted from the lesson.

Daddy drove home in our new __ .
Mother was glad to see it. We were
glad to see the new __ too. We wanted
to take a ___ in it with Daddy.
Daddy said, "Jump in and we will
go for a ride around the ____."

Instructional Input: The teacher explains that the new words are covered but that by reading the other words there is a good chance that the new words can be figured out. The teacher proceeds to read the chart aloud slowly touching each word and placing a "hmmm" in place of each omitted word. The pupils follow. Then, the teacher starts to explain why she thinks a certain word will fit because of the larger meaning and the beginning letter cue. The teacher proceeds to read the whole chart as the pupils watch.

Guided Practice: For guided practice, the teacher reveals a second page for the pupils to join with her in reading and predicting. She encourages pairs of pupils at each cluster to guess what the word might be and whisper it among themselves. Each word is inserted until the full page is read. A third and fourth page make up the guided practice.

Independent Practice: For independent practice, a fifth page is left on the screen or chart rack for all to practice on their own. A new page will be revealed each day so that the story may continue as well as the practice. Of course, they will practice the strategy each time they come to a new word in reading.

Closing: For the closing the teacher asks each group to discuss what they learned from this lesson. Group leaders summarize for their group and the teacher writes up the summary that she wants them to leave with which is:

New words can be figured out by reading ahead and using the first letter cue.

Lesson 2: Predicting other titles

Behavioral Objective: After reading narrative paragraphs and stories, the pupil will predict other titles that convey the main character or idea of each paragraph or story. (This can be a main idea organizing lesson when the pupil selects the best title from a group of three titles.)

Anticipatory Set: On a chart or transparency the teacher has a short paragraph or story without a title. After briefly reviewing that a title should tell what the content is about, she reads them a story and asks them to think of some good titles.

Diagnostic Check: The teacher asks those with good titles to whisper them in her ear. If the teacher likes the individuals' titles, she may release them from the lesson.

Instructional Input: The teacher reads the following selection aloud from a transparency as the pupils watch. Then, she models her thinking that leads to the formulation of a title that tells about the story.

> **This was to be Cathy's first trip to the circus and she was so excited that she could hardly sleep. She was going to see all the wild animals, the high flying people, and the man who got shot out of the cannon. Best of all, she was going to get to eat cotton candy, caramel corn, candy apples, and hot dogs.**

The teacher underlines the parts that lead her to her decision about the title, e.g. Cathy's first trip to the circus, wild animals, high flying people, men shot out of cannon. She says that the story is about Cathy but that is not enough. She elects to title the story *Cathy's First Circus.* She discusses other possibilities but tries to show the students why she chose her title and why it is more descriptive than other titles such as *Cathy Goes to the Circus, Fun at the Circus,* or *Good Things to See at the Circus.*

Guided Practice: For guided practice the teacher provides pupil pairs with the following passage, similar to the one about the circus. She then pairs up pupils and asks them to mark big ideas in their stories and come up with several titles. These titles are put on the board and evaluated.

> **Allan was crazy about airplanes. He cut out pictures of planes. He made model planes. He talked about planes all of the time. In fact, his bed was built to look like a plane.**

Independent Practice: For independent practice, two new stories are placed on the screen for the pupils to title on their own. Individual answers are then compared within the table groups as the teacher observes.

Closing: For the closing, the teacher asks each group to summarize what they have learned about predicting new titles for stories. She makes sure that they note that the title should be descriptive of the story.

Lesson 3: Predicting convergent endings

Behavioral Objective: When asked to predict a convergent (likely) ending, the pupil will use the information presented and his/her background experiences to project a likely (reasonable) ending.

Anticipatory Set: The teacher will ask what will happen if you fall into a swimming pool. She will then say that you would, at least, get wet. Other bad things could happen to you, too, but it is most certain that you would get wet. She explains that this is a likely (convergent) outcome from the given event of falling into a swimming pool.

Diagnostic Check: The teacher asks which students can predict a likely ending in terms of what might happen to John and his father. The pupils with predictions whisper them in the teacher's ear.

> **John and his father were fishing in the middle of the lake from their sailboat. Suddenly, they felt the wind blowing hard. The water became rough and the boat swayed left and right. One tall wave picked up the boat and flipped it over.**

Instructional Input: After the teacher has written some of the pupil predictions (they drown, they're rescued, etc.), the teacher states she wants **to use her experience** with boats to come up with a sentence or two that might explain what happened next. She refers back to her experience with boats and asks the children to think about anything they have read or heard about boats. Then the teacher begins to write her ending, modeling the thinking that has brought her to it. She explains that when she was a young girl her father had always taught her to stay with their sunken sailboat because it would float. She figured out that John's father probably told him to hang on to the boat and that they had both held tightly to the boat until they were rescued.

Guided Practice: An example similar to the one above is provided for guided practice. The pupils are asked to work at their clusters to come up with some likely predictions for the following story.

> **Mom and Dad and their two children were returning home from a visit to their cousins in a far away city. Halfway home, the car wouldn't run anymore. What did they do?**

Hopefully, there will be a lot of answers, varying from looking for help to trying to fix the car. The key element to impress upon the pupils is whether or not the happening is a likely one.

Independent Practice: At this point, further examples are placed on the transparency and the individuals within a cluster are asked to write their answers and then to compare them with the members of the group. The answers are evaluated by the pupils for reality.

Closing: The teacher asks each of the students to summarize until they come up with the idea that logical endings can be written by using the student's experience and best judgment.

Lesson 4: Predicting divergent endings

Behavioral Objective: When asked to predict a divergent (unlikely) ending, the student will use their knowledge of differences to generate a novel or unexpected ending.

Anticipatory Set: Using the same paragraph story that was used for the likely ending (the boat turning over), the teacher explains that many authors make money by producing things that we don't expect. The teacher then explains that she will try to think of an unexpected ending to see if she can generate a novel ending.

Instructional Input: The teacher asks the pupils to think of novel endings while she tries to come up with one. Thinking aloud, the teacher thinks first of a sad ending that might have the boy and his father drowning. Reflecting further, she has them sinking to the bottom where they discover an underwater bubble with a scientist in it. The scientist brings them into the water lock and then into the safety of his underwater world.

Guided Practice: Examples of paragraph stories are provided on the screen so that the various clusters can generate novel endings that can be shared with the larger group. The example of the car stopping along the road can be used this time for unexpected endings whereby group members may suggest things like the kids fixed it, the kids found a nearby gasoline station and got gas, a man came along and towed them home, etc.

Independent Practice: Two additional stories are provided for the individuals to generate creative endings which will be shared with their small groups first and then the larger group.

Closing: For the closing, the teacher has each group develop the main point of the lesson. The teacher compares their answers and praises the diversity of the answers. Answers shouldn't be the same if we are going after divergence. The more surprising the answer is, the more memorable it is.

Lesson 5: Predicting unknown word meanings

Behavioral Objective: When a pupil arrives at an unknown word in connected reading, the pupil will continue reading and use other clues to determine the meaning of the unknown word.

Anticipatory Set: On the board the teacher writes the word:

peregrinate

The teacher asks if anyone knows this word and no one does. The teacher then embeds the word in a sentence:

He wished to **peregrinate**.

Again, all are asked what this means.

Instructional Input: The teacher then reveals the following text with the word "peregrinate" embedded.

> Two sisters lived in a very small town. They had never been more than two miles from home. Both sisters wished to **peregrinate** to see the world. Since they were **well endowed financially**, the cost of the trip would not be a problem.

The teacher reads the sentence aloud and predicts that the word "peregrinate" probably means "travel". She looks it up in the dictionary and confirms that it does mean "wander" or travel". She further explains how a series of words like "well endowed financially" can mean rich.

Guided Practice: For guided practice, the teacher puts the following story on the board and reads it aloud. The pupils are supposed to read along silently and then work in pairs to provide synonyms for the underlined words.

> Two frogs lived in two **distinct** places. One frog lived in the town of Keenee while the other **resided** near the town of Pogat. Both frogs wanted to **peregrinate** and see the rest of the world. As chance would have it, both frogs decided to **initiate** their trip on the same day.
>
> When the two frogs came around a corner, they **collided**. Neither was hurt because their **velocity** was so slow that they merely bumped into one another. (Bereiter, Hughes, & Anderson, 1982).

After briefly discussing the answers of the pupils, the teacher provides independent practice.

Independent Practice: For independent practice, the teacher puts the following story on the board (Bereiter, Hughes, & Anderson, 1982):

Pedro the Wizard

> Once there was a boy named Pedro who lived on a farm with his father and mother. He didn't want to **labor** in the fields like his father. He **had the desire** to be a wizard.
>
> "How can I **become qualified** to be a wizard?" Pedro asked his father. "Is there a school for training in wizardry?"

After they have written in their word substitutions, the pupils are encouraged to share their thinking at their clusters before the teacher discusses the closures with the whole group.

Closing: For the closing, the teacher asks a pupil to summarize the point of this day's lesson. The student says simply that you can often figure out unknown word meanings if you keep reading and thinking.

LOCATING

Locating refers to the following subsets of skills: locating specific information, locating specific information holders (sentences, paragraphs, etc.), locating information with book parts, and locating information with reference aids.

Lesson 1: Locating specific information

Behavioral Objective: When seeking specific information from written materials, the pupil will quickly scan the material until the desired information is located. (The desired information can vary from a simple fact to an elaborate explanation.)

Anticipatory Set: The teacher explains that we need to find certain pieces of information in written material rapidly. As an example, she reveals how she scans a letter from her sister in order to find the ages of her nieces. In a second example, the teacher scans a local feature story about the girls and the schools they attend. The teacher wishes to find the name of each school that each niece attends.

Instructional Input: The teacher puts up the following written material and indicates that she wants to find out who will play the lead in the production of *Cinderella.*

> ***Cinderella* will be presented tonight at 8:00 p.m in the Riverside Theatre. Admission for the production is $7. Playing the central role of *Cinderella* in the play will be Susan Song. Playing opposite Ms. Song in the role of the prince will be Alfred Jones.**

The teacher models how she scans the material until she reaches the critical sentence that tells that Susan Song will be playing *Cinderella.* The teacher then puts a color mark over the name Susan Song.

Guided Practice: For guided practice, the teacher asks pairs of pupils or the members of a cluster to see how quickly they can find targeted information in a series of passages such as the following:

Question: Where did they find Al?

> **Al, the famous swimming pig in the New Town Springs show, wandered off Saturday. The staff and a group of**

volunteers searched the grounds for an hour. Al was found that evening in the back of a pickup truck in the parking lot.

As the students successfully answer each question, the teacher presents them with a new question and a longer passage.

Independent Practice: Similar examples are provided for independent practice so that each pupil can locate the information and highlight the answer on the text with a yellow crayon. Longer materials should be used after the scanning idea is developed.

Closing: Pupils are asked to explain how you search through printed material to find specific pieces of information. They explain how this can be used as a test strategy when they are asked questions about specific information.

Lesson 2: Locating specific information holders

Behavioral Objective: When seeking information contained in an information holder (a sentence, paragraph, or page), the pupil will recall the portion of the story that contains information and will quickly locate the specific holder (sentence, paragraph, page) that contains the information.

Anticipatory Set: For this task, the teacher has prepared a short story that has been divided into four parts. The teacher may ask the pupils to listen or to watch the screen as she reads the story. She will demonstrate how she will recall the distinct events taking place in the story.

<u>Part 1</u>

Saturday had come at last. Tom and John had been waiting for this day. This was the day that they would get on the bus and ride to the carnival that had just been set up at Sunset Mall.

<u>Part 2</u>

When the boys got to the carnival, they saw a lot of people. Every ride had a long line of fifty or more people Even the food stands and restrooms had long lines. People seemed to fill every bit of the mall.

<u>Part 3</u>

After buying their tickets, the boys waited in the line for the Tilt-A-Whirl. When their turn came, they got on the Tilt-A-Whirl and went for a wild ride. They liked it a lot, even though they felt they were about to be thrown out of it. Both boys were shaky as they tried to stand up when the ride had ended.

Part 4

Tom couldn't wait any longer. He just had to have something to eat. John was thirsty. The boys decided to get in line for hot dogs and soft drinks at one of the booths with the shortest lines. After a wait, they had their delicious hot dogs and drinks. They found a place to eat.

Instructional Input: After reading the story, the teacher will indicate a specific question such as "What did the boys see when they first arrived at the mall?" The teacher then models how she is trying to think of the events. She recalls that she remembers that they saw long lines at all the rides and food booths. She puts the story up on the screen and colors the sentences that tell this. She then tries to recall what they did after their ride. She remembers that they got hot dogs and soft drinks. She again puts up the transparency and colors the sentence that tells this.

Guided Practice: The pupils are asked to follow a four-part story like the one above that is displayed on an overhead projector as the teacher reads the story aloud. The teacher turns off the projector and asks the students to try to recall the parts of the story so that they will be able to locate specific answers later. The pupils are then paired up and asked to recall the parts of the story and their content.

Independent Practice: Another multi-part story is put on the screen, followed by a question that is shown when the story is taken off. The pupils at their desks are asked to show by a finger count whether they think the answer is in Part 1, 2, 3, 4, etc. The teacher reveals the part of the highest finger count and the search continues until the correct sentence is found and marked.

Closing: In the closing, the groups first summarize what they have learned, and then the whole group comes up with the generalization that:

> To locate specific sentences, you must remember the approximate parts of in the story where the important things happen. Then, you must turn to that part and quickly scan for the sentence that contains the information that you need for your answer.

Locating information with book parts includes a myriad of book parts that carry information: title, preface, introduction, contents, publication information, lists of illustrations, bibliographies, indexes, glossaries, appendices, and footnotes. The determination of when these are taught resides in the kinds of work that teachers are expecting of individuals or groups. Because the table of contents is usually the first book part taught to reading students, this direct teach will focus on a **diagnostic** direct teach of the table of contents. Rather than assuming that all the pupils need such a lesson, this lesson will initially determine who needs what help. In this instance, the anticipatory set takes on the role of a **diagnostic check** of each pupil's current skill with the objective. Consequently, those who are found to be skilled in the use of the table of contents will be released to do other things at this time.

Lesson 3: Locating in a table of contents

Behavioral objective: Using a table of contents, the pupils will quickly locate story titles, page numbers of specific stories, story authors, and specific sections within a storybook.

Diagnostic Check: The teacher asks each pupil to pickup one of the different books that she has brought to the session (all the books are different but all contain a table of contents). She then asks each one to try to follow the directions she will give, to the best of their ability, so that she can see what they know about tables of contents.

With their books in their hands, the teacher issues the first directive:

Open your book to the first page of your table of contents.
The teacher watches carefully to see which pupils turn to the correct page immediately as well as which pupils are watching others for their cue. This is noted with a mark by the pupils' names. Next, the teacher issues the second directive:

Put your finger on the title of the first story in your table of contents.
Again, the teacher takes her checklist to mark the names of those who quickly responded and had the story rather than something else.

For the third directive, the teacher asks the following:

Now that your finger is on the first story, point to the page that tells you where the story begins. Once again, the teacher should check to see who can correctly follow this directive. Then, the teacher makes similar checks as the students look for different sections of the contents or for certain authors.

For the fourth directive, the teacher asks the following:

Put your finger on the author of the third story in your book.
The teacher notes which pupils have placed their finger on the appropriate author's name in their books. Several may have a mystified look that suggests that they may not know what *author* means or that they do not understand where author's names are sometimes listed in tables of contents.

Instructional Input: Based on the diagnostic assessment, the teacher probably has a small group for the continued direct teach of content skills. For those that remain, the teacher displays a table of contents from a reader on the overhead screen and explains the relationship between the contents page and the actual contents of a reader. If possible, it is best for the teacher to have an actual set of books for each participant so that each one can find the contents item and then locate the actual element in the text.

If possible, all the pupils should have a copy of the same reader so that they can verify the relation between the contents and the contents page. The teacher carefully models how the contents can be used to find a story or its page number, author, and placement in a section of the book.

Guided Practice: For guided practice, the pupils are asked to work as pairs to locate specific stories, page numbers, sections, etc. in their individual copies of the readers. By taking turns in pairs, the pupils can assist each other and provide a check that ensures that the tasks are being done correctly.

Independent Practice: For independent practice, the pupils are asked to find specific elements in the contents or books. For example, the first pupil might ask the second pupil to locate a specific title in the table of contents.

Closing: Pupils indicate that the table of contents is a list of everything that is in a given book and that it is a quick place to find where a story, author, section, or page number is.

Locating information with reference aids concerns the development of skills to use dictionaries, encyclopedias, atlases, maps, globes, phone books, newspapers, magazines, and schedules. Direct teaches are often implemented on the spot with individuals because of the different times that students need such skills. Again, the **diagnostic check** format of the preceding lesson should be used so that pupils already possessing the skills aren't bored. Because reference skills demand the ability to alphabetize to the second or third letter, the following lesson is appropriate only after the students possess an efficient alphabetization skill.

Lesson 4: Locating information with references

Behavioral Objective: Using the *World Book Encyclopedia* or any other alphabetically organized encyclopedia, the pupils will be able to locate desired topics quickly.

Diagnostic Check: By providing each pupil with a volume of the encyclopedia and asking them to locate a given animal in their individual volume, the teacher can determine some of this proficiency. In advance, the teacher should make a transparency with each volume that lists the letter associated with the volume and the name of an animal that might be found in that volume (e.g., *A*—antelope, *B*—beaver, *C*—coyote, *D*—duck, *E*—elephant, *F*—ferret, *G*—goose, *H*—hyena, *I*—iguana, *J*—jackal, *K*—kangaroo, *L*—llama, *M*—monkey, *O*—opossum, *P*—panda, *R*—rabbit, *S*—salamander, *T*—tiger, *U*—unicorn,

V—vicuna, *Z*—zebra. The assigned animals need to be locatable in the available encyclopedia.
As the faster students locate the given page, they are asked to write an interesting fact about their animal. For those having difficulty in locating, the balance of the lesson would be directed toward that skill.

Instructional Input: The teacher takes the *G* volume of the encyclopedia and models her thinking processes relative to the location of the information on gorillas. She then explains the steps of a locating task for the students, perhaps like this:

1. Approximate the spelling—*g-o-r-i-l-l-a.* Even if it's wrong, you can usually get close. Emphasize the first two letters.
2. Decide where *go* will come in the encyclopedia and limit your search to entries that begin with *go-*.
3. Once you've found the *go-* entries, add on the *-r-,* so that you have the *gor-* that will allow you to find something that looks like your approximated spelling.
4. Search until you find it. If you can't find it, try the encyclopedia **index,** because some animals are listed under other listings.

Then the teacher models this search so the pupils can see the steps clearly.

Guided Practice: The pupils are asked to cluster in groups of two or three around a given encyclopedia where they are asked to plug in the steps modeled by the teacher. Each cluster chooses its own animal based upon the letter of their encyclopedia and proceeds accordingly. The teacher moves about and monitors the success and difficulty. Those pupils who find their entries quickly are asked to find other entries.

Independent Practice: Individuals are asked to identify and locate an animal on their own in the encyclopedia in which they started. As they find their answer, they can write the animal name and the page on which it's found so that the teacher can observe their success or lack of success.

Closing: Have the students summarize the presented steps for finding an entry in the encyclopedia.

ORGANIZING

Organizing requires different types of lessons for **narrative** and **expository** text. Lessons for the narrative area are: discovering schema, organizing temporal events, and summarizing. For expository text, the following lessons are included: discovering main idea, outlining, and summarizing. The expository skills can be used to develop **data charts** (organized information sets). Making data charts will be illustrated under outlining.

Lesson 1: Finding Main Characters

Behavioral Objective: TLW will identify the main characters in a story as those who the story is mostly about.

Anticipatory Set: In books, plays, and movies we find main characters. For instance, in the story of Snow White and the Seven Dwarfs, some might say that Snow White is the main character while the bad queen and the seven dwarfs are not main characters. How do we find out ?

Instructional Input: Before reading the story *Where The Wild Things Are*, the teacher asks the pupils to listen to identify the main characters, the ones that the story is mainly about. After completing the story, the teacher puts up the following chart:

Characters

First Part — Max, Max's mom, dog

Middle part — Max and the Wild Things

End — Max

The teacher models the thinking that shows that Max is what the book is mainly about. Thus, she circles Max's name as the main character. Subsequently, the teacher will see if the pupils identify the "wild things" as main characters also. For this discussion, she can circle the "wild things" also and thus include Max and the wild things as main characters. The teacher explains that we don't always have to agree as to who the main characters are.

Guided Practice: The teacher passes out the book *Dr. DeSoto* to each pair of students and asks them to read the story and list the main characters. Each pair should write down for later comparison their main character identifications. Most pupils will include Dr. Doolittle, his wife, and the fox.

Independent Practice: Each pupil will be asked to identify the main characters in the last narrative story that they read.

Closing: The teacher asks the pupils to tell that main characters are the ones that the story is mainly about.

Lesson 2 Finding Main Characters and Settings

Behavioral Objective: TLW list the main characters and settings that occur in the course of the narrative.

Anticipatory Set: The teacher will remind the pupils of the story *Where The Wild Things Are* and the fact that they previously agreed that Max and the wild things were the main characters, The teacher will add a new word - settings - to the board and say that they are going to see what settings the main characters find themselves in through the story.

Instructional Input: Once again, the teacher asks the pupils to listen for the various settings or places that occur as she reads *Where The Wild Things Are*. She asks them to raise their hand whenever the setting changes. In the course of the story, the teacher notes:

Main Characters	Settings
Max	Sent to his room
	Gets on boat
	Land of wild things
	Gets on boat
	Back in his room

Guided Practice: The teacher gives the pupils a copy of *Swimmy* and asks pairs of pupils to construct a chart of the main characters and setting for that story. The teacher monitors the groups and directs the comparisons at the end.

Independent Practice: Each pupil is asked to apply a main character and setting chart to the latest narrative that s/he has read.

Closing: The teacher asks the students to restate that settings are the various places that a story takes place. It's possible that a story may take place in a single setting and that the 1) problem and 2) time become the critical elements.

Lesson 3: Finding Main Characters, Settings, and Problems/Main Events

Behavioral Objective: TLW list the main characters, settings, and problems that occur in the course of the narrative.

Anticipatory Set: The teacher summarizes what the pupils have previously learned about main story characters and main settings. She explains that the thing that makes these characters and settings are the problems or main events. Sometimes it's not easy to identify the problems or main events. For example, she notes that *Where The Wild Things Are* has two main problems. The first occurs when Max is sent to bed be without his supper for acting up. He escapes in his mind to the land of the wild things. After he's there awhile, he's not happy. This is his second problem and he wishes to go home. He does.

Instructional Input: Prior to reading *Dr. DeSoto* to the group, the teacher asks them to think about the problems or main events in the story. After finishing the story, the teacher puts up the following chart and illustrates the problems from the story.

Main Characters	Main Settings	Problems/Main Events
Dr. DeSoto and wife	Dr. DeSoto's office (first day)	Fox had a bad tooth. Fox wanted to eat DeSotos. DeSotos didn't want to be eaten.
Fox	Dr. DeSoto's office (another day)	

The teacher explains that the fox's problem is the tooth that is hurting him. The DeSotos' problem is how to avoid being eaten by the fox. The teacher explains that Dr. DeSoto solves the fox's problem by pulling his tooth and making a replacement. Dr. DeSoto and his wife solve their problem by gluing the fox's mouth shut so that he can't eat them.

Guided Practice: The teacher pairs up the children and asks them to identify the main characters, settings, and problems in *Tikki Tikki Tembo.* After each pair identifies the these elements and charts them, the teacher presides over a sharing session of all who did the task.

Independent Practice: For their next narrative story, each pupil is asked to chart the main characters, settings, and problems.

Closing: Pupils relate the concept that stories are built around problems or events and that those events can usually be identified.

Lesson 4: Finding Schema (main characters, settings, problems, resolutions) in a Simple Story

Behavioral Objective: When students read narratives with main characters, settings, problems, and problem resolution, the students will accurately identify each of these four elements.

Anticipatory Set: The teacher should open the lesson by stating that being able to remember the main things about stories is a big help if you want to be able to retell the stories accurately.

Instructional Input: On the blackboard or overhead projector, the teacher writes:

Main Characters	Settings	Problems	Resolutions

Next, the teacher reads a shortened version of *Goldilocks and The Three Bears.* After she finishes, the teacher models her thinking about the story in terms of the four headings. She begins with the **main characters**—Goldilocks, Mama Bear, Poppa Bear, and Baby Bear. She notes that the **setting** was the Three Bears' house. Next, she suggests that the theme tells the main problem of the story. She decides that the main problem is that Goldilocks is trying out the Three Bears' furniture and food, and that Goldilocks always likes the small bear's things best. After this idea is written under **problem**, the teacher suggests that the **resolution** is how things are solved in the end. In this version of the story, the bears discover what Goldilocks has done and chase her away.

Main Characters	Settings	Problem	Resolution
Goldilocks Mama Bear Poppa Bear Baby Bear	Three Bears' house	Goldilocks tries out the Bears' food and furniture.	Bears chase Goldilocks out of their house.

Guided Practice: Leaving the preceding information on the board, the teacher reads a brief story about *Little Red Ridinghood.* She then asks the pupils to think about the main characters, setting, problem, and resolution. They work in pairs to see what they can come up with. After some think time, she begins to record the pupils' thoughts under the appropriate headings. Agreements are reached that the **main characters** were Little Red Ridinghood, Grandma, the wolf, and the woodsmen; the **settings** were the woods and Grandmother's house; the **problem** was the wolf trying to eat *Little Red Ridinghood* and her grandmother; and the **resolution** (in this version) was when the woodsmen chased the wolf away.

Main Characters	Settings	Problem	Resolution
Little R. R. Grandmother Wolf Woodsman	Woods Grandmothers house	The wolf wants to eat Little Red Ridinghood and her grandmother.	The woodsman chases the wolf away and saves Little Ridinghood and Grandmother.

Independent Practice: The story of *Cinderella* is read for the students in order that they can attempt to discover the main characters, settings, problem, and resolution. After all have had an opportunity to do so, the teacher writes up the answers in order that the pupils can choose the most accurate.

Closing: Pupils are asked to remember that most stories have main characters, settings (where things happen), problem (the main action of the story), and resolutions (usually problem solutions at the end).

Lesson 5: Finding Schema (main characters, settings, problems, resolutions) in a Multi Problem Story

Behavioral Objective: When students read narratives with main characters, setting, problem, and problem resolution, the students will accurately identify each of these four elements.

Anticipatory Set: The teacher should open the lesson by building on the previous lesson where the students dealt with a simple problem and solution. The teacher explains that books sometimes have more than one problem. Consequently, it is important to identify the different problems and how they are or are not solved.

Instructional Input: On the blackboard or overhead projector, the teacher writes the following four headings:

Main Characters	Settings	Problems	Resolutions

Next, the teacher reads a shortened version of *The Three Little Pigs.* After she finishes, the teacher models her thinking about the story in terms of the four headings. She begins with the **main characters**— 1st Pig, 2nd Pig, 3rd Pig, and Big Bad Wolf. She notes that the **settings** were the straw house of 1st Pig, the stick house of Pig 2, and the brick house of Pig 3. Next, she suggests that the big **problem** was to build a house safe from the Big Bad Wolf. The teacher suggests that the **resolution** is that 1) the straw house was blown down, 2) the stick house was blown down, and 3) the brick house was the one that kept Pig 3 safe.

Main Characters	Settings	Problem	Resolution
1st Pig	1st pig's straw house	The main problem was to build a house safe from the Big Bad Wolf.	1) The straw house was blown down.
2nd Pig	2nd pig's stick house		2) The stick house was blown down.
3rd Pig	3rd pig's brick house		3) The brick house was not blown down.
Big Bad Wolf.			

Guided Practice: Leaving the preceding information on the board, the teacher reads a brief story about *Stone Soup* She then asks the pupils to think about the main characters, setting, problems, and resolutions. They work in pairs to see what they can come up with. After some think time, she begins to record the pupils' thoughts under the appropriate headings. Agreements are reached that the **main characters** were the soldiers and the towns' people. The **setting** was the kitchen where the soldiers were going to make the stone soup. The **first problem** was that the soldiers were very hungry but the town's people didn't want to share their food. The **second problem** was that the soldiers had to think up a way to get food for themselves.The **resolution** (in this version) was when the woodsmen pretended to make stone soup but actually got the people to bring out their food for it.

Main Characters	Settings	Problems	Resolutions
Soldiers town's people	The kitchen of the town's people.	The **first problem** was that the soldiers were very hungry but the town's people didn't want to share their food. The **second problem** was that the soldiers had to think up a way to get food for themselves.	The **resolution** (in this version) was when the soldiers pretended to make stone soup but actually got the people to bring out their food and share it.

Independent Practice: The story of *The Boy Who Cried Wolf* is read for the students in order that they can attempt to discover the main characters, settings, problems, and resolutions. After all have had an opportunity to do so, the teacher writes up the answers in order that the pupils can choose the most accurate.

Closing: Pupils are asked to summarize that most stories have main characters, settings (where things happen), problem (the main action of the story), and resolutions (usually problem solutions at the end).

Lesson 6: Finding Schema (main characters, settings, problems, resolution) On a Page by Page Basis

Behavioral Objective: When students read narratives with main characters, settings, problem, and problem resolutions, the students will accurately identify each of these elements as the story unfolds.

Anticipatory Set: The teacher should open the lesson by building on the previous two schema lessons where the students dealt with characters, settings, problems, and solutions. The teacher explains that it's sometimes useful to chart the action on a page by page basis in order to understand the whole story.

Instructional Input: On a storyboard or an overhead projector, the teacher writes 1) the following four headings and 2) reveals a page of text.

Main Characters	**Settings**	**Problems**	**Resolutions**

Next, the teacher reads from text and models how she identifies the main elements. She writes down each element or draws an arrow to it. This process is continued through to the end of the story where the full story grammar should be complete.

Page 5- Sam and his little brother Tommy watched the rain from their living room. Almost all of it was falling into the creek near the house. As the boys watched, the creek grew higher and higher. Soon, the water had reached the edge of the yard.

"Let's make a raft and ride down the creek," said Sam.

Tommy nodded as if to say "Cool!"

Page 6- When the rain stopped, the boys went to the tool shed. That found two hammers, a saw, and some nails. They then found the scrap wood pile. Soon they were building their raft. They nailed old fence boards to two by fours. After awhile they had built their first raft.

Page 7 - Sam and Tommy carefully pushed their raft into the creek. First, Sam crawled onto the raft. It bobbed in the water a little. When Tommy slid onto it, the raft sunk. As it sunk the boys turned the raft over. Soon, they were in the water. The boys were apart, trying to stay up. The water carried them down the creek.

Page 8- Both boys had mouths full of water as they tumbled. They were very scared. Then, they saw that the creek became wide. It also became shallow. The boys were able to get up and walk home. They saw their raft laying on the bank.

Main Characters	**Settings**	**Problem**	**Resolution**
5.Sam and Tommy	living room	to make a raft to go down creek	
6. (same)	tool shed, wood pile	(same)	
7. (same)	in the creek	to stay alive and get out of the creek	
8. (same)	(same)	(same)	creek becomes shallow and they walk out

Guided Practice: Leaving the preceding information on the board, the teacher gives each pair of pupils a similar story and a story grammar sheet like the one above and asks the pupils to carry out a page by page story grammar to find the main characters, settings, problems, and resolutions.

Independent Practice: Pupils are asked to repeat this process with the story that they read for their challenge reading.

Closing: Pupils are asked to summarize that most stories have main characters, settings (where things happen), problem (the main action of the story), and resolutions (usually problem solutions at the end).

Lesson 7: Recalling temporal events

Behavioral Objective: After this lesson, students will observe stories closely so that they can discover the time or events order of that story. They will be able to retell those major events.

Anticipatory Set: The teacher asks how many students remember the nursery school story about *The Three Little Pigs.* She then asks them to think about exactly what happened and when it happened in the story.

Instructional Input: On the board the teacher writes the following:

Event 1:
Event 2:
Event 3:
Event 4:
Event 5:

The teacher explains that she could write a long series of events because stories have differing numbers of events. She refers them back to the story and begins to recount it and record the main events as follows:

Event 1:The wolf blew down their main house and they ran away.
Event 2:Each built a different house.
Event 3:The wolf destroyed the straw house.
Event 4:The wolf destroyed the wood house.

Event 5:The wolf couldn't destroy the brick house and the three pigs were safe together in the brick house.

It is a good idea to give practice with other stories too so that pupils can see that the units of time can be events, hours, days, etc.

Guided Practice: The story of *The Little Boy Who Cried Wolf* is read to the group with the express purpose of remembering the events and their order. The children, working in pairs or small groups, discuss and list the events of the story. The teacher then seeks a consensus from the group.

Independent Practice: The story of *Henny Penny* is provided for the pupils' independent work. After each pupil has finished working alone, the teacher leads a class discussion in which the students compare their results.

Closing: For the closing, the teacher summarizes the concept that most narrative stories have a temporal order of events that can be discovered by careful listening and reading.

Lesson 8: Summarizing Narratives

Behavioral Objective: Using main characters, settings, problems/main events, and resolutions, the pupils will summarize a narrative story. This is very much like the story grammar lesson except that it adds the main events that happen while the problem is being dealt with in the story.

Anticipatory Set: Start to tell about a movie or TV program that everyone has seen, such as the following:

> Last night I saw this movie called *Cinderella*. Well, it's about this girl, Cinderella. Oh, it's about a prince, too. Anyway, Cinderella has to do all the work and her lazy sisters don't do anything. Well, Cinderella is real pretty. Anyway, she goes to the ball and meets the prince. He looks for her and finally finds her.

Make sure that the retelling is long and disjointed. Finally, when the teacher sees that she is annoying the class, she stops and gets their feedback on why her retelling is not easy to understand. The pupils are quick to relate about the lack of organization.

Instructional Input: The teacher agrees with the student assessment of her retelling. She then suggests that many stories can be retold more accurately if we remember to tell the listeners certain things about any story. She then puts the story grammar and the following elements on the board:

Main Characters	Settings	Problems	Solutions
Cinderella Mean sisters Mean step mother Fairy godmother	Cinderella's house	Cinderella has to do all the work and can't go to the ball.	Fairy dresses C. up and sends her to ball.
Cinderella and Prince	Castle	C. and Prince fall in love but she must leave before 12. Loses slipper.	
	Cinderella's House	The prince tries to find the beautiful girl who lost the slipper.	Finally, he tries it on Cinderella and they marry and live happily ever after.

Using this format, the teacher quickly summarizes the show that she had begun previously to tell about and writes the details in the structure used for the story of Cinderella.

Guided Practice: For guided practice, the teacher reads the story *The Three Little Pigs* from a reader and asks pairs of pupils to fill out the structure, using the pattern demonstrated. Answers are compared within cluster groupings and then discussed in the group as a whole.

Main Characters	Settings	Main Events	Resolution
Three little pigs Big Bad Wolf	Mama's house	Pigs leave Mama's house to build own houses.	
	Straw house	Wolf blows down straw house.	
	Wood house	Wolf blows down wood house.	
	Brick house	Wolf tries to blow down brick house.	Wolf can't blow down brick houses.

Independent Practice: Pupils are asked to apply the structure to their story for instructional level reading this day. The teacher will then determine each pupil's understanding of the summary concept as developed.

Closing: For the closing the teacher asks each pupil to write the summary structure (setting, main characters, main events, resolution) on their paper in anticipation of using it during their written comprehension on their next story.

Expository Lessons

Lesson 9: Identifying Expository Main Ideas

Behavioral Objective: After this lesson, the pupil will be able to locate and identify **stated** or **unstated** main ideas in expository paragraphs. They will also be able to identify paragraphs that have **no main idea** .

1. **STATED:** The main or controlling idea is clearly stated in a topic sentence at the first or end of the paragraph and the other sentences.
2. **IMPLIED:** There is no stated main idea but the reader can readily discern and verbalize it because all the sentences imply the main idea.
3. **NO MAIN IDEA:** There is no main idea in the paragraph.

Anticipatory Set: On the board, the teacher puts the following paragraph and asks the class what its main idea is.

> **The three main trees in the region are oak, cedar, and mesquite. Oaks are large and shade producing. Cedars are spindly. Mesquite trees are thin and provide little shade.**

The teacher then puts up the following chart so that the pupils can have an organizer for the various types of main idea, and explains what those types are.

Main Ideas (Expository Paragraphs)

STATED	IMPLIED	NO MAIN IDEA
First Sentence		
Last Sentence		

Instructional Input: The teacher reads the sentence aloud and answers her question about the main idea with the identification of the first sentence—*The three main trees in the region are oak, cedar, and mesquite.* She then reasons that this main idea is an example of the first kind of main idea (stated) because the first sentence tells that the paragraph is about the three main trees in the region. The teacher then goes through the previously provided chart (stated, implied, none).

Next, the teacher presents the following paragraphs representing the three types of paragraphs and models how the main idea of each is found.

MAIN IDEA TYPES

1. **STATED:** Main idea is clearly stated in a topic sentence or ending sentence and other ideas relate to and develop that single main idea, as in the following example:

> **Fall decorations brighten up the classroom.** Colored leaves are pasted in the windows. Orange pumpkins sit on the table. Leaf collections are gathered on the back table.

2. **IMPLIED**: There is no stated main idea, but the reader can readily discern and verbalize it. All the sentences are unified around the one implicit main idea, as in:

> The **lake looked like** it was made of **glass**. The slick water began to develop a pattern. The pattern grew larger. Soon, **gentle waves** could be seen. In time, **they grew higher and higher.**

(Main idea: The lake changes from slick to rough.)

3. **NO MAIN IDEA:** There is really no apparent main idea in a paragraph such as the following:

> The goose wandered into the barnyard. A small boy played with his toy soldiers. A rooster crowed loudly. The train whistle sounded nearby.

Guided Practice: On a chart, the teacher provides a listing with an example of each main idea type. On a transparency, the teacher reveals the following five paragraphs and the students are to work in table groups of four to identify the type of each:

The storm had begun. Dark clouds raced across the sky. Giant patches of black intermingled with wispy white clouds. The trees began to whip badly in the increasing wind.

First, Pippi hoisted herself up the ladder. Then she dropped lightly on the deck. Moving quietly, she tiptoed along the deck. At last, she had boarded the pirate's ship.

The small boy took the rounded stone. Without any warning, he let the stone fly in the direction of the dog. The dog squealed and put his tail between his legs and ran.

Each step becomes harder and harder. It's like you're always working to take a step. The trees become fewer and it's hard to breathe because the air is thinner.

A big dog was standing in the road. A man walked home. A small boy had a rubber gun across the street.

Each of the paragraphs is subsequently discussed and the classifications of the various pupil groups heard. It is agreed that the classifications are as follows: 1) the first paragraph has the stated main idea—**The storm had begun**—at the start; 2) the second paragraph has, at its end, the stated main idea that **Pippi had boarded the pirate's ship**; 3) the third paragraph about the boy and the dog **implies that the boy was hurting the dog**; 4) the fourth selection has an **implied main idea that is about climbing a mountain**; 5) the fifth paragraph has no apparent main idea.

Independent Practice: The pupils are directed to analyze a series of paragraphs in a content text to determine what kinds of paragraphs are usually found in such an informative book.

Closing: The teacher summarizes that expository writing may have two basic main idea types (stated or implied) or may have no main idea.

Lesson 10: Outlining (Data Chart Skill)

Behavioral Objective: The pupils will be able to utilize the subheadings of an encyclopedia (or content chapter) as an outline for obtaining the most significant information about specific topics. The pupils will locate and record the most significant facts about a given country's government, people, land, climate, economy, and history.

Anticipatory Set: The teacher explains that she wants to prepare a lesson on Iraq from the *World Book Encyclopedia* and wants to be sure that she covers the main points. She asks the pupils how they might do this if they were called upon to give a five minute talk about Iraq. After a brief discussion the teacher illustrates how she did the task.

Instructional Input: Using the *I* volume from an alphabetically organized encyclopedia, the teacher uses the outline organization of the book and puts up the following pattern:

1. **Government**
2. **The People**
3. **The Land**
4. **The Climate**
5. **Economy**
6. **History**

The teacher illustrates the key information she has found out about each country and how she can speak briefly about each point from her study. In the process, the teacher details why she selected the information she did under each of the topics. Some explanation of the topics will be necessary for pupils who have not encountered words like *economy* before.

1. Government They have a president and two councils. One council forms policies and passes laws while the other council carries out the laws.

2. The People Eighty percent of the people are Arabs who practice the Muslim religion. About half the people live in cities.

3. The Land It has four main regions: 1) the upper plains; 2) the lower plains; 3) the mountains; 4) the desert.

4. The Climate Little or no rain falls in most of the country. Except for the mountains, most of the country is hot.

5. Economy Oil provides most of its income although half of the people make their living farming and herding.

6. History The written history dates back to 3000 B.C. Arab rule and British rule preceded independence in 1932. Ruled originally by King Faisal and later Prince Abdullah, the country became a republic.

Guided Practice: Each group of four pupils is given an encyclopedia or geography book and asked to look up a different country, read about it, and use the subheads to prepare a brief outline or a data chart from which to talk.

Information Sources:	WORLD BOOK	GROLLIERS
1. Government		
2. The People		
3. The Land		
4. The Climate		
5. Economy		
6. History		

Independent Practice: Each pupil selects a country from the encyclopedia, prepares a subheading outline, and writes down some information about their country. The information must be important and must be summarized.

Closing: The pupils note that the subheadings in content books

REMEMBERING

Remembering is a skill that is the byproduct of organizing. It is necessary to remember before you can organize things. Likewise, it is necessary to organize things so that you can remember them. Consequently, pupils who have problems remembering need clear purposes for reading and remembering as well as the organizational strategies of discovering schema, recalling temporal events, summarizing, identifying main ideas, and outlining.

Three skills for sharpening remembering skills include: setting purposes; monitoring your remembering; and monitoring your understanding. All of these skills are used in narrative and expository reading.

Lesson 1: Setting Purposes

Behavioral Objective: Before reading narrative and expository materials, the reader will set the following specific purposes for reading, which are either **narrative** (to summarize the story, to tell the highlights of the story, to tell the characters, setting, problem, and problem resolution) or **expository** (to recall the main points or structure, to recall the main points or structure and add detail to each part).

Anticipatory Set: The teacher explains that if she is going to read a story or content book, she may find that she can't recall the story or the content. She explains that this happened because she didn't have a set purpose in mind before she began reading. Thus, the current lesson provides direction about how one should approach both types of materials for purposes of organizing and remembering.

Instructional Input: When we want to remember, we set purposes for remembering. Those purposes are largely determined by the type of material we are reading and how much we want to remember. For **narrative** materials, we must remember the normal story parts like characters, settings, problem, and resolution. For **expository** materials, we need to see if the meanings are stated or implied. In the charts which follow, readers can note how the two different strategies are utilized with a narrative story about the **elephant monkey** and a content story with stated main ideas about the topic of **hibernation**.

Narrative (Main Characters, Settings, Problem, Solution)

Main Characters- elephant /monkey

Setting- the forest

Problem - quarrel about whether it is best to be strong or quick

Solution - not yet

Once an elephant and a monkey had a quarrel. Both animals were very proud. The huge elephant was proud because he was so strong. The little monkey was proud because he was so quick.

"I can pull down the biggest tree," said the elephant.

"Well, I could climb that tree before you could take one step," replied the monkey.

The elephant shouted, "It is better to be strong than to be quick."

"No", cried the angry monkey. "It is much better to be quick!"

Expository (Stated, Implied) This has stated main ideas underlined.

Hibernation

Getting Ready for Winter

This grizzly bear is getting ready to sleep for four months. He will sleep through the winter. This sleep is called hibernation.

To get ready for winter, the grizzly bear eats a lot. He gets fat. This fat helps keep him alive during hibernation. His furry coat helps him keep warm.

The Long Sleep

The grizzly bear does not always stay still when he hibernates. He moves around a little bit. Sometimes he looks for food. But he is fat. He does not need to look for much food.

When spring comes, the bear wakes up. He is hungry and looks for food again.

The teacher then tells the students that she wants to identify the *main characters, settings, story problem,* and *story resolution* of the brief **narrative** story about the elephant and monkey, and proceeds to read the story aloud. As she identifies each feature, she underlines it on the text. For the **expository** modeling, the teacher puts up a transparency of an article about the grizzly bear and reads the main subtitles and a few sentences under each subtitle. She then underlines the key words in the selection that will help her to summarize the article.

Guided Practice: The teacher gives each cluster group stories similar to the example in order that they may practice identifying the main ideas of narrative and expository selections. After each story or article is read, the pupils attempt to construct in writing the narrative and expository structures previously outlined.

Independent Practice: The teacher asks the pupils to apply the narrative structure to their instructional level story for the day. A science page, written at a level at which all the pupils can read it, is handed out so that the pupils can read the page and underline the key thoughts.

Closing: Pupils summarize the importance of having purposes for reading narrative and expository materials and demonstrate how these structures will hold important information for the reader.

Lesson 2: Monitoring your remembering

Behavioral Objective: While performing the previous purpose-setting tasks for narrative and expository reading, the pupil will strategically pause during reading to reflect on what he remembers. When he senses that he can't remember significant events (like the characters in a narrative or the subtopics in an expository piece of text), the reader will go back to the start and begin again.

Anticipatory Set: The teacher explains that we all get distracted and sometimes can't remember what we have read. To avert this possibility, the teacher stresses the importance of periodic stops every few paragraphs or pages for determining whether or not we remember the significant structures we set out to remember. The teacher explains how she pauses to remember things written on her grocery list.

Instructional Input: The most effective means of teaching this is for the teacher to read some material that the children can also see.

After she reads a few sentences, the teacher pauses and models her thinking, and openly admits that she can't remember some things. By going back to find those things, the teacher models the **metacognitive tasks** necessary for better remembering. She then continues to read, periodically repeating the reflective process as she goes.

The desert is a place that gets very little rainfall. The ground is rocky and sandy. In the day, it gets very hot. It doesn't seem like anything could live there. (**With little rain, doesn't seem like anything could live in desert.**) Still, there are things alive in a desert. These things get food and shelter to survive. **(But they do.)** Cactus plants are found in the desert. These plants spread their roots close to the ground to get rain when it comes. It then saves the water for dry days. **(Cactus saves water.)** A desert tortoise lives in the desert too. It gets most of its water from the plants it eats. Like the cactus, it also stores water under its shell so it can go a long time without water. **(Tortoise saves water under shell.)** The kangaroo rat is a desert animal. It makes water from the dry seeds it eats.	It never has to take a drink of water. **(kangaroo rat gets water from seeds.)** Food and water are not enough for survival. Plants and animals must be able to protect themselves. **(Plants and animals need protection.)** A cactus protects itself with its sharp spines. Many animals would eat the cactus if it didn't have these spines. Most animals will stay away from cactus.**(Cactus have sharp spines for protection.)** The tortoise has a shell to hide under. It can pull its legs into the shell and the strongest animal can't bite through it. **(Tortoises have hard shells for protection.)** Kangaroo rats don't have hard shells or spines. They can jump high in the air. This is how they get their name - kangaroo rat. It is because they jump high like a kangaroo. **(Kangaroo rats can jump high for protection.)**

Guided Practice: The teacher pairs up pupils so that they can simultaneously (and silently) read a given amount of text (for example, about two paragraphs), and then pause and ask each other what they are remembering about the text that they are reading. This process is repeated with various lengths of text selected by the teacher.

Independent Practice: Materials are provided for individual pupils to do this on their own with the benefit of feedback from the teacher as to what things should probably be remembered. Ideally, the materials used for this task should have blank spaces between adjacent main passages, in order that the student can write a summary of the main ideas of the passage just read in the space that follows it.

Closing: Pupils state the importance of periodically stopping and asking yourself what you remember about a passage that you are reading, and of asking yourself what important information you don't remember.

Lesson 3: Monitoring your understanding

Behavioral Objective: While performing the previous purpose-setting tasks for narrative and expository reading, the pupil will strategically pause in route to reflect on what he understands. When he senses that he doesn't understand significant events, the student will isolate the things that he does not understand and will re-read key passages or think further about what he has read until he feels that he is no longer confused.

Anticipatory Set: The teacher demonstrates how she might not understand a difficult story if she fails to go back and sort out the characters and what they are doing. She also reveals how she might ruin a piece of equipment if she continues forth without understanding the consequences of doing something out of order.

Instructional Input: Continuing from the anticipatory set, the teacher models with a well-known children's novel, pausing to state her confusion and then modeling her thinking and searching back in the book for clarification. For expository materials, the teacher reads aloud from the science book about how to hook up batteries in such a fashion as to ring a bell. As she becomes confused, she reads passages and verbalizes until she understands.

Guided Practice: The teacher continues the same type of modeling with narrative and expository materials as illustrated in the anticipatory set.

Independent Practice: This is best done with material selected from the students' content area textbooks. Pairs of pupils attempt to read the same passage, and then explain what they think they are reading. Pupils are encouraged to apply this in their daily instructional reading as well as in their content subject reading assignments.

Closing: The teacher explains that reading is thinking and understanding. If you don't understand, you often need to go back to build your structure of understanding for narrative or expository materials. At times, you may be so confused that you may wish to skim ahead to get the larger picture of what you are reading.

EVALUATING

Evaluating deals with **narrative** and **expository** forms of text. In the narrative text, the students make judgments about the desirability of a character, story, or ending as well as its reality. They also make convergent and divergent predictions about titles, endings, etc. In expository text, the pupils find discrepancies through internal and external evaluations. They also identify propaganda devices in text, such as *plain folks* or *glittering generalities.*

Narrative Lessons

Lesson 1: Judging the desirability of characters, stories, or endings.

Behavioral Objective: When asked to judge the desirability of a story character or story ending, the pupil will use his own value system to produce a stated, rational judgment.

Anticipatory Set: The teacher puts the following headings on the blackboard or transparency:

Stories I Like   Stories I Dislike

At this point, the teacher starts writing the names of stories with which the children are familiar under the two listings.

Instructional Input: The teacher explains that it's easy to like or dislike things because we have different value systems. She explains that while it's easy to list likes and dislikes, it's important to tell why we feel the way we do about the things we like or dislike. She starts telling why she likes or dislikes particular stories. She then asks for some opinions different from hers. It is especially important to show that we all don't have to share the same values.

Guided Practice: Erasing her story entries under the two categories, the teacher puts up the title of a story that was recently read to them (perhaps *Charlie and the Chocolate Factory.* (Dahl, 1973) and asks each pair of pupils to see whether they can determine why they like or dislike that book. After the groups have decided how they feel about that book and why they feel that way, each group records an explanation of their feelings. Then the teacher asks for a listing of the reasons for liking or disliking the book.

Independent Practice: Dahl's *James and the Giant Peach* (1978)is offered for each person to make a judgment and supporting argument about. The teacher subsequently has the pupils compare answers.

Closing: The teacher asks pairs of pupils to what they had learned in this lesson. Most pairs should agree that they have learned how to tell why they like or dislike a book. They should also discuss parts of books that they liked and disliked because liking and disliking should not be the only options. It's relevant to discuss character traits that you and the students might admire such as honesty, hard work, truthfulness, helpfulness as well as the opposites of these things. Pupils need to see that different people have different value sets as to what they admire.

Lesson 2: Judging the realism of characters, stories, or endings

Behavioral Objective: When asked to make a judgment whether a story is realistic, the pupils will cite evidence from the story that suggests either realism or fantasy.

Anticipatory Set: On the board or transparency, the teacher writes the headings for two columns, labeling them **Real** and **Make-Believe.**

Instructional Input: The teacher then reads a series of four short paragraphs—two of which are realistic and two of which are in the realm of make-believe. After reading each paragraph, the teacher determines what kind of story it is and puts its title under one of the two categories.

> John, a fourth grader at Green School, likes to ride his bike when he gets home from school. He rides the bike on the hills near his house.
>
> Mary, a third grader, likes to take her friends flying in her airplane after school. She has had her pilot's license since she was 6, and flies the space shuttle on weekends.
>
> Sammy has been building model airplanes for a long time. When he was ten years old, he got an engine powered model. Since that time, he has built and flown eight different planes.
>
> Alex, the mouse, told his wife Mabel that he wanted to learn to fly. His wife laughed at him. She wondered where he got such crazy ideas.

Now the teacher goes back to each paragraph and explains the clues that made it either real or make believe. The teacher then writes those clues under the appropriate headings for each of the paragraphs.

Real	**Make-Believe**
Could happen	Could not happen
Characters are real	Characters aren't real
Animals were animals	Animals can't talk aloud
People could do this	People can't do this
Possible events	Impossible events
Possible	Impossible

Guided Practice: The teacher asks the pupils to work in pairs to classify short paragraph stories that she reads to them or hands to them. Each pupil pair discusses each selection and applies the previously discussed criteria of real and make-believe to them. When agreement is reached, the pair labels each paragraph as *Real* or *Make-Believe* and tells why they think that category fits that story. At this point the teacher has the total group share their decisions to see the extent of agreement on the paragraphs.

Independent Practice: Each pupil subsequently reads or listens to two more paragraphs and makes judgments about the real or make-believe nature of what they have heard. Once again, they compare answers to see how well they have done with the task.

Closing: The teacher erases the dimensions for *Real* and *Make-Believe* and asks for the students to recall what the critical factors were for each. As the pupils recall, the teacher records the factors under the original listings of *Real* and *Make-Believe.*

Expository Lessons

Lesson 3: Finding internal contradictions

Behavioral Objective: When asked to locate contradictory statements in a single text, the pupil will accurately find them.

Anticipatory Set: On the blackboard or transparency, the teacher reads aloud from the following text:

> Joe and Bob started their cross country hike early that morning. Soon, Bob said that he was hungry and wanted to eat. Joe said, "Me, too," so the two boys sat down to eat supper.

Instructional Input: The teacher notes that this story probably didn't sound exactly correct. She reads the story again and models her thinking about the boys starting their hike early that morning. She circles *early that morning* and *soon* and then discovers that the boys are eating their *supper.* She reasons that, unless they are eating the supper that they packed, this meal is not supper. The teacher then explains that they will be looking for things in stories that don't seem to make sense in terms of what's already been read.

Guided Practice: The pupils are asked to read the following paragraph from the overhead or blackboard and determine in pairs what might be wrong with it.

> Victor is the name of the fastest-flying aircraft in the Simian Air Force. This craft has been clocked at over 600 miles per hour. As the newest member of the force, this craft stands only behind their RAF-16 in speed.

The pupils search for the differences and discuss them as a group.

Independent Practice: Similar stories with conflicting information are provided for each pupil. The pupils are directed to take a colored pencil and mark the statements that are in disagreement. The differences are then discussed by small cluster groups.

Closing: The pupils note that it is possible to have conflicting pieces of information in a story or other written material.

Lesson 4: Finding external disagreements

Behavioral Objective: When asked to find disagreements in facts in reference materials, the pupils will locate the same facts in two or more reference materials and compare the facts, choosing the most accurate.

Anticipatory Set: The teacher explains that she wants to know approximately how many people live in Saudi Arabia. She asks if anyone knows. When no one responds, she takes out the 1980 *World Book Encyclopedia* and looks for the answer.

Instructional Input: The teacher writes the answer down from the *Facts in Brief* section—estimated 8,361,000. The teacher asks if everyone is satisfied with that figure. Several children reply that the figure was taken from a 1980 book so it has probably changed. The teacher agrees and she produces a recent news article that lists the population at approximately 9,500,000.

Guided Practice: Using a current *World Almanac* and the 1980 *World Book Encyclopedia*, clusters of pupils are to determine the populations for Kuwait, Iraq, Iran, Egypt, Syria, and Israel. The answers are compared.

Independent Practice: The pupils are to locate a population figure in a volume of the classroom copy of the 1980 *World Book Encyclopedia* and check that figure with a more recent source (encyclopedia, almanac, magazine article, etc.).

Closing: The pupils explain that facts change, and that facts found in more recent materials are more likely to be more accurate than those recorded in older materials.

Lesson 5: Identifying propaganda devices

Behavioral Objective: When asked to identify propaganda devices, the pupils will identify such examples in advertisements with beautiful young people. Students will also note such propaganda devices as *bandwagon* (everybody else is doing it), *glittering generalities* (selected words of praise about a product), and *plain folks* (the people in the advertisement are just plain folks like us).

Anticipatory Set: The teacher takes out a cigarette and holds it up proudly. "These are Camel longs," she says. Holding up a colorful magazine advertisement, she shows some attractive people in an advertisement that features these cigarettes.

Instructional Input: The teacher asks the children what the magazines are trying to do with their advertisement. This launches a discussion that unveils the fact that the advertisers are trying to get you to like their beautiful people who presumably smoke their cigarettes. The teacher then reveals other advertisements for soft drinks and other products that feature attractive people drinking beer or soft drinks, wearing certain kinds of clothes, and praising great movies.

Guided Practice: The teacher passes around some popular magazines with examples of these forms of propaganda and ask pairs of pupils to identify advertisements that demonstrate these appeals.

Independent Practice: Each pupil looks through a magazine to identify an advertisement that appears to us by virtue of the people who are pictured using the product.

Closing: The pupils generalize that advertisers are trying to make us buy their products by identifying them with "beautiful" people who are supposedly using the product and having fun.

SUMMARY

Direct teach lessons for PLORE (Predicting, Locating, Organizing, Remembering, and Evaluating) were presented in a lesson format consisting of a behavioral objective, an anticipatory set, an instructional input, a guided practice, an independent practice, and a closing. A diagnostic check was featured in some of the lessons to determine whether some of the students already possessed the skill to be taught.

Lessons presented in this chapter included:

Predicting Lessons

1. Predicting new words
2. Predicting other titles
3. Predicting convergent endings
4. Predicting divergent endings
5. Predicting unknown word meanings

Locating Lessons:

1. Locating specific information
2. Locating specific information holders
3. Locating in a table of contents
4. Locating information with references

Organizing Lessons

1. Finding Main Characters
2. Finding Main Characters and Settings
3. Finding Main Characters, Settings, and Problems
4. Finding Schema in a Simple Story
5. Finding Schema in a Multi Problem Story
6. Finding Schema on a Page by Page Basis
7. Recalling temporal events
8. Summarizing narratives

9. Identifying expository main ides
10. Outlining (data chart skill)

Remembering Lessons:
1. Setting purposes
2. Monitoring your remembering
3. Monitoring your understanding

Evaluating Lessons:
1. (Narrative) Judging desirability
2. (Narrative) Judging realism
3. (Expository) Finding internal contradictions
4. (Expository) Finding external disagreements
5. (Expository) Identifying propaganda devices

STUDY SUGGESTIONS

1. Read a story or short book to a pupil and ask her to predict such things as another title, another likely ending, or an unlikely ending. You may have to prompt the pupil a lot, as some children feel uncomfortable with predicting.
2. Ask a pupil to perform the locating tasks with a table of contents illustrated in this chapter. Determine which, if any, contents locating skills that they possess.
3. Choose one of the organizing lessons and attempt to teach it to a pupil for whom it seems appropriate. (You might want to teach the lesson that deals with discovering the setting, theme, and resolution of a story.)
4. Determine what is worth remembering in a given story and try to write up a set of a few such questions. Try your questions out on a pupil who has read the story to see if the pupil remembers those things.
5. Choose one of the evaluating lessons and try it on a pupil. Making judgments about reality is a very useful exercise for younger readers, although older readers might prosper from expository tasks such as identifying propaganda devices.

11

OPERATING A PERSONALIZED READING ENVIRONMENT

In the previous chapters, you have seen the development of a special environment for pupils with special reading needs that was built on the basic principle that:

> **Reading is caught, not taught, from books that fit, are read regularly and are shared.**

In this chapter, you will be reunited with Stan, Mary, Robbie, Tanya, Greg, and Sam as they work with nineteen other pupils in Mr. John's third-grade reading and writing program.

The organization for this view of the reading-writing program is as follows: The Classroom (a diagram of which is shown below), The Students, The Behavioral Management System, The Weekly Schedule, The Reading Schedule, The Writing Schedule, One Typical Day.

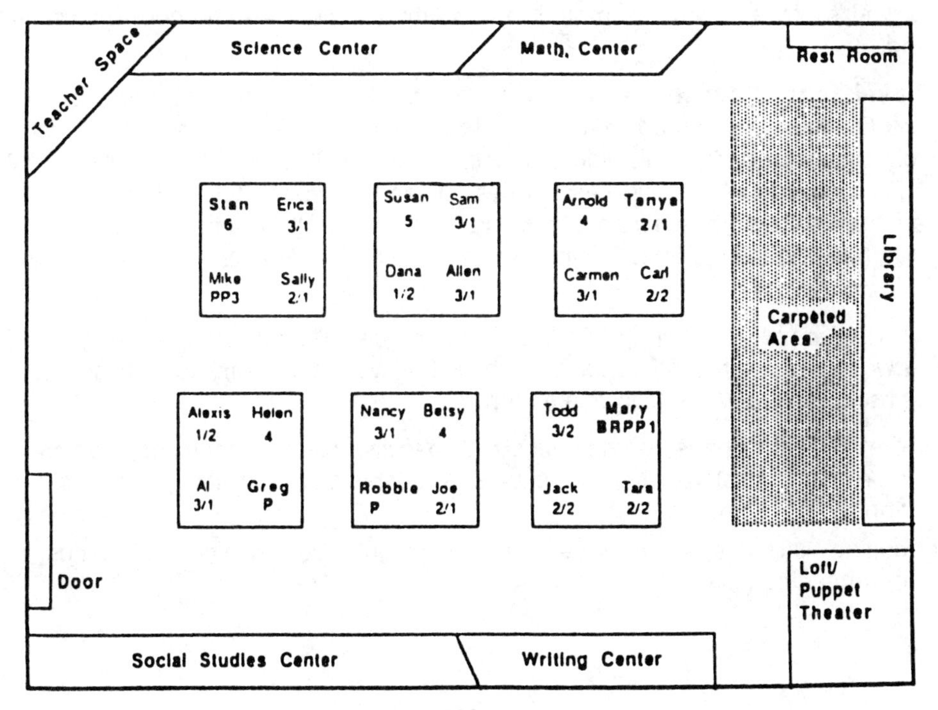

The Classroom

Some may feel that the location of pupils' desks is of minor consequence in terms of a reading program, but I believe that it is of paramount concern (see Chapter 6). You will note that this class presents the four-pupil-cluster seating arrangement, in which the pupils are strategically located so that the more skilled might be able to help the less skilled in academic and behavioral concerns. This design facilitates collaborative learning, as the more able pupils can assist the less able pupils in their reading and writing while gaining something for themselves in terms of their assistance skills.

The room presents an illusion of greater space because the space is not cluttered by the spaced desk patterns of the traditional classroom, in which rows of desks take up most of the valuable floor space. With greater space available, there is room for the many things that you can see in this classroom drawing.

If you look closely, you can see the names of the special students who are seated in the cluster arrangement. Nearby, you see the pupils who will be their immediate family in this classroom arrangement.

Special features of this classroom are a class library, a basal reader center, a class writing center, a mathematics center, a social studies center, a science center, and a loft with a puppet theater.

The **class library** contains mostly paperbacks of popular children's authors such as Beverly Cleary, Judy Blume, Roald Dahl, Steven Kellogg, Tomie de Paolo, Patricia Reilly Giff, Arnold Lobel, and others. The books began with some that Mr. John bought at garage sales for approximately 10 cents each. Pupils donated books from their own personal holdings until the library contained approximately 300 books. A checkout system was organized by a homeroom mother and a simple honor-system checkout was implemented.

The **basal reader center,** a part of the library, houses three different sets of basal readers. One set is the last adopted set, and contains a full range of books from first grade through third grade in the following amounts: 3 PP1, 3 PP2, 3 PP3, 4 P, 4 1/2, 4 2/1,4 2/2, 6 3/1, and 6 3/2. A second basal series contains approximately the same number of readers but also has 5 titles for each of the levels through fifth grade. A third set contains only 4th, 5th, and 6th readers. A generous supply of supplementary readers is also available.

The **writing center** shown in the illustration was established to support pupils in their writing workshop efforts. Students can do all the work necessary to publish their own stories here. It contains the following materials:

For drafting—draft paper of various sizes, pencils, rulers, paperclips, scotch tape, glue, staplers, staple removers, scissors, date and stamp pad, stationery, envelopes.

For editing—scissors, scotch tape, paste, white out, spelling lists, dictionaries, proofreading aids.

For publishing—flat publishing materials, book publishing materials, book cover materials, glue, tape, author pictures, work space, directions for book making, models of publications.

For sharing—The author's chair is placed near the library on a carpeted area.

In order to check the status of each pupil daily, this teacher has the steps of the writing workshop posted on the wall with a clothespin with each pupil's name on it. Daily or whenever it's necessary, the pupil moves his/her clothespin to the proper chart so that all can know precisely what task they are doing in the daily workshop. This teacher keeps a status check on a clipboard so that he can see how many days each pupil is involved in a given task.

DRAFT	PAIR SHARE	PEER EDIT	TEACHER EDIT	PUBLISH	ILLUSTRATE

A **math center** holds math menus, manipulative devices, place value charts, abaci, pattern cards, dominoes, a series of word problems, hand computers, and a variety of measurement units and instruments.

A **social studies center** provides an organized holding area for a large globe, small globes, maps (local, city, state, national, international), outline maps and colored pencils, reference encyclopedias, and a collection of *National Geographic* magazines.

A **science center** contains materials for experiments in weights, measures, and fulcrums, as well as the animal cages. Daily observations of the animals' behavior are made by various students.

Mr. John constructed the **loft with the puppet theater** so that the pupils could have a place for doing special things. The loft is a special place for pupils to do their independent reading and writing activities, drafting, plays, games, and a myriad of other activities. Working and playing in the loft is a special privilege.

The Students

Mr. John has a heterogeneously grouped, self-contained classroom. This means that he has pupils whose abilities vary over a wide range, and that the pupils essentially stay with him all day except for physical education and music. Because our interests are directed at the reading and writing curriculum, the following profile reveals what Mr. John has found out about the students' reading skills. For purposes of recalling which pupil is which, the students are ordered from highest to lowest in terms of their reading skills. Names of the special students who were first described in Chapter 1 are printed in bold for easy identification. Their presumed label is also shown.

Pupils' Instructional Levels in Reading

Through the highlighting in this list, it is apparent that there are readers like Mike who are not substantially different from the special needs students in terms of the problems they experience. Although the composition of this classroom appears to be very diverse, the range of reading levels found here is not unusual for a heterogeneous class of third graders.

Stan (gifted)	**6th**
Susan	5th
Arnold	4th
Helen	4th
Betsy	4th
Todd	3/2
Nancy	3/2
Carmen	3/1
Alan	3/1
Steve	3/1
Erica	3/1
Al	3/1
Sam	**3/1**
Connie	2/2
Jack	2/2
Carl	2/2
Tara	2/1
Sally	2/1
Tanya (ADD)	**2/1**
Dana	1/2
Alex	1/2
Greg (MR)	**Primer**
Mike	PP3
Robbie (DX)	**PP2**
Mary (LD)	**PP1 Buildup**

Behavioral Management

Mr. Johns has set up an assertive discipline system (Canter 1976, 1981). Posted clearly on one of his bulletin boards are the three rules:

> **Rule 1.** Pupils will respect their neighbors and their teachers.
>
> **Rule 2.** Pupils will do what their teachers tell them to do.
>
> **Rule 3.** Pupils will be kind to one another.

The first week of class, Mr. John explained these rules to his class so that the pupils might know how they would pertain to every interaction. Below the list of rules, each pupil's name was assigned to a cutout figure that could be moved to the right or left in terms of the following outcomes:

Lunch Club	Free Time	Praise	**Pupils**	Warning	Time Out	Note home
			Al			
			Alan			
			Arnold			
			Betsy			

Beyond the individual system, a table system was in effect whereby each table earned marbles toward a table group reward.

The Weekly Schedule

The weekly schedule reflects what presumably happens at every hour within the week. Such schedules are invariably altered by fire drills, special assemblies, special programs (drug awareness, sex education, bus safety, etc.), picture taking, special PTA programs, presentations by different school staff, and a host of other things.

Mr. John's principal has placed a priority on reading and writing and attempts to avoid interruptions in the first two hours of the morning when reading and writing are taking place.

On the written schedule, Mr. John's class had 10 hours of reading and writing weekly:

HOUR	MONDAY	TUESDAY	WEDNESDAY	THURSDAY	FRIDAY
8 - 9	READING	READING	READING	READING	READING
9-10	WRITING	WRITING	WRITING	WRITING	WRITING
10-11	P.E/MUSIC	from 10:05 - 10:40——ART/HEALTH from 10:40 - 11:00——			
11 -12	MATH	MATH	MATH	MATH	MATH
12- 1	LUNCH	LUNCH	LUNCH	LUNCH	LUNCH
	——STORY TIME EACH DAY OF THE WEEK AFTER LUNCH——				
1 - 2	——SOCIAL STUDIES——				LIBRARY
2 - 3	COMPUTERS	SCIENCE	SCIENCE	SCIENCE	SCIENCE

The Reading Schedule

The reading schedule was the first thing in the morning daily from 8:00 to 9:00 after the initial matters of starting the school day were taken care of between 7:45 and 8:00.

TIME	SCHEDULED DAILY ACTIVITY
8:00-8:20	**Independent Reading (every day)**
8:20-8:40	**Instructional Reading (Monday-Thursday; on Friday, Content Reading occurs at this time)**
8:40-9:00	**Written Comprehension (Monday-Thursday; on Friday, Content Reading continues at this time)**
12:25-12:45	**Story Time: Mr. John reads to the students every day (right after lunch).**

Independent reading is a certainty every day, because the pupils have acquired the reading habit and want to read. Also, Mr. John wants them to read because he recognizes that many of them need to read in order to cultivate their ability and their interest in reading.

Instructional reading occurs for 20 minutes daily except for Friday. On Fridays, pupils would be involved in some form of content reading from teacher-made centers, encyclopedias, data charts, and so forth.

Oral and written comprehension in the form of PLORE questions and answers occurs Monday through Thursday for approximately twenty minutes each day. Fridays again find the pupils involved in their content reading work.

Story time after lunch is always one of the highlights of the day. Currently, the teacher is reading *The Black Stallion* (Farley, 1941).

The Writing Schedule

As can be seen in the weekly schedule and the writing schedule, pupils write five days a week in the writing workshop (Calkins, 1986) format.

TIME	SCHEDULED DAILY ACTIVITY
9:00-9:50	**Depending upon the stage of his or her writing project, each pupil spends this time Drafting, Revising, Editing or Publishing.**
9:50-10:00	**SHARING occurs for the last 10 minutes of the Writing Hour each day. Mr. John chooses different pupils, depending upon the state of their projects, to share each day.**

One Typical Day

What follows is a description of a typical day in this classroom. As you read it, you should be able to visualize what the teacher and children do as they go through each of the scheduled reading and writing activities. Many of the normal happenings of a given day in an individualized program are related here.

8:00—Twenty Minutes of Independent Reading

If you were to walk into Mr. John's classroom a few minutes before 8:00, you would see that many students would have already begun their independent reading session. Realizing that independent reading is the first thing of the day, nearly half of the class begins their independent reading without any directions from Mr. John. When he sets the timer for the 20 minutes of reading, those who haven't already started reading, do so.

A few students, including **Greg,** are a little slower than others in organizing their materials, and so they actually begin to read about three minutes later. Still, all are reading by 8:03 without any spoken instructions from the teacher. This happens because, early in the school year, Mr. John used table rewards to reinforce his expectation that reading should start at 8:00 A.M. Toward that end, the slower starters were taught to take out their independent reader and have it on their desk as soon as they arrived in the classroom.

At the beginning of the period, Mr. John sits on a stool at one side of the class, modeling reading for the class by reading from his novel. He appears to be truly reading and does not move about. His behavior causes the pupils to sense that he is reading and that this is a time for reading.

Because most of the readers can read silently more quickly than orally, Mr. John has given permission to half of his class to read silently. The others have been instructed to read in a low voice so that they won't disturb the silent readers. On this day, classical music is playing at a modest volume. As a result, the classroom environment is dominated by the sound of the music, rather than by the individual voices of pupils reading aloud.

A wide range of reading materials is in evidence, with the following things noted:

* The higher readers (see names at the start of the chapter) are reading short paper back novels.
* The middle readers are reading primarily from a variety of basal or supplemental readers.
* The nine lower readers are reading exclusively from basals or buildup readers.

Mary, the lowest reader, is reading the first preprimer buildup on pages 1, 2, 3, 4 to improve her fluency with the new words *get,do,* and *bear.* The text on page 4 begins as follows:

4. Bear, bear

Bear will help you.

Will you help Bear?

I will help Bear.

I will help Bear get it.

Can Bear do it?

Bear can do it.

Can you do it?

I can do it.

She can pronounce all the words, but pauses noticeably on the word *help.* At this moment, she seems to be managing her own agenda independently.

Glancing in the direction of our targeted student **Robbie,** we see that he is rereading the primer for fluency. His rate appears to be in the high 80s and he is not having any apparent difficulty with any word.

Greg appears to be comfortable in his primer-level placement, and reads in a slightly louder voice than those around him. His rate seems to be at a comfort zone.

Tanya fidgets slightly from time to time but seems interested in her book. She reads aloud for purposes of concentration. That is, she is reading aloud because her teacher feels that the oral reading focuses her attention more on process comprehending. She is obviously working to add prosody (fluency) to her reading by giving different voices to the different characters in her story.

Stan, the high reader, is reading *A Wrinkle in Time* (L'Engle, 1963) and appears to be mesmerized by the book.

Sam, the reader with the adjusted visual problem continues to move along well in third grade material.

With everyone on task at 8:10, Mr. John leaves his high stool and takes his clipboard to begin to make his rounds of the students that he wants to check this particular day. A glance at his clipboard reveals the following information about today's stops:

Comprehension	
Susan	+
Helen	+
Todd	+
Carmen	+

Rate

Mary	**(BR)2**	**16/80**
Robbie	**P**	**50/85+**
Tanya	**2/1**	**106/96**
Greg	**P**	**62/80+**
Sam	**3/1**	**80/90**

Mr. John's first stops are inaudible, but he later explains that he is making his once-a-week **process** comprehension check of some of his better readers (Susan, Helen, Todd, and Carmen). He spends about a minute with each student, listening as he or she tells back the main happenings in the story. Mr. John spends the last five minutes on rate checks of his slower readers (Alex, **Greg**, **Robbie**, **Mary**). On his clipboard, he notes any words that are giving them trouble and jots down their page and rate figures (shown above as page/rate; e.g., Mary's 16/80 means page 16 and 80 words per minute). It's apparent that he checks these five students every day.

When Mike, another pupil, has finished his PP3, so Mr. John finds him another book that he thinks will be suitable for him. After Mike reads the first two pages aloud, Mr. John adds the new book on his clipboard checksheet. Changing books is one of the things that happens often for the lower readers with controlled vocabulary.

As the end of independent reading draws closer, some of the slower readers begin to eye the clock. When the timer sounds, no directions are given but the children quietly take their work record and record the last page that they read in their independent level book. Those caught in mid-page are allowed to finish the page and mark their copy when they are through. All of this appears to be understood. In actuality, this state of response has been reached by previous rehearsal and by Mr. John's reinforcement of the desired behaviors.

Prior to starting the time for instructional reading, Mr. John calls upon a few students to share something funny from their story this day. In this fashion, he has a few different pupils sharing something from their reading each day. The students share funny things, unusual characters, strange happenings, dull stories, and so forth.

Pupils value the brief opportunity to share something from their books and to learn about the stories that others are reading.

8:20—Twenty Minutes of Instructional Reading

Instructional reading is signaled by the shifting from one book to another by the students as they finish recording their independent level reading. It seems that everyone knows what to do except for three pupils who have their hands raised for the teacher's attention.

It turns out that each of these three pupils feels that she has finished her book, and wishes for Mr. John to help her to get a new book. He does so, moving quickly to use his knowledge of what each pupil can read as judged by what that pupil has just finished reading. These decisions generally take less than a minute.

Because nearly every pupil is reading on his own, Mr. John is able to turn his attention to the individual needs of getting new books. He will not give his attention to helping with new words at this point because he fears that would communicate a dependence message to readers who are encountering some tough words. He wants them to try to read the story through on their own before they ask for help; this desire is made evident by his application of the self-instruction rules from Chapter 6:

1. I can do most of the reading on my own.
2. I can work out unknown words and meanings.
3. If I can't get the word quickly and it seems unimportant, I can skip it.

Peer help is encouraged in the first two or three minutes when the pupils are just starting their reading. A quick look around the clusters reveals some of the pupils asking about words in their story. After this, the pupils are trying to do their reading on their own. Pupils reading the same books are encouraged to sit together to help one another as needed.

Mr. John spends the first five minutes observing to determine which pupils are asking for words from their peers. He's also trying to see if the lower readers are able to move through their story on their own with a minimum of assistance.

The distribution of oral and silent readers is about the same as in the independent reading time (about half and half). Again, Mr. John plays classical music in the background so as to mask the voices of individual readers as well as his later contacts with individual pupils.

Stan, the gifted reader, is absorbed in a *Junior Great Books* (Trevise, 1984) novel on this day. He seems oblivious to the presence of anyone else in the class. He is now able to read more books of his liking. He will chat once or twice a week with Mr. John and Susan, who is reading the same novel.

After the five minute observation period, Mr. John takes his clipboard and starts his rounds. Because it's instructional or challenge reading, his rounds begin with the lower-level readers to see if they are able to meet the challenges of reading new vocabulary. Thus, Mr. John's agenda is from the lowest to the highest.

Pupils	**Books**	**Page/Rate**
Mary	BR2	19/44
Robbie	P	60/70
Mike	P	8/65
Tanya	2/2	56/84
Greg	P	71/74

Once again, Mr. John's contacts are brief. As he observes the individual performances, he is applying the one-to-one techniques described in Chapter 7.

Mary is asked to reread each page twice as she moves through her first preprimer buildup. Mr. John times her on the first and second readings of her new page (page 19 with the new word *did.* He records the information as follows:

Mary	**PP1(BR2)**	**19/34**	**1**
		19/44	**2**

Mr. John feels that Mary needs a **tape assist** program in order that she might have a better model of the reading than he can give her in the course of the day. He decides to take his portable tape recorder home that evening and tape the next 10 pages for her so that she may listen and track as he reads at about 80 words per minute. She will then be taught to turn off the tape recorder and practice reading the page on her own. Mr. John will check her rate at the end of the period.

Robbie is on the fifth story in his primer. Mr. John times him and finds that his rate is in the range of 70 words per minute with good comprehension. He informs Robbie that he will move through this book quickly if he keeps up this pace. When Robbie demonstrates continued difficulty with "help" and "here" , Mr. John writes the following two sentences out on a card for Robbie to study and use as a prompt for this page and others.

I can help you.

Come here.

Mike finished his PP3 during the independent reading instruction time and Mr. John gave him another preprimer for practice at an easy level. Now, Mr. John wants to see how Mike can fare with the primer that follows the preprimer he just finished. He listens as Mike reads the first page with some difficulty (a rate of 50 words per minute and difficulty with the word *tomorrow.* Mr. John tells Mike the word and has him practice the page until he gets it down. On his third reading, Mike surpasses 60 words per minute and is allowed to continue on his own, trying to figure out new words on his own. Impressed with the fact that he has a hardback book, Mike works diligently.

Greg continues to read in the same primer that he was reading for his independent level. When he has trouble understanding the dialogue story about *The Five Silly Bears.* Knowing the story and the subtlety of the humor, Mr. John avoids an explanation and tells Greg that it's about some silly bears that didn't count each other. Some stories have meanings that are not completely accessible to Greg, and may simply have to be dealt with in this fashion.

Tanya appears to have little difficulty in her rate and word recognition. Mr. John decides to take a **process check** by asking her to tell him what has happened so far in her story. She briefly tells some of the details from the story. Mr. John plans to return to her during the written PLORE over the story to see what else she knows.

For the balance of the instructional reading period, Mr. John will troubleshoot the problems that are identified by raised flags. As he moves to respond to each question, Mr. John is helping with word pronunciations, word meanings, and clarifications of story meanings.

Because **Stan** never asks for words or clarifications, Mr. John decides to do a brief **process** check on him via a brief tellback of his story. Stan explains that it's pretty complicated but it has to do with these boys finding a bombed out city from a great nuclear war. Mr. John's passing familiarity with the story allows him to have a brief interaction with Stan about it.

With the end of the 20 minutes of instructional reading rapidly approaching, Mr. John looks over his notes from the previous day to see if he has some folks that he needs to visit for any reason. To his surprise, he finds that he has managed to see all of the pupils that he wanted to reach except **Sam**. He makes a quick check and finds that he's doing well.

During instructional reading, some of the pupils finish the story that they started yesterday or the day before while others finish a whole story in this day. There is a rule that if you finish a story before the time is up, you must reread it or reread parts of it. This rule was established so that the pupils wouldn't start their written work before others, close their books and set off a chain reaction of book closers, or do anything different that would cause the others to unduly press their reading. Thus, everyone remains reading up until the timer sounds the stop. Even then, some may continue so as to finish their page or story as necessary.

As the timer sounds the end of instructional reading, most of the pupils quietly close their books and take out their question folders and spirals to start their written comprehension work. Those readers who are near a stopping point continue until that stopping point.

8:40—Twenty Minutes of Written Comprehension (PLORE)

Mr. John has taught his pupils to do the range of questions involved in the PLORE spectrum. On this day, each student will be demonstrating **product** comprehension by working on a question from each of the following three question types:

PR (PREDICTING)
LO (LOCATING)
OR (ORGANIZING)

On some days they will do RE and EV questions. On other days, the pupils may be asked to do one of each question type for a story. Some stories lend themselves particularly well to certain types of PLORE questions and such opportunities should be used; for example, a sequence question is well-suited to a story that has a well-defined sequence.

Basically, Mr. John wants the questions to be answered well. This translates to the following expectations that the students have come to understand by reading the explanatory wall charts.

Comprehension Requirements

1. The answer must use the question stem to form a freestanding question. (This means that anyone who reads the answer must be able to infer the question from it.)
2. The answer must be complete. (That is, if the answer is explicitly given in the text, the student's answer must be accurate, and, if the student must infer the answer from the text, that answer must be plausible.)

Writing Requirements

1. First words in sentences are always capitalized.
2. Periods or exclamation marks are always put at the ends of answers.
3. Words in the question must be spelled correctly in the answer.
4. Unknown spelling words should be circled, to show that you know that you're unsure of the spelling.
5. Answers must be readable by most humans.

Mr. John attaches point penalties for transgressions of each of the above requirements so that each of his pupils knows precisely what will happen if an answer falls short of Mr. John's expectations.

The pupils are to do their LO answer first because it requires them to use their books. Consequently, the students are starting these answers and are busy locating specific sentences or paragraphs in text for the most part. Some, however, are locating with book parts like the table of contents or glossary. A few are locating things with the aid of reference books.

One of the first things evident to the observer of this class is the rapidity with which some pupils work as well as the slowness shown by others. All of the pupils have headed their paper prior to this time (during the time before school) so that their attention can be concentrated on answering questions. Still, some of the pupils are working on their third answers before some of the others have written the first word of their first answer.

To combat the normal happening of slow responses by some pupils, Mr. John has instituted a plan whereby he gives five minute notices like the following:

> Five minutes have passed and you should have your first answer completed. Hold up your hand if you have your first answer completed.

While he doesn't get every hand up, Mr. John has found that such time monitoring has helped to assist many pupils with their time management. He helps them further by directing his attention to their initial efforts in such a way that they speed up their operations.

To avoid a gigantic buildup of written questions to grade, Mr. John attempts to check off as many as he can as he moves about his classroom. He seems to realize that the optimum time for checking is when there is time to do something about it on the spot. Such a situation occurs when he looks at **Tanya's** answer to her first PR question. The question and her answer are as follows:

PR Question: Write another good title for the story, *The Great Hamster Hunt.*

Tanya's answer: "Harvey."

Mr. John reads the answer *Harvey* aloud and says, "I don't get it."

"That's another good title," says Tanya.

"I have two problems with it," says Mr. John. "The first one is that it violates our comprehension rules 1 and 2, and the next one is that 'Harvey' is just a name. How can you fix these things?"

Tanya, looking at the chart on the wall, says, "Well, I guess I could say that another good title for the story would be *Harvey.*"

"Now you're cooking," replies Mr. John. "Can you add some more that tells me about Harvey?"

"He's a hamster," notes Tanya.

"Yes, yes, put that in your answer," says a departing Mr. John.

Because Mr. John has his superstars pretty well identified, he generally does not check their answers during class time. He can check them individually during his work period and enjoy looking at the nice work.

Another feature of Mr. John's PLORE time is the presence of pairs of pupils who do their PLORE together. Discussed previously as "shared PLORE" the two pupils discuss the questions and form common answers to the questions. Four pairs are working in Mr. John's classroom this day. Each pair will submit a set of answers with each participant's name on it. On some days, Mr. John will have the pair tell their answers orally rather than writing them. These days are particularly appealing to the pupils. Such sessions are also appealing to Mr. John because they allow him to see much deeper answers. Some of the greatest depth is revealed by listening to the pupils discuss their probable answers and the reasons for such answers.

Mr. John has noticed a need for a **direct teach** on predicting convergent endings so he has planned a session following the lesson plan from Chapter 8. Identified for the lesson are five pupils who have been having the greatest difficulty with coming up with something that wasn't stated precisely in their story. The five pupils—Alan, Carmen, Jack, Joe, and **Tanya**—gather around their teacher on the carpet for the direct teach lesson.

DT Plan - Predicting Convergent Endings

Behavioral Objective: When asked to predict a likely (convergent) ending, the pupil will use the information presented and background experiences to project a reasonable ending.

Anticipatory Set: On a chart or transparency, the teacher will present a story without an end and ask the pupils to speculate about the known information and a likely ending.

> John and his father were fishing in the middle of the lake from their sailboat. Suddenly, they felt the wind blowing hard. The water became very rough and the boat swayed left and right. One tall wave picked up the boat and flipped it over.

Instructional Input: At this point the teacher tries to come up with a sentence or two that might explain what happened next. The teacher refers back to personal experiences with boats and asks the students to do the same. The teacher begins to write the ending, modeling the thinking. The teacher explains that he learned that you should always stay with the boat because it will probably float.

Guided Practice: Another example is provided of a boy who falls off a horse. The group will discuss and decide what the likely ending would be for the boy.

Independent Practice: The students are asked to infer a likely ending for this paragraph:

> The boys had worked in the hot summer sun all day. When it was time to go, they decided where they wanted to go.

Conclusion: The teacher notes that we can take what has happened and use our experience to predict what will likely happen.

For his actual lesson, Mr. John uses the plan just illustrated in the following manner.

Behavioral Objective: At this point, Mr. John states that the lesson will be about predicting likely outcomes and that they will be able to predict a likely ending by using the information in the story and their own experiences.

Anticipatory Set: Mr. John gathers the group on the carpet and reads the story about the boat turning over and asks them to think about what will likely happen next.

Instructional Input: Mr. John rereads the story about the boat turning over and carefully models how he learned what to do when a boat turned over when he was a young boy. He tells about learning to stay with the boat because it will probably float and keep you afloat.

Guided Practice: Now, Mr. John reads a brief story about the boy who wants to be a cowboy and falls off the horse the first time he tries to get on. Mr. John then asks the group to discuss what might likely happen next in the story. The pupils present likely happenings from their backgrounds and the teacher writes them down. The pupils select the most likely possibilities.

Independent Practice: For independent practice, the teacher poses the situation of the boys who have worked in the hot sun all day. The pupils are to generate likely endings as to what the boys might want to do at the end of the day. The predictions are compared and discussed.

Conclusion: Mr. John explains that our experiences can help us to predict likely happenings.

As the direct teach ends, Mr. John notices that the time is nearing 9:00 and the end of the oral and written comprehension lessons. This means that the children who have completed their questions for today will put their spirals on his desk for checking. Those who have not finished their questions must present a piece of paper with the following information:

Name: ____________________
Book: ____________________
Story: ____________________
Last Question finished: _______

This information allows him to know where each pupil is working.

9:00—One Hour of Writing Workshop

Writing workshop includes all aspects of writing (composition, grammar, usage, spelling, handwriting). Each pupil has two folders containing work. One folder is a **storage** folder, where previous drafts are stored, while the other folder is a **working** folder, and contains the pupil's latest three or four drafts.

The following rules for the writing workshop are based on those in Atwell's (1987) book, *In the Middle: Writing, Reading, & Learning with Adolescents:*

1. Do not erase. Save your record of thinking.
2. Write on one side of the paper only.
3. Save everything.
4. Date and label everything.
5. Speak in quiet voices only.
6. Work really hard.

As the pupils store their reading materials and get out their **working** folders, the teacher briefly goes over what each pupil will be doing on this particular day (Atwell, 1987; Calkins, 1986). Essentially, the divisions of labor at the start of this day will include edit teams, drafting, and publishing.

Beginning with edit teams, the teacher lists the following edit teams as well as their immediate tasks for this day:

Edit Teams and Tasks

Arnold, Erica, Jack	Editing Erica's draft for sentences.
Helen, Al, Joe	Editing Helen's story for accuracy.
Dana, Sally, Carl	Editing Carl's story for ideas.
Stan, Susan	Editing Susan's story for sentences, punctuation, and spelling.

Drafters and Topics

Betsy	Her pet fish
Todd	His weekend
Alan	His dog
Mary	Her new sister
Alex	His latest bike wreck
Tara	Going to church
Connie	Her mother's surprise party
Sam	Fishing
Nancy	Camping

Publishing

Carmen	*Dance school*
Steve	*Hunting for deer*
Tanya	*Uncle Leo*
Greg	*Boots, the Dog*
Mike	*Football*
Robbie	*His cat*

Mr. John has an alphabetized log of the pupils in order that he can quickly see what they are doing each day as well as what they have done on the previous days. This log helps him to see whether a pupil needs special assistance in the form of his time or a support group. This log looks more like a journal because it has jottings about what each student is doing. Only Mr. John would understand his notes.

The fact that a student is assigned to one of the three tasks only suggests that this is the activity that they will be doing at the beginning of the period. It is understood that edit groups will finish their tasks and that the member who was having his draft edited might continue on to the development of a final copy. The other members of the group would turn back to their individual works (drafting, editing, or publishing). Similarly, the pupils occupied in drafting and publishing might change their activities depending upon the completion of their tasks at hand.

Mr. John likes to establish himself as the final editor before the pupils prepare their final copy of something they have chosen to publish. Therefore, the pupils who wish to publish need to sign up for a conference with Mr. John before they publish their final draft.

To cut down on pupils wanting to publish everything they have written, Mr. John requires that his third graders must have a minimum of four drafts in their folder from which to select a single one for further work and publication. This rule can be modified for the pupils who have major difficulties in writing but it serves as a means of getting pupils to reflect upon their writing before publishing.

After the pupils have worked for approximately fifteen minutes on their initial tasks, Mr. John requires that all the pupils work silently for fifteen minutes on their own. This allows for Mr. John to model writing for the drafters and revisers who need to see a model and also need to be spared any extraneous stimuli.

When the fifteen minutes is over, students may share, edit, draft, publish, or confer with him for the next fifteen to twenty minutes. From Mr. John's perspective, this time goes very rapidly as he attempts to see a lot of different students.

The final ten to fifteen minutes is usually saved for the "author's chair", a time in which one or two pupils a day are called upon to share a draft or a published work with the class. The teacher uses the author's chair as an opportunity for pupils to learn to share each other's work and benefit from a non-ending series of lessons that they can learn about writing. The author's chair is a special privilege and the pupils look forward to the opportunity to sit and read their work.

Although Mr. John has many reasons for having his pupils share their work and experience, he's particularly interested in having the pupils learn from different types of writing and in teaching the pupils how to view writing from a supportive, but analytical, view.

On this day, Mr. John has asked Tanya to share the story she is publishing about her Uncle Leo.

In preparation for the "author's chair", the children have gathered on the floor in front of the special chair. Because she is aware that she'll be sharing, Tanya is already seated in the chair. She waits until everyone is paying attention. Each author has learned not to share a story until everyone is attending. She begins reading her story aloud:

Tanya: (Showing the cover) My book is called *Uncle Leo.*

(Reads from the first page.)

I have an uncle.
His name is Uncle Leo.
He is a funny guy.

(Reads from the second page.)

We go to Dallas to see him.
He lives with Grandma and
Grandpa.

(Reads from the third page.)

His room is really weird.
He has stuff everywhere.
He has old newspapers.

(She reads from page 4.)

Uncle Leo won't clean up his room.
Grandma tells him to clean it.
But he won't clean it.
He's nice but he's still weird.

After Tanya finished her story, Mr. John asks pupils to recall what happened in the story. Several pupils relate the details of the story in the sequence that they were heard. At this point, Mr. John asks the pupils to tell what they liked about the story. This sets off a lively discussion on how weird Uncle Leo is and how they have a weird friend, neighbor, or relative who sounds something like Uncle Leo.

The fact that her story is apparently valued is important to Tanya, who appears to beam. As the expert on Uncle Leo, she is asked for more information about some of his other strange habits. These things may furnish her with ideas for further developments. The same things will also furnish others with ideas for writing about strange characters in their own lives.

Mr. John decides that he will take the idea of Uncle Leo and lead off tomorrow's writing workshop with a direct teach about details that make a character interesting. He will illustrate with a story of his own about a funny uncle he had. He will show how unusual things make a person seem very different.

Tanya will add her book to the growing collection of pupils' books. Other authors will read her book and get ideas for their own books.

SUMMARY

This chapter reveals the operation of a personalized reading environment where all students are special. The program operates on the basic principle that pupils catch reading from books that fit and are read regularly and shared.

Initially, the students are grouped in such a fashion that they might assist one another to complete their various reading and writing tasks in the classroom. Copying is not a primary concern because pupils who read their own books and write their own stories seldom have a need to copy from someone else. Rather, they have needs for help from those who can provide it. The best help comes from good neighbors.

One typical Tuesday reveals two hours of language arts. The first reading hour is devoted to equal amounts of independent reading, instructional reading, and written comprehension. The second hour is devoted to drafting, editing, publishing, and sharing in the writing workshop where pupils choose their own topics. Their favorite pieces are shared, edited, and published for others to read and appreciate.

While Mr. John's teaching is mostly involved with individuals, he does devote some of his time to teaching specific reading and writing skills to those pupils who need them. At times, Mr. John will gather small groups of pupils for these direct teach sessions in comprehension and writing. He also manages to read a selection from a quality children's book to the whole class every day of the week during the lunch hour.

Our five special students are thriving in a classroom where each of them functions at an appropriate independent level and an appropriate challenge level. Stan, the gifted reader, functions well in his self-selected library books, which tend to be on a rather high level, and in the *Junior Great Books.* At the same time, his classmates continue to develop their reading and writing skills with material suited to their level

STUDY SUGGESTIONS

1. To practice the elements described in this chapter, you need your own classroom. If you do not, as yet, have your own classroom, it would be useful to plan for the day that you do have one by doing the following:
   a) creating a proposed floor plan indicating desk arrangements, book locations, materials centers, etc.;
   b) developing a list of the reading materials that you would want to have available for the grade level that you want to teach;
   c) writing a behavioral management plan;
   d) creating a detailed schedule of your reading and writing activities;
   e) designing forms that could help you and the pupils chart daily reading performance.

2. In the event you have access to a classroom as a student observer or student teacher, you may wish to request that the teacher allow you to implement the things you have learned with a small group of children. The group of children could be one of the reading groups. You could ask if you would be able to provide for self-selection and the subsequent placement in independent and instructional level reading, PLORE , and Writing Workshop. Lacking access to a classroom, these activities might be conducted with neighborhood children or with children in a day care center.

3. If you have your own classroom, you might start with self-selection of independent reading books and continue this for a week or two. This will allow you to be comfortable with each child's placement. Once you feel that things are operating smoothly and that every pupil is staying on task through the whole fifteen or twenty minutes, you may elect to start instructional level reading followed by generic questions such as:

   Monday: Tell the *who, what, why, when,* and *where* of your story.

   Tuesday: Briefly summarize your story (less than a page)

   Wednesday: Describe the setting, main characters, problem, and problem resolution of your story.

   Thursday: Make an illustrated drawing of your story.

Bibliography

Aaron, E.B. (1990). Inmates captured by literature. *Journal of Reading, 33,* 433-435.

Adams, E. (1991). Texas Reading Report, Volume XII, No. 4 (May 1990).

Adams, E. (1990). *The relationship between reading skills as measured by a basal reader placement test and reading skills as measured by a basal reading subskills test.* Doctoral dissertation, The University of Texas at Austin.

Adams, M.J. (1990). *Beginning to read: Thinking and learning about print.* Boston: MIT Press.

Allen, R., & Allen, C. (1966). *Language experiences in reading: Teacher's source book.* Chicago: Encyclopedia Press.

Allington, R. (1977). If they don't read much, how they gonna get good? *Journal of Reading, 21,* 57-61.

Allington, R. (1980). Poor readers don't get to read much in reading groups. *Language Arts, 57,* 872-865.

Allington, R., (1983) The reading instruction provided readers of differing reading abilities. *Elementary School Journal 83*: 548-559.

Altwerger, B., Edelsky, C., & Flores, B. (1987). Whole language: What's new? *The Reading Teacher, 41,* 144-153.

Anderson, R.C., Hiebert, E.H., Scott, J.A., & Wilkinson, I.A. (1985). *Becoming a nation of readers.* Urbana-Champaign: University of Illinois, Center for the Study of Reading.

Anderson, R.C., Wilson, R.T., & Fielding, L.G. (1988). Growth in reading and how children spend their time outside of school. *Reading Research Quarterly, 23,* 285-303.

Armbruster, B.B., Anderson, T.H., & Ostertag, J. (1989). Teaching text structure to improve reading and writing. *The Reading Teacher, 43,* 130-137.

Ashton-Warner, S. (1963). *Teacher.* New York: Simon & Schuster.

Atwell, N. (1987). *In the middle: Writing, reading, and learning with adolescents.* Portsmouth, NH: Boynton/Cook/Heinemann.

Au, K., & Mason, J. (1990). *Reading instruction for today's children.* Glenview, IL: Scott, Foresman.

Austin, M., & Morrison, C. (1967). *The first R: The Harvard report on reading in the elementary school.* New York: Macmillan.

Badderly, A.D., & Lewis, V. (1981). Inner active processes in reading: The inner voice, the inner ear, and the inner eye. In A.M. Lesgold & C.A. Perfetti (Eds.), *Interactive processes in reading* (pp. 107-129). Hillsdale, NJ: Erlbaum.

Bales, J. (1985, January). Attention disorders need better measures and theory. *American Psychological Association,* p.13.

Barr, R., & Johnson, B. (1991). *Teaching reading in elementary classrooms.* New York & London: Longman.

Beck, I.L. (1981). Reading problems and instructional practices. In G.E. MacKinnon, & T.G. Waller (Eds.), *Reading research: Advances in theory and practice* (Vol. 2). New York: Academic Press.

Becker, W.C., & Gersten, R. (1982). A followup of follow-through: The later effects of the direct instruction model on children in fifth and sixth grades. *American Educational Research Association Journal, 19,* 75-92.

Becker, W.C. (1977). Teaching reading and language to the disadvantaged: What we have learned from field research. *Harvard Educational Review, 4,* 508-541.

Beldin, H.L. (1970). Informal reading testing: Historical review and review of the research. In W.D. Durr (Ed.), *Reading difficulties: Diagnosis, correction, and remediation.* Newark, DE: International Reading Association.

Bereiter, C., Hughes, K., & Anderson, V. (1972).*Catching on. Book 2.* Reading Comprehension Series. LaSalle, IL: Open Court.

Berliner, D.C. (1981). Academic learning time and reading achievement. In J.T. Guthrie (Ed.), *Comprehension and teaching: research review.* Newark, DE: International Reading Association.

Betts, E.A. (1946). *Foundations of reading instruction.* New York: American Book.

Blachman, B.A. (1984). Relationship of rapid naming ability and language analysis skills to kindergarten and first grade reading achievement. *Journal of Educational Psychology, 76,* 610-622.

Blair, E. (1980). *A descriptive study of patterns of beginning readers' rate, miscue frequency, and miscue patterns.* Unpublished master's thesis, The University of Texas at Austin.

Bradley, L., & Bryant, P.E. (1983). Categorizing sounds and learning to read—A causal connection. *Nature, 301,* 419-421.

Brecht, R.D. (1977). Testing format and instructional level with the informal reading inventory. *The Reading Teacher, 31,* 57-59.

Brookover, V., Schweitzer, J., Beady, C., Flood, P., & Weisenbarker, J. (1978). Elementary school social climate and school achievement. *American Educational Research Association Journal, 15,* 301-18.

Brophy, G. (1982). Successful teaching strategies for the innercity child. *Phi Delta Kappan, 13,* 522-530.

Brophy, J., & Good, T. (1990). *Looking in classrooms* (3rd ed.). New York: Harper Collins.

Brown, M., Cromer, P., & Weinberg, S. (1986). Shared book experiences in kindergarten: Helping children come to literacy. *Early Childhood Research Quarterly, 1,* 397-406.

Burmeister, L. (1983). *Foundations and strategies for teaching children to read.* Reading, MA: Addison-Wesley.

Burns, M. (1981). Groups of four: Solving the management problem. *Learning, 10,* 46-51.

Calkins, L.M. (1986). *The art of teaching writing.* Portsmouth, NH: Heineman.

Calfee, R., & Drum, P. (1986). Research on teaching reading. In M.C. Wittrock (Ed.), *Handbook of research on teaching* (pp. 804-849). New York: Macmillan.

Canter, L. (1976). *Assertive discipline: A take-charge approach for today's educator.* Santa Monica, CA: Canter & Associates.

Canter, L. (1981). *Assertive discipline follow-up guidebook.* Santa Monica, CA: Canter & Associates.

Carbo, M. (1987). Reading styles research: What works isn't always phonics. *Phi Delta Kappan, 68,* 431-435.

Carbo, M. (1978). Teaching reading with talking books. *The Reading Teacher, 32,* 267-273.

Carver, R. (1983). Is reading rate constant or flexible? *Reading Research Quarterly, 17,* 190-215.

Carver, R., & Hoffman, J. (1981). The effect of practice through repeated reading on gain in reading ability using a computer-based instructional system. *Reading Research Quarterly, 16,* 374-390.

Cazden, C.B. (1965). *Environmental assistance to the child's acquisition of grammar.* Doctoral dissertation, Harvard University, Cambridge, MA.

Chall, J. (1985). *Learning to read: The great debate.* New York: McGraw-Hill.

Chall, J. (1983). *Stages of reading development.* New York: McGraw-Hill.

Chomsky, C. (1976). After decoding: What? *Language Arts, 53,* 288-296.

Chomsky, C. (February, 1972). Stages in language development and reading exposure, *Harvard Educational Review, 42,* 1-33.

Chomsky, C. (1978). When you still can't read in third grade: After decoding, what? In J. Samuels (Ed.), *What research has to say about reading instruction* (pp. 13-30). Newark, DE: International Reading Association.

Clark, M., & Gosnell, M. (1982, March 22). Dealing with dyslexia. *Newsweek,* p. 79.

Clay, M. (1976a). Early childhood and cultural diversity in New Zealand. *The Reading Teacher, 29,* 333-341.

Clay, M. (1976b). *Young fluent readers.* London: Heinemann.

Clay, M. (1979). *What did I write?* Auckland, New Zealand: Heinemann.

Clay, M. (1985). *The early detection of reading difficulties.* Portsmouth, NH: Heinemann.

Cline, R.L., & Kretke, G.L. (1980). An evaluation of long term sustained silent reading in the junior high school. *Journal of Reading, 23,* 503-506.

Coleman, E.B. (1971). Developing a technology of written instruction: Some determiners of the complexity of prose. In E. Rothkopf & P. Johnson (Eds.), *Verbal learning research and the technology of written instruction.* New York: Teachers College Press.

Cromer, P. (1970). The difference model: A new explanation for some reading difficulties. *Journal of Educational Psychology, 61,* 471-483.

Cullinan, B. (1989). *Literature and the child* (2nd ed.). San Diego: Harcourt Brace Jovanovich.

Cunningham, P. (1978). Mumble reading for beginning readers. *The Reading Teacher, 31,* 409-411.

Cunningham, P., Moore, S., Cunningham, J.W., & Moore, D.W. (1989). *Reading in elementary classrooms* (2nd ed.). New York: Longman.

Curwin, R., & Mendler, A. (1988). Packaged discipline programs: Let the buyer beware. *Educational Leadership, 46,* 68-71.

Dahl, P., & Samuels, J. (1979). An experimental program for teaching high-speed word recognition and comprehension skills. In J.E. Button, T. Lovitt, & T. Rowland (Eds.) *Communications research in learning disabilities and mental retardation* (pp. 32-65). Baltimore, MD: University Park Press.

Dahl, R. (1964). *Charlie and the chocolate factory.* New York: Knopf.

Dahl, R. (1978). *James and the giant peach.* New York: Bantam.

dePaolo, Tomie. (1975). *Swimmy.* New York: Simon & Schuster.

Daniels, H. (1994) *Literataure circles: voice and choice in the student centered classrooms.* New York: Stenhouse Publishers.

Dowhower, S. (1987). Effects of repeated readings on second-grade transitional readers' fluency and comprehension. *Reading Research Quarterly, 22,* 389-406.

Dufflemeyer, F.A., & Dufflemeyer, B.B. (1989). Are IRI passages suitable for assessing main idea comprehension? *The Reading Teacher, 42,* 358-363.

Durkin, D. (1974-1975). A six-year study of children who learned to read in school at the age of four. *Reading Research Quarterly, 10,* 9-61.

Durkin, D. (1987). *Is there a match between what elementary teachers do and what basal reader manuals recommend?* (Reading Education Report No. 44). Urbana-Champaign: University of Illinois, Center for the Study of Reading. (also, *The Reading Teacher, 37,* 734-744.

Durkin, D. (1983). *Teaching them to read* (3rd ed.). Boston: Allyn & Bacon.

Durkin, D. (1989). *Teaching them to read* (4th. ed.). Boston: Allyn & Bacon.

Durkin, D. (1978-1979). What classroom observations reveal about comprehension instruction. *Reading Research Quarterly, 14,* 481-533.

Dyson, A. (1990). Weaving possibilities: Rethinking metaphors for early literacy development. *The Reading Teacher, 44,* 202-213.

Dworetzky, J. (1990). *Introduction to child psychology.* (4th ed.) St. Paul, MN: West.

Edwards, P.A. (in press). Fostering early literacy through parent coaching. In E. Hiebert, Ed., *Literacy for a diverse society: Perspectives, programs, & policies.* New York: Teachers College Press.

Elley, W. (1989). Vocabulary acquisition from listening to stories. *Reading Research Quarterly, 24,* 174-187.

Elley, W., & Mangubhai, F. (1983). The impact of reading on second language learning. *Reading Research Quarterly, 19,* 53-67.

Ekwall, E., & Shanker, J. (1983). *Diagnosis and remediation of the disabled reader* (2nd ed.). Boston: Allyn & Bacon.

Emmer, E., & Aussiker, A..(1987, April). *School and classroom discipline programs: How well do they work?* Paper presented at the annual meeting of the American Educational Research Association, Washington, DC.

Englemann, S., & Bruner, E.C. (1969). *DISTAR* (Direct Instruction Systems for Teaching Arithmetic and Reading). Chicago: Science Research Associates.

Fader, D. (1971). *The naked children.* New York: Macmillan.

Fader, D., & McNeil, E. (1968). *Hooked on books: Programs and proof.* New York: Berkley.

Farley, W. (1941). *The Black Stallion.* New York: Random House.

Fitzgerald, G. (1979). Why kids can read the book but not the workbook. *The Reading Teacher, 32,* 930-932.

Fielding, L.G., Wilson, P.T., & Anderson, R.C. (1986). A new focus on free reading: The role of trade books in reading instruction. In T. Raphael (Ed.), *The contexts of school-based literacy* (pp.149-162). New York: Random House.

Flesch, R (1955). *Why Johnny can't read.* New York: Harper & Row.

Flesch, R. (1981). *Why Johnny still can't learn to read.* New York: Harper & Row.

Flood, J., & D. Lapp. (1986). Types of texts: The match between what students read in basals and what they encounter in tests. *Reading Research Quarterly, 21,* 284-297.

Freyd, P., & Lytle, J. (1990, March). A corporate approach to the 2 R's: A critique of IBM's Writing to Read program. *Educational Leadership.*

Gatengo, C. (1969). *Words in color.* Chicago: Xerox.

Gambrell, L., Wilson, R., & Gantt, W. (1981). Classroom observations of task-attending behaviors of good and poor readers. *Journal of Educational Research, 74,* 400-404.

Glasser, W. (1969). *Schools without failure.* New York: Harper & Row.

Goodman, K. (1965). A linguistic study of cues and miscues in reading. *Elementary English Review, 42,* 639-643.

Goodman, K. (1976). Reading: A psycholinguistic guessing game. In H. Singer & R. Ruddell (Eds.), *Theoretical models and processes of reading* (2nd ed.). Newark, DE: International Reading Association.

Goodman, K. (1986). What's whole in whole language? Portsmouth, NH: Heineman.

Goodman, K., & Goodman, Y. (1977). Learning about psycholinguistic processes and analyzing oral reading. *Harvard Educational Review, 47,* 317-323.

Goodman, K.S., Bird, L., & Goodman, Y. (1991). *The whole language catalog.* Santa Rosa, CA: American School Publishers.

Gonzales, G., & Elijiah, D. (1975). Rereading: Effect on error patterns and performance levels on the IRI. *The Reading Teacher, 28,* 647-652.

Greenwood, C.R., Delquardi, J., & Hall, R.V. (1981). *Code for instructional structure and student academic response. CISSAR.* Kansas City: University of Kansas, Bureau of Child Research, Juniper Gardens Children's Project.

Grossman, H.J. (1977). *Manual on terminology and classification in mental retardation.* Washington, DC: American Association of Mental Deficiencies.

Guszak, F.J. *Diagnostic reading instruction in the elementary school* (2nd ed.). New York: Harper & Row.

Guszak, F.J. (1985). *Diagnostic reading instruction in the elementary school* (3rd ed.). New York: Harper & Row.

Guszak, F.J. (1989, May). *Preservice reading teacher preparation.* Paper presented at the annual meeting of the International Reading Association, New Orleans, LA.

Guszak, F.J. (1968). Teacher questioning and reading. *The Reading Teacher, 21,* 227-234.

Guthrie, J.T. (1983). Letter to the editor. *Reading Research Quarterly, 19,* 124.

Herman, P.A. (1985). The effect of repeated readings on reading rate, speech pauses, and word recognition accuracy. *Reading Research Quarterly, 20,* 553-564.

Hiebert, E.H., & Colt, J. (1989). Patterns of literature-based reading programs. *The Reading Teacher, 43,* 14-21.

Hochberg, J. (1970). Components of literacy: Speculation and exploratory research. In H. Levin & J. Williams (Eds.), *Basic studies in reading* . New York: Basic Books.

Hoffman, J.V., Baker, C. (1981). Characterizing teacher feedback to student miscues during oral reading. *The Reading Teacher, 34,* 907-913.

Hoffman, J.V., O'Neal, S.F., Clements, R.O., Segel, K.W., & Nash, M.F. (1984). Guided oral reading and miscue focused verbal feedback in second grade classrooms. *Reading Research Quarterly, 19,* 367-384.

Hoffman, J.V., & Crone, S. (1985). The oral recitation lesson: A research-derived strategy for reading in basal texts. Issues in Literacy: a research perspective. *Thirty-fourth yearbook of the National Reading Conference* (pp. 76-83). Rochester, NY: National Reading Conference.

Holdaway, D. (1979). *The foundations of literacy.* Sydney, Australia: Ashton-Scholastic (Heinemann).

Hoskisson, K. (1975a). Successive approximations and beginning reading. *Elementary School Journal, 75,* 442-451.

Hoskisson, K. (1975b). The many facets of assisted reading. *Elementary English, 52,* 312-315.

Huck, C., Helper, S., & Hickman, J. (1987). *Children's literature in the elementary school* (4th ed.). Fort Worth, TX: Holt, Rinehart & Winston.

Hunt, L. (1969 May). *The effect of self-selection, interest, and motivation upon independent and frustration reading levels.* Paper presented at the fourth annual meeting of the International Reading Association.

Hunter, M. (1979). Diagnostic teaching. *Elementary School Journal, 80,* 41-46.

Irwin, O.C. (1960). Infant Speech: Effect of systematic reading of stories. *Journal of Speech and Hearing Research, 3,* 187-190.

Jones, B.F., Friedman, L.B., Tinzmann, M., & Cox, B.E. (1985). Guidelines for instruction-enriched mastery learning to improve comprehension. In P. Levine (Ed.), *Improving student achievement through mastery learning programs.* San Francisco, CA: Jossey-Bass.

Juel, C. (1980). Comparison of word identification strategies with varying context, word type, and reader skill. *Reading Research Quarterly, 15,* 358-376.

Kilgallon, P.A. (1942). *Study of relationships among pupil adjustments in language situations.* Doctoral dissertation, The Pennsylvania State University, State College. (Cited in Betts, 1946).

Kolers, P. (1972). Experiments in reading. *Scientific American, 227,* 84-91.

Kurth, R.J., & Kurth, M.K. (1987,). *The use oAprilf time in formal reading instruction in elementary schools.* Paper presented at the annual meeting of the American Educational Research Association, Washington, D.C.

LeEngle, M. (1962). *A wrinkle in time.* New York: Dell Yearling.

Lehr, F. (1986). Direct instruction in reading. *The Reading Teacher, 39,* 706-713.

Leu, D.J. (1982). Oral reading error analysis: A critical review of research and application. *Reading Research Quarterly, 17,* 420-437.

Lieberman, I.Y., Rubin, H., Duques, S., & Carlisle, J. (1985). Linguistic abilities and spelling proficiency in kindergarteners and adult poor spellers. In D.A.B. Gray & J.F. Kavanaugh (Eds.), *Biobehavioral measures of dyslexia* (pp.163-171). Parkton, MD: New York Press.

Link, M., Thompkins, G., & Shaw, B. (1980). Can you read without a book? *Language Arts, 57,* 857-865.

Madden, N.A., & Slavin, R.E. (1983). Mainstreaming students with mild handicaps: Academic and social outcomes. *Review of Educational Research, 53,* 519-569.

Martin, B. (1983). *Brown bear, brown bear, what do you see?* New York: Henry Holt.

Martinez, M., & Roser, N. (1985). Read it again: The value of repeated readings during storytime. *The Reading Teacher, 38,* 782-786.

McCracken, R. (1976). Initiating "sustained silent reading". *Journal of Reading, 14,* 521-529.

McCracken, R. (1978). Modeling is the key to sustained silent reading. *The Reading Teacher, 31,* 406-408.

McCracken, R. (1966). *Standard reading inventory.* Klamath Falls, OR: Klamath Falls.

McCracken, R. (1967). The informal reading inventory as a means of improving instruction. In T. Barrett (Ed.), *The evaluation of children's reading* (pp. 79-96). Newark, DE: International Reading Association.

Mackenzie, G. (1979). Data charts: A crutch for helping pupils organize reports. *Language Arts, 56,* 784-788.

Meyer, L.A. (1983). Increased student achievement in reading: One district's strategies. *Research in Rural Education, 1,* 47-51.

Mills, H., & Clyde, J. (1990). Portraits of whole language classrooms. Portsmouth, NH: Heinemann.

Moore, J.C., Jones, C.J., & Miller, D.C. (1980). What we know after a decade of sustained silent reading. *The Reading Teacher, 33,* 445-450.

Moyer, S. (1976). *Multiple oral rereading: A descriptive study of its effects on reading speed and accuracy in selected first grade children.* Doctoral dissertation, The University of Texas at Austin.

Moyer, S. (1982). Repeated reading. *Journal of Learning Disabilities, 15,* 619-623.

Nagy, W.E., Herman, D., & Anderson, R. (1985). Learning words from context. *Reading Research Quarterly, 20,* 233-253.

Neil, K. (1980). Turn kids on with repeated readings. *Teaching Exceptional Children, 12,* 63-64.

O'Shea, L., & Sindelear, P. (1983). The effects of segmenting written discourse on the reading comprehension of low- and high- performance readers. *Reading Research Quarterly, 18,* 458-465.

Obrzut, J.E., Obrzut, A., Hynd, G.W., & Pirozollo, F.J. (1981). Effect of directed attention on cerebral asymmetries in normal and learning-disabled children. *Developmental Psychology, 17,* 118-125.

Olson, W. (1952). Seeking, self-selection and pacing in the use of books by children. *The Packet* (Vol. 7). Boston: D.C. Heath.

Osborn, J., Wilson, P.T., & Anderson, R.C. (1985). *Reading education: Foundations for a literate America.* Lexington, MA: D.C. Heath.

Pearson, P.D., & Fielding, L.G. (1994) Reading comprehension: what works. *Educational Leadership* 62-68

Pearson, P.D., Barr, R., Kamil, M.L., & Mosenthal, P. (1984). *Handbook of reading research.* New York: Longman.

Pelham, W.E. (1977). Withdrawal of a stimulant drug and concurrent behavioral intervention in the treatment of a hyperactive child. *Behavior Therapy, 8,* 473-479.

Piccolo, J. (1987). Expository text structure: Teaching and learning strategies. *The Reading Teacher, 40,* 838-847.

Public Law 94-142 (1975). The education for all handicapped children. Washington, DC.

Public Law 99-457 (1986). Washington, DC.

Perfetti, C.A., & Lesgold, A. (1979). Coding and comprehension in skilled reading and implications for reading instruction. In L.B. Resnick & P. Weaver (Eds.), *Theory and practice in early reading* (Vol. 1). Hillsdale, NJ: Erlbaum.

Perfetti, C.A., & McCutcheon, D. (1982). A speech process in reading. In N. Lass (Ed.), *Speech and language: Advances in basic research and practice* (Vol. 4, pp. 237-269). New York: Academic Press.

Powell, W. (1968, May). *Reappraising the criteria for interpreting informal reading inventories.* Paper presented at the annual meeting of the International Reading Association, Boston, MA.

Powell, W. (1970). Reappraising the criteria for interpreting informal reading inventories. In D.L. DeBoer (Ed.), *Reading diagnosis and evaluation* . Newark, DE: International Reading Association.

Powell, W. (1980, Winter). Measuring reading performance informally. *Journal of Children and Youth, 2*, 28.

Rashotte, C.A., & Torgenson, J.K. (1985). Repeated reading and reading fluency in learning disabled children. *Reading Research Quarterly, 20,* 180-188.

Read, C., Yun-Fei, Z., Hong-Yin, N., & Bao-Quing, D. (1986). The ability to manipulate speech sounds depends upon alphabetic writing. *Cognition, 24,* 31-44.

Reeder, G., Padilla, J., & Krank, H. (1989). What research really shows about assertive discipline. *Educational Leadership, 47,* 72-75.

Roberts, T. (1974). "Frustration level" reading in the infant school. *Educational Research, 19,* 41-44.

Trelease, J. (1985). *The read aloud handbook* (rev. ed.). New York: Penguin.

Trevise, R. (1984). Teaching reading to the gifted. In A. Harris & E. Sipay, (Eds.), *Readings on reading instruction* . New York: Longman.

Turkington, C. (1987, September). Special talents. *Psychology Today,* 42-46.

Vacca, R., & Vacca, J. (1986). *Content area reading* (2nd ed.). Boston: Little, Brown.

Veatch, J. (1978). *Reading in the elementary school* (2nd ed.). New York: Ronald Press.

Weber, R.M. (1970). First graders' use of grammatical context in reading. In H. Levin & J.P. Williams (Eds.), *Basic studies in reading* . New York: Basic Books.

Whitehurst, G.J., Falco, F.L., Lonigan, C.J., Fischel, J.E., DeBaryshe, B.D., Valdez-Menchaca, M., & Caulifield, M. (1981). Accelerating language development through picture-book reading. *Developmental Psychology, 24,* 552-559.

Wixson, K. (1979). Miscue analysis: A critical review. *Journal of Reading Behavior, 11,* 163-175.

Wubbena, R. (1983). *WILSAD. A Reading Report.* Weslaco, TX: Weslaco Independent School District.

Wubbena, R. (1990). *Annual Report of Reading Progress.* Weslaco, TX: Weslaco Independent School District.

Wulbert, M., & Dries, R. (1977). The relative efficacy of methylphenidate (Ritalin) and behavior-modification techniques in the treatment of a hyperactive child. *Journal of Applied Behavioral Analysis, 10,* 21-31.

Ysseldyke, J.E., & Algozzine, R. (1982-1983). Where to begin in diagnosing reading problems. *Topics in Learning and Reading Disorders, 2,* 60-68.

Author Index

Keyword Index